D0204948

CASES IN CONSUMER BEHAVIOR

Hale N. Tongren
George Mason University

PRENTICE-HALL, INC., Englewood Cliffs, N.J. 07632

Library of Congress Cataloging-in-Publication Data

TONGREN, HALE N., (date)
    Consumer behavior cases.

    1. Consumer—Case studies.   2. Consumers—
United States—Case studies.   I. Title.
HF5415.3.T64 1987   658.8′342   86-25547
ISBN   0-13-115346-3

Editorial/production supervision and
  interior design: Allison De Fren
Cover design: Lundgren Graphics, Ltd.
Manufacturing buyer: Ed O'Dougherty

© 1987 by Prentice-Hall, Inc.
A Division of Simon & Schuster
Englewood Cliffs, New Jersey 07632

Printed in the United States of America

10   9   8   7   6   5   4   3   2   1

ISBN 0-13-115346-3 01

Prentice-Hall International (UK) Limited, *London*
Prentice-Hall of Australia Pty. Limited, *Sydney*
Prentice-Hall Canada Inc., *Toronto*
Prentice-Hall Hispanoamericana, S.A., *Mexico*
Prentice-Hall of India Private Limited, *New Delhi*
Prentice-Hall of Japan, Inc., *Tokyo*
Prentice-Hall of Southeast Asia Pte. Ltd., *Singapore*
Editora Prentice-Hall do Brasil, Ltda., *Rio de Janeiro*

CASES IN CONSUMER BEHAVIOR

Hale N. Tongren

George Mason University

PRENTICE-HALL, INC., Englewood Cliffs, N.J. 07632

of Congress Cataloging-in-Publication Data

WREN, HALE N., (date)
Consumer behavior cases.

1. Consumer—Case studies.   2. Consumers—
United States—Case studies.   I. Title.
HF5415.3.T64 1987   658.8'342   86-25547
ISBN   0-13-115346-3

Editorial/production supervision and
  interior design: Allison De Fren
Cover design: Lundgren Graphics, Ltd.
Manufacturing buyer: Ed O'Dougherty

Printed in the United States of America

10   9   8   7   6   5   4   3   2   1

ISBN 0-13-115346-3   01

Prentice-Hall International (UK) Limited, *London*
Prentice-Hall of Australia Pty. Limited, *Sydney*
Prentice-Hall Canada Inc., *Toronto*
Prentice-Hall Hispanoamericana, S.A., *Mexico*
Prentice-Hall of India Private Limited, *New Delhi*
Prentice-Hall of Japan, Inc., *Tokyo*
Prentice-Hall of Southeast Asia Pte. Ltd., *Singapore*
Editora Prentice-Hall do Brasil, Ltda., *Rio de Janeiro*

To my wife,
Sally S. Tongren

Contents

Cases and Related Concepts

Case	Primary Area(s)	Secondary Area(s)
Ultra Mart, Inc.	*Segmentation*	*Attitude Measures*
Olde Odeon Theater	*Motivation and Needs*	*Segmentation* *Life Styles*
Nike, Inc.	*Motivation and Needs*	*Culture* *Communications*
Source Perrier	*Pyschographic* *Characteristics*	*Price-Quality* *Perceptions*
Dollars and Scents	*Psychographic and* *Self-Concept*	*Culture* *Consumer Research*
Atari Corporation	*Perception and Image*	*Positioning*
Image Strategy and E. J. Korvettes	*Perception and Image*	*Attitude* *Attitude Change*
The Fairfax County Bottle Bill	*Learning*	*Consumer Choice*
Which Coke is It?	*Learning*	*Brand Loyalty* *Attitude Measure*
The Sport of Kings	*Attitude* *Attitude Change*	*Life Style*

Case	Primary Area(s)	Secondary Area(s)
Procter & Gamble	*Attitude* *Attitude Change*	*Sub Cultures* *Beliefs*
Mary Kay Cosmetics	*Situational Factors*	*Opinion Leaders* *Life Style*
Pearl Travel Service	*Communications*	*Advertising* *Information Processing*
Soviet Central Department Store	*Communications*	*Cultural Factors*
Bridge-O-Matic	*Reference Groups*	*Self Concept* *Consumer Profiles*
Old Spaghetti Mill	*Family Decision* *Making*	*Opinion Leaders* *Diffusion*
Riverside Savings	*Family Life Cycle*	*Demographics* *Social Class*
Hatton and Mayer	*Subcultures*	*Segmentation* *Life Style*
The Profit Cemetery	*Cultural Factors*	*CB Models*
Polaroid Corp.	*Cultural Factors*	*Innovation*
Radley Development	*Social Class*	*Motivation* *Positioning*
Campbell's Soup and Nonsoup	*Diffusion of Innovation*	*Life Styles*
Merriwether Distillery	*Consumer Tastes*	*Culture* *Life Styles*

Preface

The cases in this book have been prepared so that students will benefit in the following four areas:

1. Learning about different types of businesses and organizations.
2. Learning to recognize and analyze the important aspects of case situations and to isolate the major problem.
3. Learning how to apply the theories, concepts and techniques of consumer behavior in solving marketing-related case problems.
4. Learning to write clearly, concisely, logically and convincingly, in presenting case analyses.

In our economy today, consumers are kings. It is they who decide which products and services will be successful and which ones won't. Because consumers are so important, producers spend billions of dollars to find out what kind of attitudes consumers of their goods and services have about them and their products. They also want to know how consumers go through the process of making up their minds to buy something, how they get the information they need to decide if the product will do what they want it to, and how they actually go about buying it. These, and many other aspects of how all of us behave as consumers, are the basis for the study of consumer behavior.

But much of the learning process in our college environment consists of remembering facts and terms, and repeating them on examinations, using true-false and multiple choice questions. While these methods are useful in some courses, they don't perform well in more flexible fields. In marketing, and in consumer behavior specifically, there aren't always "right" or "wrong" answers. The important thing is to know the concepts and techniques of these subjects, and when and how to apply them to solve problems. When you go to work in the marketing business, it isn't very likely that your manager will ask you to recite the four functions of attitude. But you will certainly be asked to work out solutions to problems that may involve applying the functions of attitude. Only by practice analysis of situations and problems can students learn to use the concepts, apply them collectively and judiciously, recognize the real versus the apparent problems, and suggest logical courses of action. It is for these purposes that the case analysis method is used to simulate real life situations and to try to come to conclusions about them.

One of the most challenging aspects of case analysis is defining the central problem that needs to be analyzed and solved. A decline in sales, for example, is likely to be a symptom rather than the problem itself. Once the problem is identified, the major factors and data in the case that influence it should be examined by applying marketing principles and concepts from the course. Cases require very careful reading because important factors may be disguised in remarks made by individuals in the case. For example, a prospective home buyer, after talking with people who have already moved into a new development, may observe, "These people are just like us." If this buyer is upwardly mobile, the remark may be a derogatory one, indicating a desire to live in a higher social class area. A common pitfall in case analysis occurs when students, having decided upon the central "problem," also decide upon its solution. They then accumulate only the data and information from the case that support their solution, often ignoring information or indications that do not support it. A good analysis includes both the pros and cons of the situation and suggests how the cons may be overcome or why they may not be important. If a case has been carefully analyzed and prepared, the reader should be able to predict the solution or recommendations before they are actually presented.

The cases in this book are designed to provide a wide spectrum of consumer behavior situations and problems. They range from the giant Procter & Gamble to a tiny rural motion picture theater, and they include both profit and nonprofit oriented organizations, as well as service firms. An effort has been made to vary both the style and presentation of the cases, and to provide different approaches to their analysis and solution. Generally, all data and information needed for analysis is available in the case and its exhibits, and from texts or lectures relating to the topic.

The cases and related concepts section have been arranged so that both the major area of emphasis in the case, and the secondary areas are listed. But for most of the cases, the secondary areas are of sufficient importance that they may be used separately. One of the purposes of case analysis is to provide data and information as a basis for students to make decisions. Particular attention should be paid to the data, and to the need for sorting the relevant from the irrelevant. Often, as in real situations, important aspects of the case may be found in an obscure group of data, or in an off-hand remark by a case figure.

Of those who have been helpful in the preparation of this book, I want to express my appreciation to the three reviewers: Wayne D. Hoyer from the University of Texas at Austin; Bruce Stern, Portland State University; and Peter B. Turk, University of Oklahoma, who provided insight, and most useful comments and suggestions. I also want to thank the students who have provided feedback for these original cases, and to my wife, Sally Tongren, an author in her own right, who gave both assistance and understanding.

HALE N. TONGREN

Case 1

Ultra Mart, Inc.

In the early 1980s, Glenn Golden was working as a research assistant in the Washington, D.C., office of the secretary of a large U.S. government agency. A young bachelor, he lived in a modest but comfortable apartment across the Potomac River in a nearby Virginia suburb. His work was varied and interesting, but quite demanding. More often than not, he had to work late—sometimes until midnight or later. Many times, when the Congress was in session, he worked a seven-day week. With this schedule, he found it hard to cope with all the regular chores involved in keeping up his apartment and running necessary errands. The one task he found particularly troublesome was grocery shopping, since he often had to do it late in the evening on the way home.

One evening about nine o'clock while filling his shopping cart after a hectic 12-hour day, Glenn wondered if there wasn't an easier way to shop. He thought how simple it would be if he could just phone his order in to a store and have it delivered after he got home. His mother had often told him about phoning in her order and having it delivered by a boy in a wagon, when she lived in a small town. Or, if the groceries couldn't be delivered, he could stop in front of the store, have the order put into his car, pay, and drive away! Maybe it would cost a little more, but it would be worth it. Surely, he thought, there must be a lot of people who don't have time to shop—busy singles and families where both members work. There might be a market, too, for older people who can't get out to shop but would be willing to pay for delivery.

He looked around the store where he was shopping and noticed the attractive decor, the wide expanse of fully stocked shelves, the extensive refrigerated cases, and the enticing displays of fresh produce. He thought about the battery of people who kept the shelves stocked and the line of checkers who ran the registers, all of whom were paid the wage rate negotiated by the Retail Clerks Union. Maybe his phone-in and pick-up idea need not be more expensive after all. It wouldn't have to be an actual store; it could be just a warehouse that customers would never enter—no soft lights or fancy fixtures, no decorations or display cases, no item or shelf pricing, no high-cost labor.

PLANNING AND EARLY RESEARCH

The more Glenn thought about his idea, the more obsessed he became with it. Little by little the details began to form in his mind and he jotted down a general outline of how such a "phone-supermarket" would work:

> It will be located in a warehouse district as near as possible to a major freeway access. Customers will buy a membership for $2.00 entitling them to an account number and a catalog listing all items carried, with an order number for each. When a customer dials the supermarket's phone number, a recorded voice will ask for the order number of item one. The customer will punch in the number using the phone dial, followed by the quantity. If an item is out of stock, a recorded voice will say so and the customer will be given a short time to make another selection. When the list is complete, the account number will be entered together with the estimated time of pickup. Later, the customer will drive into a loading lane at the warehouse, give the account number, pay by cash or check, and the order will be immediately loaded into the car.

He spent what little spare time he had drawing warehouse layouts and working out the most efficient methods of storing and picking the merchandise. Instead of a chore, shopping now became part of his research and, as he shopped, he compiled lists of the kinds of items the warehouse store would have to carry. He enlisted several friends who helped to estimate costs for rent, equipment, inventory, and personnel to operate such a business. Most interesting and enlightening, though, were the population data he gathered that showed the "baby-boom" population segment was moving rapidly into the household formation stage. Exhibit 1-1 shows changes from 1960 with projections to 1990.

Glenn calculated that the oldest of the baby-boomers were just over 30 and that, far from being an anachronism, marriage still flourished. Even with a high divorce rate, he found that most people eventually remarried; the proportion of the married population age 18 and over in 1983 was 66.6 percent, just about the same as it was in 1950. He also discovered that over half of all married women were working outside the home (50.7 percent). At the same time, one- and two-person households of singles were forming at a rapid rate. They accounted for 8.5 percent of all U.S. household expenditures in 1983. This information confirmed Glenn's hunch that the time was ripe for innovation in the grocery business, even if the innovation involved moving the clock back to his grandmother's day. The data indicated at the very least the existence of a potential market for a new and different way for busy people to buy groceries. If the service could be provided at a price less than that charged by conventional supermarkets, Glenn could provide prospective customers with both motivation and rationalization to use the phone-in service.

GATHERING CONSUMER INFORMATION

Up to this point, Glenn's quest for information had been a kind of game for him and the only investment he had made was his time. He realized that he had gone as far as he could in treating the idea as a hobby and he would have to either get serious or abandon it altogether. If he decided on the former course, it was time to put up some money. He had gathered the basic secondary data on population and household formation trends, but he still did not know much, if anything, about the shopping habits of the new generation or about their life-styles, and he had neither the time nor the expertise to get it.

He asked one of the executives in his agency about these matters, since they often used marketing research firms to do opinion polling and other research work. Several research firms were recommended and Glenn talked with two that seemed most suited to his needs. After checking with a few of their clients, he chose Peterson Associates, a small firm with a good reputation and reasonable hourly rates. Glenn had a general idea of the kind of information he wanted but in his first business meeting with Mr. Peterson he found out how hard it was to zero in on exactly what he needed to know. Fortunately, Mr. Peterson knew the right questions to ask and how to construct a set of research objectives from Glenn's description of the type of business he had in mind. Because Glenn had only limited funds for the project, some tailoring had to be done, but they finally agreed on this objective: Determine the shopping habits of younger grocery shoppers in households in the northern Virginia area adjacent to Washington, D.C., including the following:

1. Attitudes and objections of shoppers toward shopping
2. How often people shop and how many grocery stores they visit
3. How shoppers know what grocery items to get at the store(s)
4. The time shoppers spend on the several phases of grocery shopping, including travel; shopping for meat, fresh vegetables, baked goods, dry and canned groceries; and the total time spent in the store

5. The proportion of the average grocery bill spent for fresh meat, fresh vegetables, bakery goods, and all other items
6. Average adult family sizes, the extent to which adult members are employed full-time, and who normally does grocery shopping
7. Limited demographics: age group, zip code, sex

A description of the questionnaire design is shown in Exhibit 1-2. The survey form and the data actually gathered with it are in Exhibit 1-3.

SURVEY RESULTS

Mr. Peterson analyzed the survey results and prepared a market research report for Glenn, who spent all his spare time for two weeks going over it. He thought the average total time for a shopping trip was not surprising since he calculated his to be a little under an hour. But he lived closer to the store than the average respondent, and, as a single, he probably bought fewer items. He did note the large proportion who said they did not like shopping and found it "simply troublesome, a hassle that takes too much time." Most important, though, was the 19 percent who wanted an easier way to shop— that was nearly one out of five. If he could only get half of that market, or 10 percent, the venture would be assured of success.

These two questions were about as close as the research could come to attitude determination within the survey's cost limits, but there were many other things it would have been helpful to know. Some of these are whether grocery shopping is seen as a "personal" activity, whether or not the buying process evokes any favorable reaction such as pleasure or gratification, how shoppers cope with financial constraints (fitting the purchases to a budget), the type of life-styles the shoppers in each category pursue, and similar behavioral information. Glenn wasn't sure which of the subgroups of shopping habits would provide the most fruitful target market. Are those who make a list and buy only what is on it most likely to use a catalog? By cross-referencing the questions in the three shopping habits groups, he found that the first groups in all three questions are essentially the same people, the organized shoppers. The store-loyal buyers are also the "listers" and the "buy all at once" customers. It seems that if only a part of this group had a problem with shopping, they would certainly be potential customers.

Glenn was not really sure how much time customers would actually save, so he and his friends conducted some simulated telephone tests using a sample catalog he put together. See Exhibit 1-4. Most of his test subjects did not prelist what they wanted, but made the phone call and selected items by simply going down the list. The average time was about 20 minutes. Glenn made some "dummy runs" to find the time it took to leave the freeway, pick up the order, and return to the freeway. The average time during several rush-hour periods was about 18 minutes, or a total of 38 minutes including calling in the order.

He also knew that there were changes taking place in the food marketing industry and that experts were predicting substantial increases in the proportion of total meals that consumers will buy away from home. One report indicated in part:

> Population trends, more families where both adults work, less leisure time, and an increase in the number of eating establishments compatible with a casual life-style, support further growth in the food service industry. Younger adults eat out more frequently than the rest of the population, and the 18–44 group will show the largest increase in the 1980s.

There were also a number of social questions about the life-styles of younger married consumers. Economic and real estate forecasts suggested that home ownership goals are paramount for this group. But in most large urban areas, new housing is in the outer suburbs; moreover, it is very expensive and becoming more so. To afford it, both spouses must work and, to do so, they usually commute. If the couple has children, time at home becomes even more valuable and demands on it are resented. For young professionals, therefore, time is often perceived as having more value than money.

STARTING THE BUSINESS

By the fall of 1983, Glenn found the right sized space on the ground floor of a new warehouse under construction less than one-half mile off the freeway. He applied to several banks and to the Small Business Administration for loans, but was turned down because he had no business track record, even though the loan officers thought his idea was promising. Glenn had about $30,000 in securities that he inherited from his grandmother, which he had been saving for a "nest egg" when he married. He decided to use this, and he also cajoled his father into cosigning a $40,000 bank loan. Since that wasn't nearly enough to finance the inventory and provide working capital, he had to get outside capital. After a full day on the telephone, he located two college classmates who agreed to invest $20,000 each. One of them had experience in the retail grocery business and expressed interest in coming into the firm as an employee. During the next several months Glenn was able to raise nearly $50,000, mostly in small-lot stock subscriptions from friends, relatives, and associates. He planned to buy some of this back as soon as he could afford it, to assure himself of full control. Together with his inheritance, and the loan from his father, he had accumulated what he calculated would be needed for the initial costs of setting up the business as well as working capital for the near future.

He met with the sales representative of a large grocery products wholesaler and together they decided upon the range and depth of inventory needed to open the store. The wholesaler, Beckett and Co., agreed to finance one-third of the inventory for 90 days, but the remainder would be sold on standard terms of 2% 10/net 30. Beckett recommended an opening inventory valued at about $140,000, which was somewhat higher than Glenn estimated on the pro forma balance sheet and income statements he had furnished to the bank and to the wholesaler. By a little judicious cutting of items he thought might not have much demand, he was able to reduce it to about $125,000. Beckett would finance $40,000, Glenn would pay the balance in 30 days, and he expected to replenish stock with the income from sales.

Glenn thought his working capital would be enough to carry the business for about six months, and by that time it should begin to be self-supporting. He thought it might be profitable in a year. The only unknown in the equation was whether or not a large enough segment of the market would actually use the new service initially, and eventually become regular customers.

After about six grueling months of 12- to 18-hour days, Ultra Mart finally opened. Catalogs were in the hands of about 2,500 potential customers, the shelves were stocked, a delivery truck was waiting to be loaded, and a roller-conveyor system for filling orders was in place. Glenn gazed thoughtfully out the window as he waited for the telephone to ring.

Analysis Questions

1. What do you think about Glenn Golden's initial demographic research? Did it suggest a potentially viable segment for his proposed business?

2. When all the information collected in the survey is reviewed, what did Glenn Golden really find out about attitudes of younger consumers toward his proposal? What method might have yielded more useful information?

3. Glenn Golden made some "judicious cuts" in the number of items the wholesaler suggested he carry, because his inventory funds were limited. Considering the kind of service he planned to operate, would a few out-of-stock items make much difference?

4. Do you think his new business will succeed? What consumer behavior research might he do now?

ULTRA MART, INC.

EXHIBIT 1-1

Population Changes in 18–45 Age Groups (000s)

Year	18–24	25–34	35–44
1960	15,600	22,800	24,100
1970	23,000	24,900	23,200
1975	27,735	31,314	22,760
1980	30,100	37,426	25,824
1982	30,151	39,379	28,113
1983	29,897	40,146	29,424
1985	28,739	←————73,792————→	
1990 (est.)	25,794	←————81,376————→	

ULTRA MART, INC.

EXHIBIT 1-2

Questionnaire Design and Data

Questionnaire Design

The basis of the design is the objective of the research and the accompanying details as outlined in the case. The number, sophistication, and scope of the questions are, of course, functions of the time and financial constraints of the project. No direct questions are asked about the respondent's probable behavior under a hypothetical set of circumstances. For example, we did not ask if a respondent would shop from a catalog, would like a delivery service, or would buy a prepackaged selection. Such questions, we believe, would not produce reliable answers since the concept itself is likely to be outside the respondent's frame of reference. What we are saying here is that the consumer would have to know all about the procedures for the proposed type of grocery shopping service if the questions are to be answered intelligently.

We also avoided rhetorical questions such as "Would you like lower grocery prices?" or "Would you prefer stable prices?" Most people reply affirmatively to questions such as these.

This research attempts to find out what consumer grocery shopping habits are, what consumer's feelings are toward grocery shopping, and how they spend their time while shopping. Also important is whether or not they consider both the time spent and the shopping chore itself to be excessively cumbersome to the point where they would accept a substitute for it. Using this information, we hope to make some assumptions that could help in assessing the probable success of the concept.

EXHIBIT 1-2 (*Cont'd.*)

Sample Selection

Again, because of time and financial constraints, we were not able to design a truly valid and reliable sample. A sample size of about 387, randomly selected, is needed to give a representation of the entire population with a confidence level of .95 and an error of .05. We did, however, conduct a judgment, convenience sample in parking lots, by intercepting shoppers about to enter supermarkets in locations picked randomly. They were asked to jot down the times spent in specified areas of the store on a card furnished to them, to agree to let the researcher see their sales slip, and to answer a few short questions when they came out. A total of 181 replies was obtained.

ULTRA MART, INC.

EXHIBIT 1-3

Mean Replies to Questionnaire

1. **a.** Time normally spent on grocery shopping trip?   1 hour 36 minutes
   b. About how far from home to your store?   3.4 miles
2. **a.** Of total spent, about how much for fresh meat? $16.20
   b. Of total spent, about how much for fresh vegetables? $6.57
   c. Of total spent, about how much for fresh bakery goods? $4.94
   d. What is your total bill for an average shopping trip? $58.54
3. Of total time in the store, how much did you spend in:
   a. Fresh meat selection (meat counter)?   12 minutes
   b. Fresh vegetable selection?   10 minutes
   c. Fresh bakery goods selection?   3 minutes
   d. About how long did you actually spend shopping for groceries from the time you entered until you left with your groceries?   46 minutes
4. Which of these statements best describes how you know what to buy at the grocery?
   a. I make a list and buy only what is on it.   21%
   b. I just walk through the store and pick up what I need.   48%
   c. I pick up what I need but buy other things as well.   31%
5. Which of these statements best describes how often you shop?
   a. I make a major trip (weekly, monthly, etc.) and I try to buy very little else in between times.   23%
   b. I make a regular trip but I often need one or two other items every several days.   67%
   c. I shop for what I need in small lots every few days.   10%
6. Which one of these statements best describes how you shop?
   a. I usually shop at only one store and get all I need.   21%

b. I watch the ads and may shop at several stores to get the lowest prices. 19%

c. I usually shop at one store but may pick up convenience items at other stores now and then. 60%

7. Which one of these statements best describes how you feel about shopping?
   a. I don't mind shopping. 24%
   b. It's a chore I don't like but it has to be done. 48%
   c. I wish there were an easier way to shop. 19%
   d. I rather enjoy grocery shopping. 9%

8. Number of adults in the household: 1–22% 2–59%

   3–12% 4+–7%

   How many of these work full time: 0–3% 1–79%

   2–72% 3+–44%

   (*Example*: 79% of the one person households, 72% of the two person households, etc., worked full time.)

   Who does most of the grocery shopping? Female adult 51%

   Male adult 14%

   Yourself (single) 22%

   We trade off 13%

9. Which of these statements best describes how you feel about your main objection to shopping? (Of those who had objections to it.)
   a. It's such a hassle. 38%
   b. It takes so much time. 53%
   c. Too many decisions. 2%
   d. Any others? 3%: Difficult to park   Can't find items
   Too long at checkout   Crowded, congested

ULTRA MART, INC.

EXHIBIT 1-4

Sample Catalog Page

			Size	Value	Price
	Tea				
16601	McCormick Tea Bags		48 's	0.024	1.15
16610	McCormick Tea Bags		100 's	0.024	2.39
16629	Lipton Instant Tea		3 oz	0.897	2.69
16638	Lipton Instant Tea, Lemon Flavored		4 oz	0.498	1.99
16647	Lipton Iced Tea Mix, Lo-Cal, Lemon Flav.		6 oz	0.415	2.49
16656	Lipton Tea Mix, Lemon & Sugar Added		24 oz	0.094	2.25
16665	Lipton Tea Mix, Lemon & Sugar Added		36 oz	0.083	2.97
16674	Lipton Tea Mix, Lemon & Sugar Added		54 oz	0.074	3.99
20561	Nestea Instant Tea		3 oz	0.897	2.69

EXHIBIT 1-4 (*Cont'd.*)

Toaster Pastries

20938	Kellogg's Blueberry Pop-Tarts, 6's	11 oz	0.075	0.83
20947	Kellogg's Cherry Pop-Tarts, 6's	11 oz	0.075	0.83
20956	Kellogg's Strawberry Pop-Tarts, 6's	11 oz	0.075	0.83
20965	Kellogg's Frosted Dutch Apple Pop-Tarts, 6's	11 oz	0.075	0.83
20974	Kellogg's Frosted Blueberry Pop-Tarts, 6's	11 oz	0.075	0.83
20983	Kellogg's Frosted Cherry Pop-Tarts, 6's	11 oz	0.075	0.83
20992	Kellogg's Frosted Chocolate Fudge Pop-Tart	11 oz	0.075	0.83
21001	Kellogg's Frosted Choc-Vanilla Creme Tart	11 oz	0.075	0.83
21010	Kellogg's Frosted Sugar-Cinnamon Pop-Tart	11 oz	0.075	0.83
21029	Kellogg's Frosted Concord Grape Pop-Tart	11 oz	0.075	0.83
21038	Kellogg's Frosted Strawberry Pop-Tart, 6's	11 oz	0.075	0.83
21083	Kellogg's Danish Rings—Apple	12 oz	0.079	0.95
21092	Kellogg's Danish Rings—Blueberry	12 oz	0.079	0.95
21111	Kellogg's Danish Rings—Cherry	12 oz	0.079	0.95
21267	Kellogg's Danish Rings—Strawberry	12 oz	0.079	0.95

Tomato Paste & Sauce

10478	Contadina Tomato Sauce	8 oz	0.034	0.27
10487	Fine Fare Tomato Sauce	15 oz	0.026	0.39
10496	Hunt's Tomato Sauce	8 oz	0.034	0.27
10506	Hunt's Tomato Sauce	15 oz	0.034	0.51
10515	Hunt's Tomato Sauce	29 oz	0.032	0.93
10542	Hunt's Tomato Sauce Special	15 oz	0.039	0.59
10560	Contadina Quality Tomato Paste	6 oz	0.065	0.39
10579	Contadina Quality Tomato Paste	12 oz	0.061	0.73
10588	Fine Fare Tomato Paste	6 oz	0.052	0.31
10597	Hunt's Tomato Paste	6 oz	0.065	0.39
10607	Hunt's Tomato Paste	12 oz	0.061	0.73

Toppings & Coffee Creamers—Frozen

47465	Bird's Eye Cool Whip	9 oz	0.094	0.85
47474	Bird's Eye Cool Whip	13.50 oz	0.081	1.09
47483	Rich Coffee Rich	16 oz	0.028	0.45

T.V. Dinners—Frozen

47593	Banquet Man Pleaser Chicken Dinner	17 oz	0.079	1.35
47603	Banquet Man Pleaser Salisbury Steak	19 oz	0.071	1.35
47612	Banquet Man Pleaser Turkey Dinner	19 oz	0.071	1.35
47621	Morton Chicken Dinner	11 oz	0.075	0.83
47630	Morton Country Table Salisbury Steak	10.50 oz	0.085	0.89
47649	Morton Macaroni & Cheese Dinner	12 oz	0.058	0.69

Case 2

The Olde Odeon Theater

It was a Friday afternoon and a beautiful September day in the foothills of the Appalachian Mountains. But not much sunlight crept into the dingy inner office of the Olde Odeon Theater where the governing board of the Preston County Cultural Association was holding a special meeting. Bob Kozaki, president of the association, had called today's meeting because he and others were concerned about the mounting losses from operating the Olde Odeon. Since it had been renovated and opened under the sponsorship of the association last year, it had operated in the black for only about half of the 16 months it had been running.

At least five of the eight-member board were anxious to close what they saw as a worthy but unsuccessful venture that they had hoped would bring motion picture entertainment (some of it cultural) into Preston County. But Bertrand (Bat) Weaver, who had spearheaded the project, was equally determined to keep the theater running, at least through the coming winter season. He had come prepared to make a proposal, and while he listened to the various members drone on about why the theater ought to be closed, he thought about it. He would have his say when they finished.

PRESTON COUNTY—THE NEW AND THE OLD

Preston County, North Carolina, is located in rolling hill country near the Virginia border, roughly an equal distance (about 60 miles) from the Raleigh/Durham and the Winston-Salem/Charlotte metropolitan areas. It is mainly a community of small to medium-sized farms, with only three small towns—Wingate, Sutterville, and Monson—none of which have a population of over 500. The farms had provided comfortable, if not outwardly profitable, livings for the families that worked them. But the 1940s and 1950s had brought economic changes that had adverse effects on smaller farms, particularly those from several hundred to a thousand acres. They could no longer provide enough income to pay for the necessities and conveniences that the U.S. population was beginning to demand. While older county farmers continued to work their land and lived in reduced circumstances, younger men and women often took seasonal or full-time jobs in stores, construction, or factories in one of the metropolitan areas. Most of them continued to live in Preston County, commuting the 50 to 70 miles each way to work. They continued to operate their farms, with the help of their children and other family members, or rented their land to others.

In the late 1960s, as the next generation moved out of its teens and was ready to form its own households, two things happened that were to make irreversible changes in the character and life-style of Preston County. First, as members of the new generation began to follow their fathers and mothers into the stores and factories of Durham and Winston-Salem, they quickly tired of the hundred-odd-mile daily drive. In addition, many of them had carried the brunt of farm work as they were growing up, and they had little interest in continuing it as a part-time occupation. So they began to move to the cities and the exodus from Preston County began. Over the next ten years, their parents grew older, some farms lay fallow, and, when the old folks died, with only limited demand for land in the county, farmhouses sat empty.

At the end of the 1970s Preston County was "discovered" by an increasing number of older families from the large metropolitan areas in central North Carolina. Land prices were quite low compared to those closer to the cities and most of the farmhouses were salvageable. For example, a 400-acre farm with an older brick house could be had for not much more than $35,000. But for many, the price was secondary to the idyllic countryside with its rolling hills, the many picturesque small farms that were still operating, and the pleasant, generally mild climate.

Among the first "outsiders" to buy property in Preston were Bat and Elsie Weaver, who bought a decrepit farm from its absentee owner who worked at Bat's metal cabinet factory in Charlotte. The brick house had been empty for about five years, and was basically sound although it needed some extensive repairs. The Weavers, who were both in their early fifties, planned to use the farm as a summer home and a place where their children and grandchildren could spend summer vacations. But in 1980, Bat received an attractive offer for his business, and after some family discussion, he and his wife decided to sell and move to Preston County.

They had lived there about six months, the remodeling of the old house was nearing completion, and Bat was getting restless. He was accustomed to working long hours, but now he had more leisure time than he really wanted. So it was only a matter of time until he began looking for a new occupation. Both he and Elsie noticed the increasing demand for Preston County real estate. Yet only one realtor from Wingate handled most of the property that was for sale.

After investigating the potential of the real estate business, Bat and Elsie took some courses in Charlotte and passed the examination for their broker's licenses. He set up a small office in Sutterville and she shared space with a stationery and gift store in Wingate, about 12 miles away. They were aggressive in tracking down owners of vacant farms and houses and visiting them to get listings of the property. The summer of 1981 was successful beyond their wildest dreams, with over 30 properties sold, most of them at asking prices. Many of the buyers were about the same age as the Weavers, or slightly older, and they were all thinking of eventual retirement, since few were interested in commuting to the larger cities. Also, prices had risen considerably and the area was attracting a number of well-known and prominent people from the two heavily populated areas to the south. One of the well-known ones was Georges Lyes, a long-time friend of Bat's, who had owned and operated the successful Paris Soir restaurant in Raleigh for many years. At lunch there one day, Georges confided in Bat that he was losing his location in an urban renewal project, and wanted to locate in the country where he could run a small, quiet restaurant. Bat was quick to see the advantages to the real estate business of a first-class restaurant in Preston County, and quickly convinced Georges that it was the spot for his peaceful country restaurant. But this was not to be. Because of Georges's culinary reputation, people from the metropolitan areas flocked to "quaint" Sutterville on weekends to dine at his excellent but expensive table. They often drove around the county and recognized the attractive possibility of buying property there.

THE PRESTON COUNTY CULTURAL ASSOCIATION

By 1982, Preston County had become one of *the* places to live, and it was even attracting some business executives whose hours were flexible enough to permit commuting. Real estate sales statistics showed nearly 225 property sales in the past two years, most of them to "outsiders," and the extensive remodeling of old farmhouses made the countryside resemble an old-time Hollywood movie set.

But as these new arrivals settled down, Bat could see that they, too, needed some activity to occupy themselves. Many were interested in music, books, the theater, and art, but had to make "expeditions" to the cities for them. So Bat and Elsie took it upon themselves to do something about it. With a few well-planted suggestions, these uprooted urban families decided to band together in a group where they could discuss cultural topics and other things of interest. Although it began with informal small group meetings at each other's homes, it soon evolved into a formal organization with officers, a board of directors, and dues-paying members. By early 1983, the "cultural association," with Elsie as president, had helped to renovate the small Wingate library and to buy 250 new books, had organized a small chamber orchestra from its own membership, and had put on a Christmas play in the high school auditorium to a full house.

The Olde Odeon Theater

Flushed by these successes, the association members looked around the county for other projects that would benefit the community and would absorb their spare time. Bat Weaver, who succeeded Elsie as president, came up with the answer. Over in Sutterville, which was about in the center of the county and which had once been a much larger town, was an old, 230-seat movie theater. While it needed paint, a little carpentry work, and a monumental cleaning, the screen seemed to be in fair condition, as were the seats and heating plant. The town had taken the theater for unpaid taxes several years ago, and had made several unsuccessful attempts to sell it. Bat thought the association could use it, for the price of cleaning and renovating. "There's no movie or any place else to go around here, except for the drive-in at Ravenal, 30 miles away," he pointed out. "If we could get some good films, we should be able to attract a sizable number of customers if our price is right, even here in Preston County."

Committees were formed and work schedules were set up. An ex-corporation president worked alongside an electronic engineer and the retired editor of a national womens' magazine, with mops, paint brushes, and hammers. There was no lack of expertise; one member designed the lobby, while another experienced retail chain executive set up the concessions. The film committee, chaired by an ex-theater owner, contacted a distributor and arranged to rent second- and third-run films at prices that would bring the estimated total cost per showing to about $50–75. The house committee found that the screen was in much poorer condition than was apparent on first inspection and needed to be replaced. Projection equipment was also needed and the cost for both these items was estimated at about $5,500. While the association's treasury could cover most of the renovation costs, $5,500 was far beyond its capabilities, so the committee asked the board of directors to launch a fund drive to buy the screen and equipment. The full amount was subscribed in only a few weeks, and a date was set for the opening ceremony, in April 1984. The following is a quotation from the association's May newsletter:

The opening day ceremony was a whopping success. We were all delighted at the number of dignitaries and other well-known personalities from Charlotte, Durham, and Winston-Salem who were there, not to mention our Senator who came all the way from Washington. The unexpected television and newspaper coverage certainly helped to put Sutterville and Preston County on the map. All this is a gratifying tribute to those who put so much work into the project.

Our new pair of 16mm projectors worked perfectly, having been checked over and over by Mary and Paul Steinberg. (They just *knew* something would go wrong.) The 12 by 16 foot screen gave us an excellent picture and the stereo sound system, donated by Grant Haskell, was ready to go about the same time the paint dried in the lobby. But the popcorn was hot and buttery and the whole theater shone like a new penny.

Altogether, our audiences have been cooperative and enthusiastic during our "shakedown" period while we try to get everything working in unison. Our projector operators have learned quickly and we hope to continue to play to the large groups we have had during our first month.

If we are to make a success of our venture, we need your help in getting the word around. As you know, we are able to rent such high-quality films at low prices because we are a non-profit group and because we agree not to advertise or otherwise compete with commercial theaters. So we cannot use radio, TV, or print media. But we must let our audience know what movies we will show, and when. We can get "publicity" announcements in the *Preston Weekly Banner* and on local radio stations, but we cannot include the names of the films. So we need to have everyone "Talk it up" wherever you go.

We thank all those who helped, and we appreciate the active and constant support of the Association Board.

THE THEATER IN OPERATION

As the season progressed into summer, attendance remained high, and the association was able to sell a number of season tickets for 12 performances, mostly to its own members. Initially, Sheila McBride, head of the theater committee, noticed quite a few local residents (as distinguished from the "newcomers") at the showings. May and June continued to be successful, although the number of "locals" declined and association members and their friends made up most of the audiences. At the end of the series, however, the Olde Odeon showed a respectable profit of nearly $1,000. Exhibit 2-1 shows the attendance and selected financial data for the 1984 spring season.

Sheila and all those involved in the Odeon were quite pleased with the results of their labors. But the problem of attracting more local customers still needed some work. So in her planning for the fall and spring series, she decided to target the younger group in the county—those who might want films with more action, and who would be most likely to travel some distance to an out-of-town drive-in theater. She also faced other problems, not the smallest of which was the growing shortage of volunteers to staff the performances. At least three were needed to sell tickets, run the concession stand, and clean up afterward. And they were needed on weekend evenings when many people had other things to do.

The fall series started off quite well, probably because of the widespread publicity the Olde Odeon received in several mid-state cities as a result of publicity releases (and influence) from a former editor of Raleigh's major newspaper. Although a few of the younger local group came initially, their numbers soon tapered off. One high school senior and his date were surprised to find her grandparents in the seats behind them during one performance. "That sure wouldn't happen at the Ravenal drive-in," he sheepishly remarked later.

As the series went on, overall attendance was spotty and it became increasingly difficult to show a reasonable profit. This was an important consideration because the association's objectives in opening the theater were not only to provide a local entertainment center, but also to generate profits that could be used for other community projects such as the health clinic and the library. This season, the Odeon was not doing very well. Exhibit 2-2 shows data for the 1984–85 series.

Sheila was concerned about overcoming these difficulties when she began planning the fall season in August 1985. She had tried a number of different strategies, none of which had done much to increase the local attendance, and she was hampered by the restriction on any advertising that mentioned the film names. It was common practice for distributors to rent films to nonprofit organizations for fund-raising purposes, but there could be no direct advertising of film names and dates so as not to compete with regular theaters who paid much higher rental fees. Nonetheless, she was still enthusiastic about the theater and was ready to plead with the board to approve it for yet another year. Her only hope was that Bat Weaver would have enough support to force that decision.

THE BOARD'S DECISION

At the board meeting, the debate finally dwindled down. Bat Weaver rose and said:

> I tend to agree with most of what has been said. But there has to be something more involved in this attendance pattern than we have been able to find up to now. Maybe there is something else we can do. Maybe not. But I'd like to make a suggestion. I've been talking with Eric Swenson who just moved here from Charlotte where he had an ad agency and market research business for twenty-five years. He can't put his finger on the problem either, but he agreed to run a small research project on his own that should suggest what we should do. He says he can do this by early October, so why don't we go ahead and start the fall series. If Eric then suggests we fold, we can vote on that. If he suggests we try another strategy or other tactics, we can vote on that. I put this in the form of a motion to the Board.

The motion was seconded and was approved by a majority vote.

ERIC SWENSON

In the year since he and his family had moved to Preston County, Eric Swenson had been intrigued with the wide gulf that separated the long-time residents from the newcomers. So his first task was to collect basic demographic data to see what changes had occurred in the county in the past 10 to 20 years. Also, he wanted to get an idea of the characteristics of the area and of the people in it. The information he collected is shown in Exhibit 2-3. In addition, with the help of several long-time residents, he was able to get information on the entertainment habits and attitudes of their friends and relatives toward the Olde Odeon. This was done in casual conversations rather than by formal interviews, so he had to get the information second hand. The results are shown in Exhibit 2-4.

While he knew that this research was neither extensive nor exhaustive, he believed it gave him a clear picture of the consumers in the target market the Olde Odeon wanted to attract. Although he had lived in Preston County a relatively short time, he fully realized how important it was to the "new" residents that the Olde Odeon remain in business and show some profit. So he was ready to make suggestions to the board at its next meeting.

Analysis Questions

1. From case information, and in terms of goals and needs, why did Eric Swenson believe the continued operation was so important to the new Preston County residents?

2. In general, would you think the selection of films should appeal to most of the "old" residents as well as the "new" ones? Why?

3. Has the Olde Odeon been reasonably successful in its objective? Support your answer with case information and data.

4. What should the board recommend?

THE OLDE ODEON THEATER

EXHIBIT 2-1

Theater Attractions, Revenue, and Expenses, Spring 1984

Date	Film	Gate[a]	Receipts[b]	Expenses	Net	Cumulative
Apr. 9, 10	Arthur	86	$117	$134	($17)	($17)
Apr. 16, 17	Diva	132	246	183	63	46
Apr. 23, 24	Diner	177	289	158	131	177
Apr. 29, 30	Ragtime	87	119	134	(15)	162
May 6, 7	Time Bandits	149	271	134	137	299
May 13, 14	My Favorite Year	163	280	158	122	421
May 20, 21	Atlantic City	76	103	159	(56)	365
May 27, 28	Pippin	63	94	108	(14)	351
June 3, 4	Reds	152	285	159	126	477
June 10, 11	Limelight	184	318	74	244	721
June 17, 18	Gallipoli	119	167	134	33	754
June 24, 25	Last Metro	54	87	105	(18)	772
July 1, 2, 4	Days of Heaven	221	361	158	203	975

Net Income: $975

[a] Gate includes number of box office sales, number of prorated season tickets, and number of complimentaries.
[b] Receipts include amount of box office sales, amount of prorated season tickets, and concession sales.

THE OLDE ODEON THEATER

EXHIBIT 2-2

Theater Attractions, Revenue, and Expenses, 1984–85 Series

Date	Film	Gate[a]	Receipts[b]	Expenses	Net	Cumulative
Fall Series 1984						
Sep. 29, 30	Tender Mercies	191	$335	$130	$205	$205
Oct. 6, 7	Year of Living Dangerously	153	297	158	139	344
Oct. 13, 14	Last Metro	204	377	183	194	538
Oct. 20, 21	Local Hero	157	288	130	158	696
Oct. 27, 28	Four Seasons	137	231	112	119	815
Nov. 3, 4	Gallipoli	142	244	184	60	875
Nov. 10, 11	King of Hearts (incl. matinee)	223	315	158	157	1032
Nov. 17, 18	Night of Shooting	131	196	183	13	1045
Nov. 24, 25	Say Amen	112	153	208	(55)	990
Dec. 1, 2	Gandhi	149	231	197	34	1024
Dec. 8, 9	Bingo Long	99	128	130	(2)	1022
Dec. 15, 16	Days of Heaven	87	112	159	(47)	975

Spring Series 1985 (though April)

Feb. 2, 3	*Bro Sun*	111	$163	$178	($15)	$960
Feb. 9, 10	*Missing*	94	128	191	(63)	897
Feb. 16, 17	*Chariots of Fire*	214	297	273	24	921
Feb. 23, 24	*Sting*	83	102	110	(8)	913
Mar 2, 3	*Mao To Mozart*	115	168	228	(60)	853
Mar 9, 10	*Tess of the D'Urbervilles*	110	159	145	14	867
Mar 16, 17	*Muppets*	76	110	80	30	897
Mar 23, 24	*Honey Rose*	45	62	56	6	903
Mar 30, 31	*Jimmy's Hand*	57	77	110	(33)	870
Apr 6, 7	*Breaker*	151	228	249	(21)	849
Apr 13, 14	*Das Boot*	137	203	259	(56)	793
Apr 20, 21	*Graduate*	62	97	93	(4)	789
Apr 27, 28	*Sophie's Choice*	121	184	177	(7)	896

[a] *Gate* includes number of box office sales, number of prorated season tickets, and number of complimentaries.
[b] *Receipts* include amount of box office sales, amount of prorated season tickets, and concession sales.

THE OLDE ODEON THEATER

EXHIBIT 2-3

Demographic Data for Preston County

Age Distribution *(1983)*		Income Distribution *(1983)*	
Under 5	361	Total households	2,250
5–14	1,005	Under $5,000	353
15–24	1,053	$5,000–9,999	418
25–34	1,072	$10,000–19,999	661
35–44	881	$20,000–24,999	254
45–54	925	$25,000–34,999	260
55–64	765	$35,000–49,999	127
65+	853	$50,000+	177
Median Age: 32			

Population		Workers Commuting Outside County	
1960	5,587	1960	590
1970	5,289	1970	746
1983	6,250	1980	1,100
Percent change 1970–83: 10.6%		Percent of population 1980: 50.1%	

Employment *(1982)*		Retail Sales *(in millions)*	
Total labor force	2,502	1975	$4.7
Number unemployed	264	1977	5.5
Unemployment rate: 10.6%		1979	6.5
		1980	6.8
		1983	8.2

EXHIBIT 2-3 (*Cont'd.*)

Type of Employment		Commercial Bank Deposits (in millions)	
Manufacturing	489	1975	$7.6
Construction	431	1977	9.1
Wholesale and retail	354	1979	10.6
Service	745	1980	11.4
		1983	12.9

Housing Values		School Enrollment	
Median owner value	$47,100	1977–78	1,207
Median rent	222	1979–80	1,175
		1981–82	1,135
		1982–83	1,071

Total Housing Units		Crimes Committed	
1970	2,024	1977	105
1980	2,704	1978	88
Percent change: 33.6%		1979	76
		1980	103
		1983	70

Residential Building Permits Authorized		Sources County Revenue		
			Amount	Percent
1981	52			
1982	37	Local	$1,096,126	41.4
1983	30	State	1,175,602	44.3
Percent change 1982–83: -42.3%		Federal	384,344	14.4

Net Migration	
1960–70	−473
1970–80	+807

THE OLDE ODEON THEATER

EXHIBIT 2-4

Interview Information from Preston County Residents Obtained by Mr. Swenson

Note: Mr. Swenson gave a list of six questions to seven local residents who agreed to bring the questions up in conversations with friends and relatives when they could, and to keep a record of the replies or expressed feelings of each person. While Mr. Swenson believed that the general trends shown by the replies are reliable, he recognized that there were likely to be some errors in recording and interpreting the information by the interviewers.

		Age Group		
$n = 38$	16–24	25–34	35–44	45+

1. About how often do you go to the movies?

	16–24	25–34	35–44	45+
More than once a month	3	4	1	0
About once a month	5	4	6	1
Four or five times a year	1	2	2	4
Once or twice a year	0	0	0	1
Very seldom or not at all	0	2	1	1

2. Where do you usually go?

	16–24	25–34	35–44	45+
Ravenal Drive-In	7	8	5	1
Randal Twin Cinema	2 (7)	1 (6)	2 (4)	4 (1)
Raleigh or Charlotte	0	2 (2)	3 (1)	2
Other	0	1	0	0

(*Note:* Parentheses are winter choices of drive-in patrons)

3. Have you ever heard of the Olde Odeon?

	16–24	25–34	35–44	45+
Yes	7	10	7	2
No	2	2	3	5

If you know it, have you ever gone?

	16–24	25–34	35–44	45+
Yes	6	8	5	2
No	1	2	2	0

If you went, would you go again?

	16–24	25–34	35–44	45+
Yes	1	3	3	2
No	5	5	2	0

4. When you do go to a movie, how important is the movie itself?

	16–24	25–34	35–44	45+
The movie is the main reason I go	2	5	7	6
I go just to go someplace	2	1	0	1
The drive-in is most important	5	6	0	0

5. Those who said they would not go to Olde Odeon again were asked, Why not? These are representative replies:

a. We'd rather go where there is something to do afterward.
b. I'd rather go to a bigger theater.
c. I don't want to go with my date where people know me.
d. We'd rather be by ourselves at a drive-in.
e. The kids like the drive-in.
f. We don't feel comfortable at the Odeon with kids.
g. We like to go to Randall or Ravenal for something different.
h. A lot of older people go to the Odeon.
i. It's hard to find out what's playing there.

Case 3

Nike, Inc.

The relatively short but meteoric history of Nike, Inc., is symbolized by the vapor-trail simulation of its own distinctive "swoosh" logo. The firm was started in the early 1970s by a former University of Oregon runner, Philip H. Knight. He and a bevy of former athletes guided Nike's growth from a small importer of athletic shoes in 1972 to a major manufacturer with a spectacular $900 million in sales for the fiscal year ended in August 1984. Meanwhile the Nike shoe had not only become the largest-selling running shoe in the United States, but it had dislodged Adidas as the status brand. Now, the firm is embarked on a campaign to outperform that $2 billion rival company in the international market as well. It was an unusual management team that orchestrated Nike's success and seized opportunities offered by the zeal with which U.S. consumers adopted fitness activities. Many company team members were also former members or associates of the University of Oregon's track and field teams, including founder Knight, former president Robert Woodell, and deputy chairman Bill Bowerman. Together, they not only brought a wealth of running expertise to Nike but they also had an uncanny knack of successfully riding the country's cultural currents.

CULTURAL CONDITIONS
AND PROMOTION STRATEGY

If the United States hadn't undergone the health and fitness craze of the 1970s, Nike might have jogged along itself, selling to a small market of serious runners. But not even the wildest visionaries could have predicted how all-encompassing the fitness pastime would become. By the mid-1970s, Nike shoes had become a major part of the official uniform of the "Me Generation," and around-the-block runners bought them by the millions. Even nonrunners sported Nikes as an effortless way to partake in the mystique of running.

Nike's initial product, running shoes, fit naturally into the succession from the self-infatuation syndrome to the immersion in health foods and physical fitness activities. Advertising was directed to the solitary runner, the "detached" personality, the self-involved spirit that transcends the stifling bonds of society. One such ad, shown in Exhibit 3-1, depicts three runners on a muddy track with the caption:

THE RACE IS ITS OWN REWARD

There was a time when people didn't run to collect T shirts.
Or race numbers.
And when the finish line was drawn in the dirt with a stick.
And all the winner collected was a cold beer and a thumbs-up.

In another ad labeled "Man vs. Machine," a radiant woman is running past two creeping lanes of exhaust-laden traffic whose drivers are gray and faceless.

Jogging actually is a highly personal, solitary, ego-building activity closely related to self-concept. What you wear while doing it sends a message to others about it and about you. A status-branded running shoe, for example, says the wearer is physically fit and that his or her mind is on higher things. Named for the Greek goddess of victory, Nike symbolizes the achievement and success that its users pursue. Nike also uses ad captions such as: "Machines have put our bodies out of a job," and "Sooner or later the serious runner goes through a special, very personal, experience unknown to most people. Some call it euphoria, others say it is a new kind of mystical experience." These expansive, cultlike statements appealed to joggers and nonjoggers alike. They also appealed to unruly high school and early college-age adolescents. For them, it captured the essence of their yearnings and rebelliousness. Nike successfully seized the opportunity to exploit this new culture and its new concepts, but did it in a supportive rather than an aggressive way.

To attract attention to its advertising messages and the product, Nike also concentrated on the use of big-name athletes. John McEnroe, according to a *Fortune* article, can command up to $100,000 a year by just lacing up a pair of Nikes. *Advertising Age* reports that Michael Jordan, star of the Chicago Bulls, was offered $2.5 million to wear Nikes for five years. The firm also solidified its position in the industry by asking athletes to help design shoes and it signed large numbers of professionals to exclusive promotional contracts. While payments cannot be made to amateur athletes, Nike donates shoes and other equipment to them and their organizations, all clearly featuring the famous vapor-trail logo. Nearly 75 percent of the firm's advertising and promotion budget goes for this type of sales promotion.

Early on, Nike firmly allied itself with amateur athletics, and with the Olympics in particular, by sponsoring Athletics West. This supportive and training operation was the first large-scale corporate program to train potential U.S. Olympic participants. Of the 90 U.S. World Track and Field participants at Helsinki in 1983, 22 were from Athletics West. Athletics West sees itself as a free enterprise alternative to the Eastern bloc regimented programs, and Nike makes a contribution of as much as $2 million a year to it. Athletes get stipends, but only for their roles as Nike endorsers. Younger athletes who are brought in for their potential receive a few hundred dollars a month and part-time jobs. Leaders in their sport, however, often get contracts that run into six figures. The close ties between Nike and the participants in Athletics West, in themselves, provide an aura of confidence in the products the firm sells. Nike's help to athletes is also demonstrated in its advertising, and one such ad offering posters is shown in Exhibit 3-2.

SALES HISTORY

Nike's phenomenal sales success is illustrated in Exhibit 3-3, which shows the sales and net income for the company since 1976. A plunge in profits for the bellwether summer quarter in 1984, and in 1985, resulted in part from the 1982 peaking and subsequent leveling off of the jogging fad. A Gallup poll in 1981 estimated that the number of joggers would stay at about 20 million and that there would be little, if any, real growth. A major adjustment in the market was a foregone conclusion. Richard Benyo, editor of *Runner's World*, estimated in 1981 that if jogging continued to increase at the rate it had since the fad began, everyone in the country would be running by 1985. Largely because of this situation, many shoe producers found themselves with surplus capacity and the market shares of marginal brands fell drastically. In 1983, Nike's shoe inventories soared to 22 million pairs, forcing it to take $27 million in write-offs through 1984. The stockpile has since been cut to 15 million against a goal of 12 million. This and other problems have affected the value of Nike's stock. The shares were first offered publicly in December 1980 at $22, and climbed to $43 in the latter part of 1982. By December 1984, however, a share was quoted at $8, but rose to $17 by June 1986.

PRODUCT STRATEGY

Spurred by the success of its uniquely designed running shoe in the early 1970s, Nike moved rapidly into basketball, tennis, and other shoes used in court sports. As sales grew, Nike moved its production from Japan to South

Korea and Taiwan, where costs were considerably lower. This move enabled the firm to introduce a moderately priced line of shoes that quickly became a status product for the teen-aged market, and an intermediate line that provided trading-up steps for novice runners.

In 1978, the company began diversifying into babies' and children's shoes, in an attempt to imitate the appeal its products had in the adult market. Brand-conscious parents bought the status shoes for their youngsters as extensions of their own self-concepts. Nike's move in 1980 to introduce a line of sports apparel aimed at lower middle-class consumers (instead of their usual target of youthful but upscale income-education buyers) lasted only six months before it was replaced by a new look trading on Nike's image. In 1984, apparel accounted for 21 percent of Nike's U.S. revenues.

With the same type of image extension in its expanded family brand strategy, the company also ventured into nonathletic leisure and work shoes, to complement the apparel line. It then moved belatedly and unsuccessfully into a special shoe for aerobics addicts.

FOREIGN EXPANSION

In 1980, after less than ten years on the market, Nike had edged out the perennial U.S. running shoe sales leader, Adidas, a feat few thought possible given Adidas's strong brand position. With this unpredicted success, Nike moved into the European and Japanese markets in 1981 with the hope of using the international arena to continue the growth that was fizzling at home. Using the strategy that brought success in the United States, the firm hoped to command the same attention among serious runners in Europe. But jogging did not become a fad there, as it had in the United States, and other shoe producers have switched to soccer, tennis, and basketball shoes to increase foreign sales. As one British observer put it, "The English don't have the mad ambitious striving—the questing Puritan fanaticism—that it takes to make a whole country run. It's really a religion, this quest for self-perfection. People don't have it here or in the rest of Europe, and without it, the Nike mystique loses force."

In contrast to European markets, in Japan, Nike and other U.S. sports producers benefited from a strong association with major U.S. sports, and the quality image of U.S. products. Also, Japanese competitive firms are smaller and are probably less of a threat than Adidas was in Europe. When the footwear line was introduced in Japan in late 1981, sales of Nikes accounted for over $11 million by May, a much stronger performance than in Europe.

The apparel line has not helped much to continue Nike's growth pattern. The line was introduced overseas in 1982, and while it produced 21 percent of Nike's U.S. revenues in the August 1984 quarter, foreign sales were a disappointing 18 percent of those revenues. The company has also been trying to find a position for its products in Asia, Africa, and Latin America. But in these locations these products are just items of clothing emblazoned with the Nike name. They have no magic, no unique self-concept qualities, and no association with being "different," innovative, and young.

FUTURE STRATEGY

Although many Americans have diversified their fitness programs, Nike executives believe that the market will continue to be strong. Nike's future strategy will include a sharpening of its identity following an image that has been somewhat downgraded by its use on a proliferation of apparel and shoe products. Exhibit 3-4 follows this philosophy. The "swoosh" label will be less of a widespread family brand and more of a quality or status symbol.

Although large numbers of people continue to jog through neighborhoods, others are joining physical fitness centers where they run a few laps around the track before heading for indoor tennis or racquetball courts. Heeding this recent tendency toward diversification of fitness programs, Nike will promote itself as a total fitness company. Deemphasizing its wide line of shoes, it plans to cut the number of Nike shoe models by 30 percent, and its recent acquisition of a maker of home lifting and other equipment will help it diversify.

But the company hopes to increase the contribution of foreign sales to total sales from the present 16 percent to 20 percent during the next year, and it will continue its use of major athletic figures to promote its products. The question is whether or not the attributes that skyrocketed Nike to first place in the U.S. market are those that are needed to compete on a three-front market that includes Europe, Japan, and the United States. Clever management and the ability to take advantage of U.S. cultural trends were the hallmark of Nike in the 1970s, but both new strategists and new strategies may be needed to map international attacks. It is unlikely that Adidas will be as vulnerable on its own turf as it was in the United States. One Adidas executive remarked, "Nike should know that the marketing strategies that led to success in the U.S. will not necessarily work in Europe."

Recent shake-ups in top management suggest that Knight is aware that different approaches are needed. In 1982, he hired Neil Goldsmith, former secretary of transportation in the Carter administration, as vice president for international marketing. Another Oregon alumnus, Goldsmith had little experience in the athletic shoe business and was shifted to the Canadian market in 1984. In another shuffle, Knight took back the company presidency from Robert Woodell in September 1984. It may be that these moves reflect an attempt to place more seasoned business executives in key positions, in response to Nike's flagging success in both domestic and international markets.

The following quotations from Nike's 1985 annual report indicate some of the recent problems, yet reaffirm the corporate image of dedication to higher goals:

> For Nike, 1985 was indeed a year of corporate transition. Many of the changes experienced this year were associated with overwhelming success in new products and market techniques. Other changes, however, led to significant inventory problems and Nike's first ever quarterly losses. . . . The reexamination by management of Nike's corporate identity, of its strategy, and long-term plans reaffirmed the values upon which Nike has built its tremendous success. The same reexamination has also provided the catalyst for meaningful internal change. . . . Now, more than ever, Nike is sports, Nike is also fitness. Nike's focus has been and continues to be athletes.

Analysis Questions

1. Were Nike's earlier running shoes innovative products? What was the primary reason for the firm's phenomenal success?

2. How did the motivating influences of social theory and self-concept operate in Nike's market? What influence did culture have?

3. What communication processes did Nike rely on to spread the word about its products?

4. Why has Nike had difficulty in using in other countries the concepts and techniques that brought it success in the United States?

Source: Photo courtesy of Nike, Inc.

NIKE, INC.

EXHIBIT 3-2

A. Roadrunning, Deschutes River, Oregon.

B. "Battle of Atlanta," the Peachtree 1978.

C. Rono.

D. Finish, N.Y.C. Marathon 1978.

BUY A POSTER. HELP AN ATHLETE.

You can have any of these big, (22"x36") full-color posters for only $2.50 apiece.

They're made from pictures of real athletes caught in the act of being themselves.

And the money goes for a good cause. We're donating the profits to the people and organizations that will best serve the interest of giving equal treatment for women athletes in the Olympics.

Simply put, we want to help convince the IOC to allow women to run the 3K, 5K, 10K, and marathon in the Olympic games.

The money will only be given to those dedicated to the runner's cause. It will be used wisely for athlete travel to some of the key foreign countries that remain unconvinced. For speaking tours and anything else that's necessary to persuade the IOC to give fair treatment to women.

We're putting up $5000 right away, and will donate any profits from the sale of these posters beyond this amount.

Send for one or more of these posters, and join our Operation Bootstrap: Athletes helping athletes.

If you don't help, who will? **NIKE**

Dear Nike:
    Please send the poster(s) I've checked below. I've enclosed my check or money order in the amount of $_____ ($2.50 per poster).

☐ A.
☐ B.
☐ C.
☐ D.

Name_____

Address_____

City_____

State_____ Zip_____

Mail to Posters/Blue Ribbon Sports, 8285 S.W. Nimbus Ave., Suite 115, Beaverton, Oregon 97005

Source: Photo courtesy of Nike, Inc.

NIKE, INC.

EXHIBIT 3-3

Sales and Net Income for Selected Years, 1976 to 1985 (in millions)

Year	Sales	Net Income
1976	$ 14.1	N/A
1977	28.0	N/A
1981	457.0	$25.9
1982	694.0	49.0
1983	867.0	57.0
1984	920.0	40.7
1985	946.0	10.2

A MATTER OF CONSCIENCE.

The day running became big business it started down a questionable, but predictable path.

We can't go along.

Maybe it's because we remember how it all began. We don't feel comfortable with mass marketing. We bristle at the idea all runners are created equal, and all shoes should be made to a single standard.

Then judged.

Because the more we learn – in the laboratory, in working with podiatrists, orthopedists, in studies of biomechanics – the less we see of this so-called "average" runner.

And the more we appreciate the different foot types, gait patterns, body weights, speeds and training schedules.

If success brought us to this crossroads, it has only strengthened our commitment.

Nike is introducing a complete new line of performance shoes. With models for every kind of athlete, every kind of foot, every kind of regimen. And we're making it easy to choose the right one. Without counting stars, stripes or anything else.

It's not important whether we live up to someone else's expectations.

What's important is whether we can help you live up to yours.

NIKE

Beaverton, Oregon

Source: Photo courtesy of Nike, Inc.

Case 4

Source Perrier

It was nearly six o'clock on a hot summer afternoon in July 1981. Bob and Les Anderson sat in the cool lounge of the Holiday Inn, just off the interstate highway leading to the downtown area of a large southern city. They had stopped for a drink on their way home from work at Anderson Bros. Bottling Co. The brothers were equal partners in the firm founded by their father in 1927, and which they inherited in 1965 upon his death. The company bottled and distributed five brands of soft drinks in the Atlanta area. They had the franchise for a brand of cola (not one of the leaders), and for a leading noncola. They also produced a local brand of club soda, quinine mixer, and a noncarbonated orange drink. As usual in hot weather, demand was heavy and the plant was running two shifts. Exhibit 4-1 shows the proportion of total annual production for each of the five products, together with the plant capacity used during the summer months, for the years from 1976 to 1980.

The Andersons were discussing the normal problems of their business: production scheduling, maintenance of the equipment, and increasing distribution costs. But foremost in their conversation was concern about the decreasing share of the market that their cola brand was getting, due mainly to the promotion and advertising battle between Coca Cola and Pepsi. Since sales of their other brands were fairly stable, the cola drop meant idle capacity, except for the summer months of June through September.

They had talked several times before about looking for another product to take up the slack and to carry them through the slow fall and winter seasons. Although they had followed several leads, they had not been able to find a profitable one. In 1980, they tried a second noncarbonated fruit punch, since they heard through their trade association that consumers were looking for more "natural" products, but it was not well received by the market and was dropped after the end of the season.

A POSSIBLE NEW PRODUCT

Just as Bob reopened the subject, he noticed a waitress passing by with several odd-shaped green bottles on her tray, which she served to a nearby table. Curious, he called her over and asked what the name of that drink was. "Perry-Aye," she replied. "We get a lot of calls for it served with a lemon twist; more all the time." The brothers were familiar with Perrier sparkling water, from radio ads and informational material from the American Bottled Water Association, one of the trade groups they belonged to. It was supposed to be quite popular in the Northeast and on the West Coast, but they had not heard much about it in their area. They seemed to remember that one of their competitors distributed it. Since Anderson Bottling serviced the Holiday Inn, the two men went to see the restaurant manager to find out more about the product and how he was supplied. "We kept getting a lot of requests for it starting a year or two ago and found it was being distributed by Dr Pepper in nearby Denton. I've been getting ten cases every two weeks, and I'm about to increase it to 15. The number of calls for Perrier isn't increasing as fast as it used to, but there are plenty of people who order it regularly, especially our younger customers. I heard a rumor last week, though, that the distributor in Denton is going to stop their service here next month, so I'll have to look for another supplier."

Bob and Les took note of this and decided, on their way to their cars, to look into the possibilities of this product. It would be their first venture into pure distribution, rather than producing the product first, then distributing it. But they had the facilities, the customer list, and the expertise. What they needed to do was find out if it was possible to get a distributorship and on what terms, and to look into the product itself, its producer, and the kind of promotion and growth it was getting. Bob volunteered to do some research on the product and its producer while Les gathered information about the distribution franchise. The following paragraphs contain information gathered by the two brothers.

A UNIQUE PRODUCT

Bob found that, unlike most carbonated soft drinks or mixers such as those Anderson Bros. made, Perrier is not manufactured at all. Instead, according to Perrier officials, "It comes from an underground volcanic spring which supplies some 21,000 gallons of carbonated water per hour, and has done so for nearly 2,000 years." They also point out that since 218 B.C. when Hannibal rested his troops in the small town where Perrier flows, the water has treated the maladies, lifted the spirits, and quenched the thirsts of some 85 generations. Also, Emperor Napoleon III is said to have ordered in 1863 that the spring waters be bottled "for the good of France," and the spring has been under the scrutiny of the French government ever since. His edict appears on each bottle of Perrier water.

Other carbonated water mixes are made by infusing purified or filtered tap water with man-made carbon dioxide. But Perrier is actually bottled at the "source" and the carbonated water in every bottle comes directly from the spring near the village of Vergeze in southern France, whether it is served in Paris, Paraguay, or Peoria.

But, as it is with many simple stories, the process is a little more complicated. Because the solution of carbon dioxide in the water is not consistent day to day, Perrier used to get complaints about too much or too little carbonation. To assure that the gas content is always the same, carbon dioxide is removed from the water at the well head, stored, and reintroduced in precise quantities when the product is actually bottled. Thus, no external ingredients are used and the firm can claim it is bottled in its pure form, at the source. This source, or the spring from which this special water "bubbles up from deep within the earth through porous limestone and cracked marls," may be seen at the imposing mansion built by Sir St. John Harmsworth, a short distance from the bottling plant. Housed in a white gazebo is a small fountain covered by a clear plexiglass half-sphere. The bubbly mineralized water flows from a pipe in the center of the fountain.

The Perrier plant is self-sufficient not only in terms of the supply of sparkling water. It also produces the bottles it needs by using sand from its own mines. With the spring at one end and the sand and bottle production at another, the final result is a filled bottle, ready to be shipped, as shown in the following diagram:

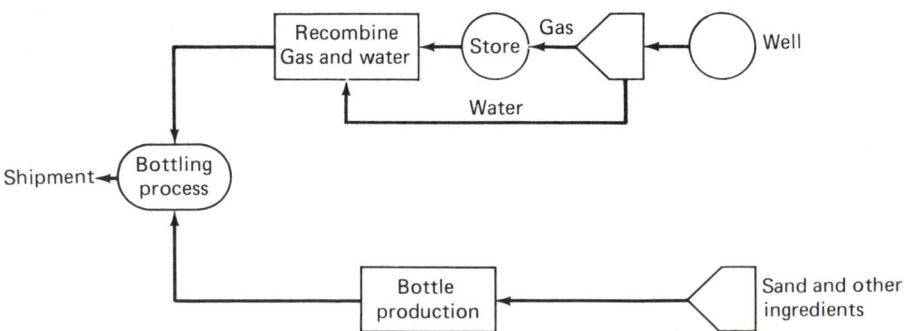

Perrier claims that its natural carbonation produces smaller bubbles, which reduce the "bloated" feeling consumers sometimes get, while man-made carbon dioxide produces much larger gas bubbles. The only naturally carbonated spring water bottled in the United States is Saratoga Mineral Water, which has been sold in relatively small quantities for many years.

HISTORY AND MANAGEMENT

The rights to the famous springs at Vergeze were owned for many years by Britain's Harmsworth family. Sir St. John Harmsworth acquired them in 1903 with proceeds he got from selling his stock in the family business, the London Daily Mail. Source Perrier's present president, Gustave Leven, bought the rights in 1948.

Mr. Leven, now in his late sixties, is not a typical business executive. He believes in a three-day work week for himself and sometimes disappears for a week or two at a time. He has made no provision for a successor in the business, although most of the company executives are in their sixties and seventies. The firm has no real structure at the top and it makes no attempt to do analytical financial accounting. The French business magazine *L'Expansion* reports that "finance man Maurice Epry has the reputation of calculating his sales prices by hand, just as he did in 1947."

In 1954, the firm acquired Contrexville, a French mineral water with a pronounced soda bicarbonate taste. Nevertheless, it is the leading mineral water sold in France. Since 1968, the firm Source Perrier has functioned as a holding company for various subsidiaries. Altogether, it operates some 18 bottling plants and warehouses throughout France. In 1969, the company took over Preval, an ailing French producer of dairy products, placing a severe strain on Perrier's resources through the early 1970s. Perrier also has the franchise to distribute Pepsi Cola and a European product, Gini, in France.

But the erratic Gustave Leven reshaped Perrier into a major worldwide producer and a household word in the United States. Through a series of moves in 1975 and 1976 he rid the company of about 70 percent of its miscellaneous holdings, thereby cutting its losses. From these moves he amassed FF250 million. By adding FF50 million more from Perrier funds, he was able to double the company's bottling capacity to about 2 billion per year. Now, he was ready to enter the potentially lucrative U.S. market.

PERRIER IN THE UNITED STATES

When Leven made overtures to U.S. distributors, they were not very interested in his "Coca Cola without sugar." It was not until he hired Bruce Nevins, fresh from a successful career at Levi Straus, that things began to happen. Nevins was appointed to head Great Waters of France, Inc., Perrier's U.S. subsidiary, with a $2 million advertising budget for the first year. His strategy was to capitalize on the health-conscious baby-boomer market by stressing the natural properties of Perrier; he promoted it as a chic drink with no calories—an alternative to sweet soft drinks and alcoholic beverages.

This part of the strategy set the stage, but the final touch was pricing. While the pre-1976 U.S. price was as much as two dollars a bottle, Nevins cut it to about 69 cents. This move had the effect of maintaining the product's premium niche (still 50 percent or more above the cost of the average soft drink or carbonated water) yet giving it appeal to affluent young adults, or those aspiring to this group. The approach was straightforward: Perrier was to imply status, and this snob appeal was aimed exclusively toward adults. This was an entirely new direction since there had never been an attempt by any brand to segment the soft drink market on a price basis or to tap the adult market to any great extent.

ADVERTISING AND PROMOTION

To market the product, Nevins unleashed a cleverly designed advertising campaign using both print and electronic media. On national television, the lofty tones of Orson Welles proclaimed the "miracle of Perrier." While he narrated the miracle, "In the south of France, near the village of Vergeze, stand gates which guard a single spring . . . blessed with waters of unusual purity and clarity," the sound of gas and bubbling water provided a tantalizing background. Print advertising featured details of how the product is naturally carbonated, how nature protects its purity, and why it is enjoyed for healthful reasons. Appealing to the health- and exercise-oriented market, another ad tells why Perrier is "the natural conclusion to strenuous exercise." Exhibits 4-2, 4-3, and 4-4 are examples of themes that Source Perrier has used in its health and life-style advertising.

There was also a rash of word-of-mouth advertising and society page photographs showing affluent younger adults drinking Perrier on various occasions. It was fashionable to wear Perrier T-shirts and to flaunt Perrier beach towels, proclaiming the owner's membership in a status group. To combat rumors that the product was actually bottled in Brooklyn, Perrier flew a group of journalists to Vergeze to show them that the water was naturally carbonated.

As the publicity hype ebbed, the company embarked on a third campaign to coin an ad "punch line" that would revive interest in the brand. The new campaign, begun in 1981, used historical or literary characters in vignettes related on radio by Orson Welles. In the one using Dracula, Welles tells how the vampire kneels beside a beautiful sleeping woman and lovingly sinks his long teeth into her white throat. This and other stories end with the line that Perrier hoped would become a household phrase: "It is good. But it is not Perrier."

PRODUCTION AND SALES

The sales push in the United States was forced by the need to cover the heavy expense of the new bottling plant that Leven built. Estimates are that the firm must produce and sell at least 800,000 bottles a year of the plant's 2 billion-bottle capacity in order to break even. And sales in the United States are expected to account for a large proportion of this figure. In Perrier's 1978 fiscal year, U.S. revenue was nearly $30 million, up from under $1 million two years earlier. About 180,000 bottles were bought in the United States in 1978, and the number grew to over 300,000 by 1979, or about 27 percent of Perrier's total sales. Although the company predicted a rise to over 500,000 in 1980, and 800,000 in 1981, actual results in 1980 showed no increase from 1979, and there was only a slight increase in 1981.

To offset the failure to meet predictions in the United States, Perrier used advertising blitzes in Britain and Germany. These campaigns brought nearly a 60 percent increase in British sales, with totals climbing to 12 million bottles. In Germany, where the heavy advertising was steered by the Benton and Bowles agency, annual sales are also expected to reach about 12 million. Bob was told that Perrier planned to test market the product in Italy and Spain in 1982. If the U.S. sales held at over 300,000, and French sales stayed at their normal level of about 400,000, Perrier would easily reach their break-even point. Financial data for the company, which include all of Perrier's products, are shown in Exhibit 4-5.

COMPETITION

In addition to the naturally carbonated Saratoga Water mentioned earlier, a number of artificially carbonated products began appearing on the market in the mid- to late 1970s. Among these was Premier, which was introduced in Chicago in November 1978 by Hinckley & Schmitt, a long-time bottler of still (non-carbonated) spring water. Premier was simply a carbonated form of the regular product, and was marketed with the slogan, "Let your guests *think* it's imported." Nestle's Deer Park division also began selling its Sparkling 100% Spring Water in New York in the fall of 1987. At the same time, Cadbury Schweppes test marketed its Schweppervescence carbonated mineral spring water in California. While this was a new product to the United States, it had been sold internationally for many years.

There are also many still bottled waters produced in Europe that are acclaimed by experts. Among these are French Evian, Italian Fiuggi, and Belgian Spa. Interestingly, in a test of sparkling waters conducted by *Savor* magazine, Perrier was placed third after Ramiosa, an obscure Swedish product, and the famous German Appolinaris.

DISTRIBUTION FRANCHISE CONSIDERATIONS

While Bob was gathering information about the company's product and history, Les contacted Great Waters of France, Inc., in New York to inquire about the availability of the distribution franchise in their area, and the terms under which it might be granted. He was told that the Denton distributor could no longer serve Anderson's area because of a recent change in Great Waters' retail strategy for Perrier. The product had been sold mainly through specialty gourmet shops, which accounted for about 60 percent of the sales. Now, distribution was being shifted to supermarkets and convenience stores, which are expected to account for 70 percent of the sales in the near future. By the next year, Great Waters planned to have the product available in two-thirds of the U.S. market.

There were a number of requirements that Anderson Bros. would have to meet, or agree to, to get the franchise. There was a basic payment and a minimum guaranteed monthly sales quota of 10,000 bottles—a modest amount by Anderson's standards. But Perrier was not yet volume competition for the better-known soft drinks or mixers, so meeting this requirement might be a problem. Perrier's price would provide a higher margin than that provided by Anderson's other products and the new product would be delivered to the same customers that were already served by the company route sales-delivery people. The Great Waters representative told Bob that the move to supermarkets would be accompanied by an advertising and promotion campaign, primarily the new Orson Welles radio spots.

Bob Anderson also made inquiries at the soft drink trade association and at a leading securities brokerage house that had a beverage industry analyst. Their comments were as follows:

> *Soft Drink Association Executives*: "I doubt that the natural craze will drive people to forsake Pepsi for Perrier." "I doubt whether the American palate is trained to enjoy carbonated spring water."
> *Beverage Industry Analyst*: "It [Perrier] may occasionally take the place of an alcoholic or a soft drink but probably not too often." "Will a sparkling water really replace a cola or a lemon-lime drink?"

During Bob's inquiries, he heard about two new products that also provided alternatives to regular soft drinks and alcoholic beverages. At that time, they were sold only in some local areas, but trade association analysts believed that they would move into the national market within the next year or two. One was the "natural soda"—a type of fizzy punch made from sparkling water and fruit juices. It was expected to appeal to the health and exercise set—the same group that Perrier was targeting. On the other hand, Bob heard rumors that Perrier would introduce lemon and lime flavors to its natural water before long. The second alternative was the wine cooler, a mixture of lightly carbonated wine and fruit juices. It had the advantage of being able to project an image of a light drink, one that contains less alcohol than wine, yet gives some of the effect, and at the same time is a taller drink, more refreshing.

After reviewing all the information they had available, they met with Great Waters' regional representative, Bob Rand. He told them that another bottler in their area was also interested in the Perrier franchise and if they wanted it they must make their decision within the next three days. That evening, the brothers got together at Les's house. "Well, Bob," he said, "considering our needs for a product that has long-term possibilities, and what the franchise offers, what do you think we ought to do?"

Analysis Questions

1. What do the three Perrier advertisements in the case tell you about Perrier sparkling water?

2. Why has Perrier become so popular in the United States, when it sells at a price far above that of ordinary carbonated waters?

3. Will the move to supermarkets and other mass outlets affect the upscale image of Perrier?

4. What should the Anderson brothers do?

SOURCE PERRIER

EXHIBIT 4-1

Proportional Product Sales and Summer Plant Capacity Used

Description	1976	1977	1978	1979	1980
% of Capacity Used (summer months)	94%	92.5%	91.1%	88.7%	88.0%
% Sales by Product					
Cola	53.0%	50.3%	47.2%	44.8%	42.6%
Non-Cola	19.5%	20.4%	21.9%	23.7%	23.4%
Club Soda	12.3%	12.9%	13.2%	12.8%	13.6%
Quinine Mixer	9.4%	9.6%	10.4%	10.8%	11.5%
Orange Soda	5.8%	6.8%	7.3%	7.9%	8.9%

EARTH'S FIRST SOFT DRINK.

When the earth was new, mountains rose and valleys were carved and there was created, in what is now called France, a spring that is now called Perrier.®

All the Perrier in the world is born in that spring.

Still clear, pure and sparkling, and minus all those additives that civilization has invented. There's no sugar. No artificial sweetener. No calories. There's no caffeine, no coloring. And Perrier is recommended for salt-free diets, as well.

In modern times, when most beverages are made with water that's been disinfected, softened, oxidated or chlorinated, it's nice also to know that Perrier is naturally filtered as it rises to the surface from its deep underground source.

And so our only concession to civilization is the green Perrier bottle. Because without it, you would never get to enjoy Perrier.

Perrier. Earth's first soft drink.™ Not manufactured, but created by the earth when it was new.

© 1982 Great Waters of France, Inc.

Source: Courtesy of Perrier/Great Waters of France, Inc.

BEFORE MAN HAD HYPERTENSION, HE HAD SALT-FREE PERRIER.

In the good old days there was lots to be tense about. The Ice Age was coming. You might be run over by a mammoth. Your cave might cave in on you. But no one suffered from high blood pressure.

Why? First, because you could work out all your anxieties by pounding rocks, chewing animal skins and running around a lot in the fresh air.

Second, because the salt-shaker had yet to be invented.

If you were really lucky, you lived near the Perrier spring, somewhere in the south of France. Because that sparkling fresh and salt-free refreshment was just the thing after a hard day's hunt. It was earth's first soft drink.

Today, civilization has introduced such amenities as canned soup, pickles, soy sauce and high anxiety. The combination of all these might very well have led to modern hypertension and all kinds of civilized problems.

But down through the ages, Perrier has kept its innocence, freshness and happy taste. And best of all, Perrier is still naturally salt-free.

Perrier. Earth's First Soft Drink.

Source: Courtesy of Perrier/Great Waters of France, Inc.

218 B.C.
HANNIBAL HAS ONE FOR THE ROAD.

Hannibal was one smart Carthaginian general. Smart enough to know you don't get tipsy when you have to drive an elephant across the Alps.

Before embarking on that trip, legend has it, Hannibal threw a rousing party in Gaul—now known as France. And toasted himself and his troops with copious drafts of the local sparkling mineral water—now known as Perrier.® The rest is history.

Many empires have declined and fallen since. But man still celebrates. And if man is smart, the beverage of choice is still Perrier. Especially before he gets behind the wheel.

In some respects, life is more exciting now than in Roman times. We still have the very same salt-free, calorie-free Perrier that Hannibal used when he wished himself *bon voyage*. But we also have Perrier With A Twist. Of lemon. Or orange. Or lime.

So if you're crossing an Alp over the holidays, or only crossing town, make sure your one-for-the-road is Perrier.   © 1985 Great Waters of France, Inc.

EARTH'S FIRST SOFT DRINK.
BOTTLED IN VERGÈZE, FRANCE. WHERE IT WAS BORN.

Source: Courtesy of Perrier/Great Waters of France, Inc.

SOURCE PERRIER

EXHIBIT 4-5

Consolidated Income Statements for Selected Years (in 1,000 French Francs)

	1977	1978	1979	1981	1982	1983
					(PROJ)	(EST)
Sales, net	912,252	1,419,737	1,804,150	2,433,757	2,841,173	3,483,596
Other Revenue	123,068	151,525	233,432	175,832	191,914	192,704
Total Revenue	1,035,320	1,571,262	2,037,582	2,609,589	3,033,087	3,676,300
Mat'l & Supp.	310,946	481,515	535,264	738,816	863,592	1,180,462
Salaries and Wages	352,465	473,222	605,281	743,387	865,180	981,599
Other Expense	342,247	582,945	825,079	1,046,917	1,185,523	1,337,477
Net Income	29,662	33,550	71,958	80,472	118,792	176,762

Case 5

Dollars and Scents: The Fragrance Industry

Leslie Saunders was vice president for corporate and consumer relations at a medium-sized Chicago bank. As a successful single young career woman, she was highly conscious of her personal appearance, not only because looking well was part of her self-concept, but because her job required her to attend a number of business and social functions.

Early in her career with the bank, she had worked with L'Endanger Laboratories, a small, but growing, cosmetics and perfume producer. The firm has been a continuing loan customer with her bank as it expanded over the years, and it repaid its obligations on time. More recently, L'Endanger had applied for another loan to finance its further expansion. The perfume part of the business captured Leslie's interest and she began reading as much about it as she could find in local libraries. She also took the time to read the loan application from the cosmetics firm, and the information the bank had collected that related to it. While the bank analyst's opinion was generally favorable, he pointed out several risks and recommended that only part of the loan request be approved.

One of the projects the loan was to help finance was a new perfume called Sextette. This product was to be positioned with the recently marketed "communicative scents". Although L'Endanger's management thought the product had considerable potential, the bank analyst considered it to be risky. Leslie agreed intuitively with L'Endanger's management, so she investigated a similar product on the market called Muskone Ph5.

In the early 1980s, a British firm introduced a new product called Muskone Ph5. Although it sounds like a cross between a mosquito repellent and a soil tester, it is a perfume. What makes it different from other scents is that it contains pheromones, a chemical that prompts a kind of sexual response in animals and could possibly produce the same effect in humans. This is one example of "communicative scents," a concept now being actively investigated by the fragrance industry.

The information that Leslie gathered intrigued her even more, and she seriously considered offering to loan L'Endanger a portion of the amount that the bank had refused to approve. At that time, she was selling her downtown apartment at a substantial sum and she had decided to invest the money where the risk and return were both high. Even the name of this firm, L'Endanger, seemed to suggest those criteria. Before making a decision, however, she reviewed some of the things she learned from her readings about the perfume business.

BACKGROUND

Perfumes, or fragrances, are usually mixtures of many different ingredients in solution. The solution most often consists of about 80 percent alcohol and up to 15 percent water. The remainder is the perfume itself. It, in turn, may contain more than 30 different ingredients of vegetable, animal, or synthetic origin. Most perfumes contain some of all three types.

Essential plant or vegetable oils come from flowers, roots, stems, or seeds, and include lavender, rose, sandalwood, citronella, and rosemary. These oils are extracted from flowers primarily by solvent extraction, using a highly volatile solvent such as petroleum ether. In this process, flower petals or other parts are mixed with the solvent in closed containers for a lengthy period of time. The essential oils dissolve into the liquid, which is then fully evaporated, leaving the oils.

The best perfumes also contain ingredients of animal origin, such as musk (obtained from the glands of deer), civet (obtained from the glands of the civet cat), and ambergris (obtained from sperm whales). These ingredients impart a warm quality to a perfume's scent and intensify the fragrance of other substances. In recent years, however, scents that previously required the crushing and extraction of a thousand rose petals to yield one ounce of expensive fragrance are being accurately reproduced in the laboratory. Most of these synthetic fragrances are used in soaps, lotions, room fresheners, and similar products.

PERFUME USE IN DIFFERENT CULTURAL ERAS

Before 1800, perfumes were produced for small, affluent groups of people, in tiny "laboratories." Manufacture in bulk did not begin until the 1800–50 period when companies were formed to provide larger quantities and to package the products, in response to increased demand. The Victorian era, about 1850 to 1900, was noted for its austerity and strict morality. Those cultural qualities were reflected in the types of perfume used. They were predominantly simple, based on natural flower essences. But perfume remained primarily a semiluxury item because of its high cost.

Around the turn of the century, the way in which perfumes were presented became increasingly important. The name and package supplemented the perfumes themselves in the marketing process. After World War I the cultural emancipation of women began, and great fashion designers dominated the scene. Perfume was representative of their life-style and originality, and became a true luxury product.

In the 1930s and 1940s, traditional perfumery houses lost their dominant position in the industry as the market sought greater individuality. This trend concentrated less on the floral base and more on perfume combinations. Around the mid-1950s, perfume products were well into the growth stage. The proliferation of products and the cost of launching new ones prohibited the positioning of fine perfumes solely for the elite. During this period and well through the 1960s, perfumery was primarily a French preserve. Although the number of fragrance producers was increasing in other countries, most of the world still looked to France for leadership.

Even so, the mass market was emerging in the United States, where consumers' purchasing power was growing at a greater rate than in Europe. Avon, Max Factor, and Prince Matchabelli all offered what consumers wanted: medium-priced products, value for the money, performance rather than sophistication, and scents that were easier to "comprehend." This meant a return to familiar, strong fragrances with little originality—a "reassuring" product.

In the early 1970s, the U.S. perfume producers began to move away from French leadership and to develop products designed to capture their own prestige market. Yves de Chris of Naarden International Fragrance Center in Paris observed: "American designers were never able to impart, by their names alone, their tastes and ideas into [the U.S.] fragrance market." In part, this was because the American woman had begun to consolidate her status and, above all, her individuality. The success of tomorrow's products will be increasingly dependent on the quality of the concept developed and the fidelity of its translation into fragrance advertising, packaging, and color scheme—in other words, the "total package".

THE PRESTIGE MARKET

Mr. de Chris was right. In the mid-1980s, U.S. perfume sales were about $2 billion a year, but much of the recent growth was caused by price increases. The number of units has remained constant. Therefore, as with other saturated markets, growth of a brand must come at the expense of others. In this market, the product itself must have appeal. The bottle and package must exude "class" and "status" but the "total package" is what is really being sold. The product's image must be carefully created through advertising and other marketing devices. As one executive put it, "The beauty business deals in people's dreams and you have to be careful how you market dreams."

The perfume industry introduced 32 new perfumes in 1984 and 23 in 1983. To make an impact in this crowded market, a new brand must be accompanied by extra-heavy promotion. When Maxim's de Paris appeared in late 1985, female models dressed as 1920's flappers passed out three million trial vials, while videotapes at cosmetic counters recounted the history of Maxim's, the restaurant from which the perfume got its name. To top it off, Macy's held a masked ball in honor of the product's debut.

Leslie knew that several cosmetic and perfume marketing firms would probably buy L'Endanger's new product and sell it under their own names, with a distinctive identifying scent. But she wasn't sure if these firms had the resources to promote their products properly, or if they could generate enough volume by selling lower-priced versions of the prestige-brand pheromone perfumes. She was also concerned about whether or not these firms had researched the middle-priced cosmetic and perfume market, as the larger firms had done. She reviewed some of the research for major perfume products.

RESEARCH RESULTS

In preintroduction market research, hundreds of women were interviewed, and many were not sure about what Maxims was. But the name did connote thoughts of beautiful people, sensuality, and drama. This perception, according to researchers, fit the notion that women's life-styles and values today suggest a resurgent interest in romance and elegance. Hard work and stress in the lives of today's women inspire self-indulgence and fantasy— which fits with Maxims's slogan, "Hearts beat faster, anticipation soars." The target customer for this new fragrance is a woman, 25 to 49 years old, with a household income of over $40,000. She reads *People* magazine and watches "Dallas" on television. To reach this consumer, Maxim's will spend $6 million on advertising and promotion, in the hopes of a $15 million yearly gross.

SYNTHETIC SCENTS

Most of the scents used in consumer products are put in simply to make the products smell better. And better fragrances are constanty appearing on the market because of technological advances in reproducing natural ones. A rose scent that previously required over a thousand rose petals per ounce of essence can now be synthetically produced in the laboratory. And this reproduction is accomplished at such a comparatively low cost that artificial fragrances are now available for use in mass-produced products.

The maturing perfume market has also driven producers such as IFF (International Flavors and Fragrances) to try to educate American consumers toward expanded uses of scented products, thereby stimulating demand. One of the newest innovations is to embed fragrances in plastic for use in furniture, automobile interiors, bags, toys, and plastic shoes. In Italy, Fiat has been experimenting with using interior parts made of perfumed plastic in its cars. A household product, Sunlight liquid detergent, depends on a special scent to enhance its image.

New scents and chemical techniques are positioning, or repositioning, room air fresheners. Formerly, these products mainly covered up undesirable odors, but they are now being introduced as "atmosphere enhancers"—much as incense has been for centuries. Furniture polish may have a mood-aroma of its own, now that good, cheap, synthetic fragrances are available. IFF's Walter also believes that people from less developed countries like stronger smells and flavors, and cites the heavy-handed use of spices in Third World foods as an example. He believes that as more people from Third World countries enter the American labor force, perfume and aroma sales will benefit.

Synthetic aromas that tempt the palate as well as other senses have also been developed. IFF and other firms have succeeded in imitating such mouth-watering aromas as candy, pizza, chocolate chip cookies, and baking ham. But the marketing and packaging of these aromas is the clever part. They are packaged in aerosol cans that come with a timing device ($35 extra) that periodically release a burst of the scent into a shopping mall. "We tried venting our cooking odors into the mall," says one restaurant manager, "but grease and other material came out, too, and they made us stop. These canned aromas are the ideal solution and they sure help bring customers in."

A boon to used car dealers has been canned, synthetic, "new car aroma" which can be sprayed inside an older car to make it smell as though it was just driven off the showroom floor. One brand, Velvet Touch, made by a Massachusetts firm, has been a good seller not only to dealers but also to owners who want to rid the car of undesirable odors, such as dog or cigar.

Leslie was also concerned about competition in the new communicative scent market, and whether or not pheromones actually have the same effect on humans that experiments suggest they do on animals. Or, in the context of consumer behavior theory, will consumers perceive that the products have that effect even if it cannot be proven scientifically that they do? She looked further at the communicative products.

COMMUNICATIVE SCENTS

Maxims, Chanel, Max Factor, and a host of others produce "decorative" scents. But the pheromone-laden "communicative" perfumes marketed by a British company, Medical Express U.K., Ltd., and Chicago's Jovan, Inc., may fulfill the unsaid promise of aphrodisiacal properties found in many standard perfume ads. The question is whether or not the chemical actually does produce a noticeable or measurable effect on humans. A few experiments claim to have shown that some people react more favorably to those wearing scents containing pheromones than to those wearing regular fragrances. An executive of Jovan says of users of their product, Andron: "We hear pretty graphic stuff from them, but such claims are not documented." See the descriptive text in the advertisement in Exhibit 5-1.

Jovan says that Andron, which comes in both male and female versions, is selling quite well at $7.50 an ounce. But fragrances containing pheromones are not new. They have been sold in sex boutiques for years, and many customers who have bought them there believe claims made for them, as do Andron customers. The future of the commercial product depends on more reliable scientific studies than have been made so far. The Fragrance Foundation is currently studying the scent–sex link.

CONTROL FRAGRANCES

Henry G. Walter, chairman and CEO of International Flavors and Fragrances, Inc. (IFF), has other ideas about the future use of "control" fragrances. He has a crystal-ball conception of people who will control their health and even their moods with scents instead of drugs and alcohol. One scent could help them sleep, another could control high blood pressure, others could induce relaxation, keep them awake, or cope with depression. "In twelve months, we will have a product on the market," he promises, "probably a stress-relieving fragrance."

To bring some of his other ideas closer to reality, Walter has instituted research at IFF into the effect that fragrances have on such basic human drives as anger, anxiety, depression, and fear. But the research in control fragrances apparently has a long way to go. At least one competitor, the French producer of Armani perfume, is skeptical of the influences of these scents. Its chairman, Fred-Henri Firmenich, says: "We do not believe fragrances have physical effects, though we do think they have psychological ones."

There are others in the industry who, although they may not envision the uses Walter does, are convinced scents have more potential uses than mere decoration. Tom Cannariation, vice president of Naarden International, USA, says: "We are encouraging marketers to do more testing of the impact of fragrance on people's emotions and attitudes." Recently, a perfume producer and a shampoo marketer worked together in an experiment where the same shampoo solution, augmented with various fragrances, was bottled under different labels. Consumers were highly favorable to only one of the test batches, reporting that it made their hair both cleaner and fresher than did the identical shampoo, bottled under other labels.

One company, Proprietary Perfumes Ltd., asks its clients, most of whom are producers of consumer products, to decide what the fragrance goals of a new product should be, such as: fresh, clean, refreshing. The firm then selects a few of the thousands of scents it produces that are most likely to work on an almost subconscious level to stimulate the desired sensations in the product's buyers.

Another venture that the bank's analyst considered risky was the proposal that L'Endanger move forward into men's fragrances and cosmetics. Leslie suspected that it was potentially profitable, but recognized that the market would have to evolve further for it to benefit from aggressive promotion. Thus, it would be a long rather than a short term venture, and she reviewed what she had discovered about its prospects.

FOR MEN?

Ideas have been changing about men wearing fragrances. Ten or 15 years ago, after-shave lotion was a new and a somewhat questionable male-directed product. Today, aftershave is a common item in male grooming, and cologne (a perfume heavily diluted with alcohol and water) is gaining in acceptance. Moreover, the newer men's scents are likely to be lighter and fresher smelling than women's perfume. Earlier ones were heavier and permeating, hence the joke, "I knew you were coming. Your aftershave got here ten minutes ago."

The newest notion put forth is that there is a link between good looks, good grooming, and success. So men, like women, are becoming more concerned with such personal detractions as lines under the eyes and blotchy skin. Cosmetic makers are responding with such products as wrinkle-removing eye cream, "color-correctors," and skin lotions. There is also a "Nails for Males" polish designed to remove ridges from nails.

Brand-naming men's products with masculine themes is a major element in market success. The aggressive striver is supposed to be attracted to Compete, while Entrepreneur is for men who would like to be one. The *Wall Street Journal* reveals that the latter product contains "a blend of exotic musk, amber, oriental spices and just a hint of cognac." Other macho-sounding names are the Gripper (football connotation), EC-17 (military), and Matrix Cellular Eye Creme (space and high-tech).

Although men seem more willing to accept lotions, colognes, and some creams, they balk at "cover-up" or color products. The only one with any degree of acceptance is a new bronzer, but it is packaged in an inconspicuous gray and white tube so it won't be noticed in the locker room. As the president of one major cosmetics firm observed: "The use of cover-up, eye shadow, or lipsticks by males is probably a generation away."

Choosing the proper location for men's fragrances and cosmetics has been a tricky decision for stores. Estee Lauder's Aramis affiliate prefers to use the spot where men's products of the English Leather variety have traditionally been sold. On the other hand, Clinique, which overtly features men's personal grooming products, sells in the women's cosmetics department. So far, according to store managers, the location seems to have very little effect on sales to men. Some give a slight edge to the women's location, since customers shopping there may pick up a man's product on impulse, as a gift.

The ultimate in men's fragrances is offered by Bijan Pakzad, a fashion designer. For $1,500 you get six ounces of perfume in a hand-blown, hand-cut Baccarat crystal bottle. (Men are reluctant to buy small bottles because such containers are not masculine enough, so the perfume comes only in elaborate six-ounce containers.) The perfume is made up of rosemary, nutmeg, black pepper, vanilla, tangerine, and 17 additional plant and flower oils. Pakzad claims that Prince Mohamed bin Fahad al Saud, heir to the Saudi Arabian throne, bought seven bottles to give to friends. Another customer says, "The perfume reminds me of the Arabian Nights. It's a heavier, spicy kind of scent. Something a man would wear."

By carefully examining her own motivations, self-concept, and expectations from fragrances, Leslie wondered how other women in the same or different social and career patterns viewed this product. She was also interested in how market researchers determined the basis for segmenting the perfume market, and how they decided on promotional themes to promote to the several segments.

DESIGNING A PRESTIGE FRAGRANCE

Up to now, little psychographic research has been conducted to determine what male fragrance consumers want in a shaving lotion or cologne, or to investigate consumers' inner motivations. And researchers have not asked men what attributes they would respond to in a women's perfume. They have talked mostly to women. They have not investigated what women want in a fragrance but instead have inquired about their dreams and what they want out of life. The replies have been: luxury, adventure, and sex—mostly sex.

This method helped Charles of the Ritz to effectively segment the perfume market. The first targeted product came in 1974 with Charlie, a perfume designed for the independent, carefree woman. The next year, there was Jontue for the romantic and Aviance for the housewife. Two years later, Enjoli was marketed for the working mother. Senchal is designed for another type of modern woman. This woman is looking for some danger. She wants the passionate, adventurous life. She's a connoisseur of luxury. Men are part of her life, but she'll have a meaningful relationship with whom she wants, when she wants. The world is her toy, she's queen of the jungle. And she's not going to marry the boy next door. At least not in the ads.

Brenda Harburger, marketing vice president for Charles of the Ritz, points out that ads used to be able to say, "Wear this perfume and you'll catch a man." Today, the buyer must be convinced that a perfume brand matches her own attitudes and life-style. Lois Ernst, of the Advertising to Women, Inc. agency, says, "We're talking about a stupid little perfume, but we're dealing with the whole texture of life and relationships."

In a nutshell, that is what the fragrance business is all about.

Analysis Questions

1. About half of U.S. women are in the labor force. How does this factor tend to increase the demand for products such as perfume?

2. How do Charles of the Ritz and other perfume companies go about designing perfumes to "match" women's life-styles or personality characteristics?

3. What social factors are involved in the so-called "communication" scents and "control" fragrances? From information in the case, do you think either of them will actually accomplish what is claimed for them?

4. What do you think the future is for men's fragrances other than colognes and after-shave lotion? What about "communication" scents?

5. Considering your answers to the questions above, do you think Leslie should invest her money in L'Endanger? Why or why not?

Source: Courtesy of Jovan, Inc.

Case 6

Atari Corporation

As Frank and Alice Morrison strolled through the Tri-City Mall, they stopped at the window of a department store and looked at the array of computer products displayed there. "We really ought to think about getting the kids a computer that will help them learn something instead of just playing those weird games," Alice remarked. "Anyway, they seem to be getting tired of the ones we got them at Christmas." "Will you look at the price?" Frank exclaimed. "$99 for the Atari 800XL! We paid $900 for our old 800 back in 1981! We should get something more like a real computer; maybe an Apple or IBM. Let's ask the kids about it. They think they are real experts."

This conversation is really a concise history of the lower-priced segment of the home computer market and the traumatic changes this market has undergone since the mid-1970s. Of all the major firms involved (Commodore, Atari, Texas Instruments, Mattel, Coleco, and Timex), Atari was the one that captured the public eye because of its meteoric rise and fall. While many of Atari's problems involved product development, poor marketing, product timing, and management style, what really happened was that Atari went one way and consumers decided to go another. It was a change in behavior that altered the thrust of how home computers would be used, almost overnight.

EARLY DAYS WITH THE PARENT COMPANY

In late 1978, Warner Communications was ready to release the first full-length movie of Superman. Since 1938, the comic book, radio, and TV serial character had earned a substantial amount of money for Warner's DC Comics subsidiary. Toys, dolls, and other products bearing his name had been highly profitable, too, but these were aimed mainly toward the children's market. A $50 million motion picture venture had to attract a substantial number of adult customers as well. To do this, Warner called upon nearly all of its divisions to lend a hand. DC Comics put out 500,000 reproductions of the original 1938 Action Comics in which Superman made his debut. Warner Books published nine products tied to the movie, including the story of how it was made, a Superman quiz book, and an original novel. Warner Bros. Records released the movie's sound track in a special album. And there were plans to have Warner's newest acquisition, Atari (a manufacturer of electronic games), develop a Superman pinball game. Richard Domer, the director of the film, said, "I'm making a picture for adults that kids will go to see."

This was one of the first ventures in which Atari, a 1976 acquisition of Warner Communications, participated. But Atari was in the right place at the right time when the video game craze swept the country in the late 1970s. In 1977, the first year after its acquisition, Atari's sales were slightly under $200 million (with a $3 million loss), but by the end of 1981 sales had skyrocketed to $1 billion with a $3 million profit. It was the overwhelmingly popular Pac-Man that brought prosperity to Atari and Warner, mainly through coin-operated games in video arcades. A home version brought out in 1982 helped to boost 1982 sales to nearly $2 billion.

THE PAC-MAN PHENOMENON

Pac-Man was not only a money maker, but he became a national figure, or fad, and was a popular topic of conversation for both adults and children. In early 1982, Norman Ricken, the president of Toys R Us, said: "We haven't even started to advertise [Pac-Man] yet, and people are buying them as quickly as they can get in the door." One securities analyst predicted that Pac-Man would sell nine million cartridges in its first year and bring Atari about $200 million. Even children's cereal manufacturers were trying to cash in on game-name popularity. General Foods began selling Smurf-Berry Crunch in February 1982 and Ralston featured Donkey Kong in July. At about the same time, General Mills introduced a new Pac-Man cereal. The question was whether or not one game name on a product might find itself "eaten" in reverse Pac-Man cannibalization by another newer fad name.

Besides its 40 percent share in the video arcade market, Atari had games in 6 million homes by 1981. It had also captured a 40 percent share of the home computer market. As shown in Exhibit 6-1 the firm contributed a huge share of its parent firm's sales and profits through 1982. Atari had been an excellent acquisition for Warner, who paid only $28 million for it in 1976.

Atari's meteoric growth was based upon a single product that caught the fancy of the American public in the early stages of hands-on computer products. It was the Video Computer System (VCS), a high-tech sounding name that consumers fantasized would transport them into the electronic age. The VCS could be programmed to play video arcade games at home, using a small computer. The computer itself was lodged in a small box that could be attached to an ordinary home television set so that the TV screen resembled that of an arcade game. The games are started by inserting a cartridge into the computer. Immediately, Pac-Man or alien armies begin rushing across the screen ready to be controlled by the player's joy stick.

The VCS was by no means a perfect product. Its graphics were inferior to those of other entertainment media, even the video arcades, and the reproduction was often fuzzy. But that did not seem to bother the customers, and by 1982 there were over 11 million Video Computer Systems in U.S. households. And Atari was counting heavily on the "Gillette syndrome" (where profits are made from selling blades, not razors)—to cash in on future profits from new game cartridge sales. Hit games were selling for about $30 and brought manufacturers a whopping 40 percent profit margin. Pac-Man itself sold nearly 7 million copies in 1982 at the $30 price—lower than the prediction, yet still an excellent performance. Both producers and market analysts foresaw a healthy games market for years to come.

In line with this apparent strategy, Atari announced after the 1981 Christmas season that the suggested retail price of its model 800 home computer would be cut from $1,080 to $899. This was the first price change since the computer was initially marketed in 1978. At the same time, prices on Atari games were hiked an average of 12.4 percent. Clearly, the company believed that VCS owners were hooked and would pay even more to support the video game habit. The price of Atari's only other system, the 400, had been cut the previous June from $630 to $399.

At the beginning of 1982, Atari had a lower, but still healthy 30 percent share in the home computer market. Although 1982 was a peak year for both computer and game cartridge sales, it also marked the maturing of the market. By the end of the year, Atari's computer share dwindled to 18 percent. Its software, designed for the Atari video game player, had cornered an 80 percent share in 1981 but slid to 56 percent in 1982. Nonetheless, both sales and profits rose rapidly for Atari until the third quarter, when the first signs of trouble appeared. The market was near the end of the growth stage of the product life cycle and competition was nipping at the complacent Atari. The phenomenal success of Pac-Man had lulled the firm into a belief that almost any other product would sell too, so it issued a number of older games that consumers rejected for more interesting ones offered by competitors. By mid-1983, Atari was still trying to dump millions of game cartridges that were left over from 1982. As if this was not trouble enough, the home computer division was beset by price cutting from aggressive competitors.

EXECUTIVE CHANGES

At Warner's instigation in late 1982, Raymond Kassar, Atari's chairman and chief executive officer, fired Perry Odak, who was head of the consumer electronics group. Odak had just come to Atari in February from Jovan, Inc., an innovative cosmetics marketer. Kassar also slashed overhead, cutting 2,000 blue collar and 1,000 white collar jobs, and moving a sizable portion of game and computer production outside the United States. Although he was strictly a marketing man with little ability to communicate with Atari's technical and development engineers, he continued in the top executive spot until June 1983, when he was replaced by James J. Morgan, who took over in September. Morgan was another marketing executive who had been vice president for marketing with Philip Morris, USA. After a two-month vacation before taking command, Morgan's first act was to declare a 30-day freeze on all product development—a risky move at best in the fast-paced computer business.

Atari's goal had been to introduce the new 1450XLD and 1400 models in the $500 to $1,000 price range to compete directly with Commodore and Apple. The freeze, which lasted into October 1982, effectively kept this line out of the 1983 Christmas market. In addition, Morgan decided to compete in the lower price range where Atari's products were being undersold by Commodore. This proved to be a poor decision. Not only was Atari unable to compete at those low prices, but consumers were already balking at what they perceived to be low-price, low-quality, game-oriented models. Atari's poor showing in 1983 had its effect on Warner's profitability, as shown in the firm's financial statements (see Exhibit 6-2). To make matters worse, by the time Morgan changed his mind in June 1983 to reinstate the 1450XLD, it was again too late, this time for Christmas 1984. The season was even more of a debacle for Atari than it might have been. First, Morgan decided to produce the low-priced 800XL in the United States instead of overseas. Then, because of production problems and higher costs, Atari could not meet demands. Also, the 800XL had to retail at $299, fully $100 more than the competitive Commodore 64. So Atari not only missed its entrance into the higher end of the computer market with its 1450XLD, but also missed its chance to compete in the tail-end of the low-priced market with the 800XL.

FUTURE MARKET FACTORS

Not only was this market acting according to classical marketing theory in the growth stage, but there were also more subtle complications related to the products themselves and to increasing consumer sophistication. While Atari was staking its future on the continuing use of computers to play electronic games, its competitors visualized a much different market. Other small computer producers, mainly Commodore and Texas Instruments, took advantage of Atari's position and reputation in games devices to establish themselves firmly in the expanding home computer market. They recognized that not only was the market undergoing a normal growth-stage shake-up but that consumers were making a clear statement of their future intentions. Instead of using a trial-and-error approach to upgrade computer games hardware and software, they were learning that computers had more potential than a games vehicle in today's expanding technological environment. People wanted a computer so that their children could understand and operate one.

But the popular notion that children will be lost in the "computer age" if they are not immersed in the technology and techniques is disputed by many scientists and educators. They fault much of the so-called educational software that has come on the market in recent years. Many say a large proportion of the programs are glorified games at best or, at worst, are "an uninspired rehash of skills that can be taught more effectively without a computer." A professor at MIT describes as "pure baloney" the notion that children will not go far in life without an intricate knowledge of computer logic and technology. With proper software, people who use a computer only to run certain types of applications (word processing, bookkeeping systems, etc.) never need to learn how the technology works. Nonetheless, many parents firmly believe that early exposure to both operational and technological aspects of computers is a pathway to success in life.

Atari might have wrung one more profitable year from game software, but its major titles for Christmas 1982—Raiders of the Lost Ark, ET, and Real Sports—offered no excitement to buyers. Also, while competitors brought out more sophisticated games and hardware, Atari simply expanded their strategy of producing licensed versions of arcade games and of popular movies. In that Christmas season, there were over 150 game titles available from 16 producers, most of which could be used on Atari hardware.

RECENT EVENTS

In 1983, Atari lost more than $500 million and around the middle of that year, Warner hung out the "for sale" sign (see Exhibit 6-3). A year later, in July 1984, Jack Tramiel bought the company for $240 million in notes. Tramiel, who steered Commodore from a small typewriter sales firm to 40 percent of the home computer market in 1983, had just been forced out of that firm. One of the first things he did after taking control of Atari was to cut the price of the 800XL from over $300 to $189, alienating retailers who originally paid more than that for the products. In November 1984, he slashed the price again to $99 for the 1984 Christmas season. A history of the 800 series and Commodore competitive pricing is shown in Exhibit 6-4. Since Warner kept the coin-operated arcade part of the business, Tramiel had to capitalize on game cartridges, home computers, and the software to run on them. For Christmas 1984, only Commodore was able to supply the demand for computers in the $500-and-below market, largely because Morgan's decisions made it impossible for Atari to jump into the gap when there were shortages. Another of Tramiel's tactics was to cut the price of game cartridges—but by then the market glut had already forced prices down from the $30 range to as low as $4. And his main problem remained: how to change Atari's image from that of a toymaker to that of a legitimate computer producer. Neither Coleco (Adam computers) nor Mattel was able to do that. And others—Timex and Texas Instruments—have also bowed out of the computer business.

In the January 1985 Winter Consumer Electronics Show in Las Vegas, Tramiel employed another tactic that worked at Commodore: using price to create excitement and attention. He announced a new line of computers, which were coined "Jackintosh," the cheapest of which would cost about $800. This model would have the same capacity as the Mac but would include a color monitor and disc drive, for about $1,000 less than a similarly configured MacIntosh. But critics pointed out that no software was available for the new line, and that it had not yet been produced in volume.

In early 1985, a leading financial magazine reported that at Christmas 1984, consumers generally ignored computers under $500 and that sales for these models were essentially flat during 1983 and 1984. On the other hand, units selling for between $500 and $1,000 nearly doubled in 1984 and were expected to triple in 1985. "Consumers are bored with home computers costing a couple of hundred dollars but good for little more than playing games. They are no longer buying computers to learn about them. They are buying them to do something useful."

In April 1985, Atari pulled out of the big June 1985 Consumer Electronics Show in Chicago. The company had promised to unveil a new computer, twice as powerful as the MacIntosh, at a German show in April and at the Chicago show in June. In May 1985, Tramiel announced that delivery of his Apple-competitive ST line, promised in April 1985, would not be available in U.S. stores until July. The company also said that a second, larger model that had also been scheduled for the spring, would not be available until late 1985 at the earliest.

LATER DEVELOPMENTS

In the fall of 1985, during the lowest ebb the electronics business had seen, and when consumers were seriously questioning the value of personal computers, Tramiel brought out the 520ST. The model was, according to experts, as easy to operate as the MacIntosh and had color graphics as well. Targeted to the small business market, it offered 512k of memory, a medium-resolution color monitor, and a 3 1/4" disc drive system, with 360k of storage—the same as 5 1/4" standard discs. But the most attractive feature was the price for the entire array: around $1,000. Comments about the 520ST's capabilities from advertisements are shown in Exhibit 6-5. The equipment began to be shipped in October 1985 and by mid-November, software was not available for it and the *New York Times* reported that no one at Atari was able to say when it would be. On the other hand, MacIntosh had the same software problems and overcame them with media blitzing and low prices.

In December 1985, *Business Week* suggested that Atari's future depended upon the success of the 520ST, and Tramiel's ability to cut operating costs ruthlessly. By the middle of December, 50,000 520STs had been shipped and predictions were that another 50,000 would be sold by the end of the year. But final success depended on three other factors: (1) software still needed to be developed for the new model; (2) retailers, distrustful of Tramiel's tactics when he was with Commodore, had to be persuaded to sell it (many top chains ignored the product); and (3) most importantly, consumers' perceptions of Atari as a games device needed to be changed.

Analysis Questions

1. Did the Pac-Man fad help or hurt Atari's image in the home computer market?

2. In 1981, Atari had games in 6 million homes and a 40 percent share of the home computer market. What happened to the market in 1983? What consumer factor(s) caused its sudden "maturity"?

3. Atari's answer to its marketing problems was to change management. How does consumer price-quality perception and risk perception fit with the strategies of both Morgan and Tramiel?

4. Atari's most recent product, the 520ST, appeared to be a price-competitive threat to MacIntosh and other higher-priced configurations, but software was not available. What effect might this have on consumer expectations and ultimate consumer perception of the product?

ATARI CORPORATION

EXHIBIT 6-1

Sales and Income: Warner Communications and Atari

	1981	1982	1983
Sales (billions)			
Warner	$3.3	$4.1	$3.4
Atari	$1.1	$2.0	$1.1
Atari Share	33.3%	48.7%	32%
Earnings (millions)			
Warner	$226	$257	($417)
Atari	$281	$400	($538)

ATARI CORPORATION

EXHIBIT 6-2

Warner Communications, Inc. Consolidated Balance Sheets 1, 1981–1983

	1981	1982
Assets		
Cash & marketable securities	184,898	206,227
Receivables net	805,547	724,039
Inventories (LCM)	470,948	589,401
Other assets	255,897	250,484
Total Current	1,717,290	1,770,151
Net property, etc.	380,968	400,532
Investments	304,463	257,989
Inventories	402,860	408,951
Accts, notes, excess acq. cost, etc.	316,725	348,732
Total	3,122,306	3,186,355
Liabilities		
Commercial paper	81,326	56,066
Notes, etc. payable	126,711	68,063
Accts. etc. payable	871,737	868,260
Income taxes	2,000	23,981
Total Current	1,081,774	1,016,370
Long-term debt	615,989	414,982
Accounts payable	315,021	300,029
Deficit revenue or inc. tax	149,475	59,0021
Common stock ($1)	66,845	65,394
Paid in capital	428,955	405,814
Retained earnings	490,508	956,877
Stockholders' equity	960,047	1,395,972
Total	3,122,306	3,186,355

ATARI CORPORATION

EXHIBIT 6-3

Consolidated Income Statements 1981–83 (000)

	1983	1982	1981
Operating revenues	3,425,272	4,090,651	3,293,748
Cost of revenues	2,963,219	2,756,866	2,230,143
Selling expenses, etc.	787,251	809,885	626,393
Corporate costs, expenses	98,446	75,446	58,991
Interest, etc.	107,458	68,554	13,028
Income tax	cr113,300	122,089	138,700
Net Income	(417,803)	257,811	226,493

ATARI CORPORATION

EXHIBIT 6-4

Prices of Atari and Competitive Commodore Products

Date	Model	Price
December 1981	Atari 800	$899 from $1,080
1982–83	Atari 800	$315 from $899
Summer 1984	Atari 800XL	$200 from $315
October 1984	New 800XL	$188 from $200
November 1984	Commodore 64	$200
	New 800XL	$119 from $188
January 1985	Atari TS (announced)	<$600
	Commodore C128	$300
February 1985	New 800XL	$99 from $119
	Commodore 64	$159 from $200
	Atari 65XE (Repl 800XL)	$100
	Atari 65XL	$120–150
	Atari ST	$400–600
November 1985	Atari 520ST	$1,000+

Atari Explodes

Atari's new computer serious threat to Macintosh. Will the Amiga survive?

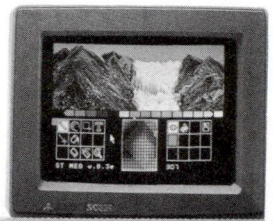

The Atari 260 ST is a serious challenge to the Apple Macintosh and will open up a major fight in the personal computer market.

By Joseph Sugarman

Imagine this. If I could offer you a Macintosh computer—(a computer that sells for over $2000)—for one third the price, you might wonder.

But what if I offered you a better computer with none of the disadvantages of the Mac and what if I added new features which improved its speed and performance? That's exactly what Atari has done in an effort to grab the ball from Apple and really explode into the personal computer market.

HEADING EFFORT

Heading the effort at Atari is Jack Tramiel—the same man who built Commodore into a billion dollar corporation, sold more computers than any other man in the world and believes in giving the consumer incredible value without sacrificing quality. The new Atari is a perfect example.

First, let's compare the new Atari ST to the Macintosh and the Commodore Amiga. Sorry IBM, we can't compare the ST to your PC because yours is almost five years old, much slower, and, in my judgement, over priced.

Price The cheapest you can get the Macintosh with 512K of memory is $1800 with a one-button mouse, a disk drive and a monochrome monitor. The Amiga sells for $1995 with a two-button mouse, a disk drive and a color monitor. The Atari ST sells for $699 with a two-button mouse, a disk drive and a monochrome monitor and for $200 more, a color monitor. Read on.

Monitor With the Mac you can only use its 9" monochrome monitor and with the Amiga you can only use its 12" color monitor. With the ST you have a choice of either a 12" monochrome or high-resolution color monitor or your own TV set.

Resolution The number of pixels or tiny dots on a screen determine the sharpness of a computer monitor. The Mac has 175,104 pixels and has one of the sharpest screens in the industry. The Atari ST has 256,000 pixels or almost a third more than the Mac. And the Atari color monitor compared to the Amiga in its non interlace mode is 128,000 pixels or exactly the same.

Power All the computers have a 512K memory with a 68000 CPU operating with a 32-bit internal architecture. But Atari uses four advanced custom chips which cause the CPU to run faster and more efficiently giving it some tremendous advantages. For example, it has a faster clock speed of 8Mhz com-

pared to the Mac's 7.83 and the Amiga's 7.16. And the speed of the unit is hardly affected by the memory requirements of the monitor which in the Amiga can eat up much as 70% of the unit's cycle time or speed.

Keyboard This is the part I love. The Mac has a small 59-key keyboard and a mouse. That's all. The 95-key Atari has both a mouse, cursor keys, a numeric keypad and ten function keys. The keyboard looks fantastic and is easy to type on. Although the 89-key Amiga has almost all the features of the Atari keyboard, it looks like a toy in comparison. (Sorry Commodore, but that's my opinion.)

Disk Drive The Mac's 3½" disk drives run at variable speeds—slowing down as they run. The Atari 3½" drives run faster at a constant speed—and quieter than any other unit.

Features The Atari ST comes equipped with the same printer and modem ports as the IBM PC—a parallel and RS232C serial port. The Mac comes only with a tiny non-standard serial and modem port. The ST has a hard disk interface capable of receiving 10 million bits per second. There are two joy stick ports and a 128K cartridge port for smaller programs or games. It has 512 colors (for the color monitor), it has a unique MIDI interface in-to which you can plug your music synthesizer and record or play back your music.

Software Right now, the Mac has more than the Atari ST and the Amiga combined. The Atari is a new system but the track record of Atari's Jack Tramiel and the potential of the new unit is causing a flood of new software titles. In fact, I'll predict that eventually the Atari will have more software than the Mac. There are now hundreds of titles, from word processing to spread sheet programs, from graphics and games to data base management—all with those easy drop-down menus and windows. There's plenty from which to select now and plenty more to come.

If you think I'm enthusiastic over the ST, listen to what the press is saying. *Byte Magazine* just called it the "Computer of the year for 1986." *Creative Computing* exclaimed, "Without question, the most advanced, most powerful micro computer your money can buy." and finally, the Atari ST is the best selling computer in Europe and acclaimed, "The computer of the year," by the European personal computer press.

I am going to make the ST so easy to test in your home or office that it would be a shame if you did not take advantage of my

offer. First, I will offer the computer itself for only $299. You will need, in addition, either one or two disk drives and either an Atari monochrome or color monitor or your own TV. If you order with your credit card during our introduction I will ship your order and only bill you for the postage and 1/3 the purchase price. I will also add a few software packages free including "Logo"—a beginners programming language, a disk for programming in BASIC and Neochrome—a graphics paint program.

COMPARE THE TWO

After you receive the Atari ST, put it next to your Mac or Amiga or even IBM. See how extremely sharp the graphics appear, discover what a perfect word processor it is, how great the keyboard feels and finally how much faster and quieter it runs.

If you're not convinced that the Atari is far superior to your present computer and a fantastic value, simply return it and I'll refund your modest down payment plus our postage and handling charges. If you decide to keep it, I'll bill your credit card account for the remaining balance and enroll you in our discount software club (a $50 value) that lets you buy software for up to 50% off the retail price.

But act fast. We have only 2,000 units and 1,000 free memberships that we will offer as part of this introductory program and we are certain they will go fast. Order today.

To order, credit card holders can toll free and ask for product by number (shown in parentheses). Please add $20 per order for postage and handling. (If you pay by check, you must pay the full amount but we will provide you with a bonus software package.)

ST Keyboard, CPU & Mouse(4060E) **$299**
Disk Drive (4056E) **199**
Monochrome Monitor (4057E) **199**
RGB Color Monitor (4058E) **399**
Note: A list of software will come with the unit.
IBM is a registered trademark of International Business Machines Corp. Commodore & Amiga are trademarks of Commodore Electronics LTD. Atari, Apple & Macintosh are trademarks of Apple Computer, Inc. Atari, ST & Logo are trademarks of Atari Corp.

JS&A PRODUCTS THAT THINK

One JS&A Plaza
Northbrook, Illinois 60062
CALL TOLL FREE 800 228-5000
IL residents add 7% sales tax. ©JS&A Group, Inc.,1985

Source: Courtesy of JS&A Group, Inc.

Case 7

Image Strategy
and E. J. Korvettes

Bob Bernstein gazed at Jean-Paul Leveque, assistant to the new president of Korvettes, Inc., with open-mouthed disbelief, as Leveque concluded the first part of his remarks to the group of store managers. From the entire 20-minute presentation, the only words that Bob kept hearing over and over were, "We're going to compete on a discount basis with national chains like Sears and J. C. Penney." He only half heard the rest of the new strategy, which involved closing unprofitable stores and cutting overhead to the bone. Bob didn't worry about his store closing—it was still profitable, but he was quite concerned about the new direction the firm was taking. This was the third strategy in about the same number of years.

It was early in 1980 and Bob was in a New York meeting of managers of the E. J. Korvettes chain of stores. The meeting had been called by Alain Mathieu of Agache-Willot, the $3.5 billion French textile and retail conglomerate that controlled such status labels as Ted Lapidus, Christian Dior, and Au Bon Marche. Agache-Willot had acquired Korvettes in April 1979 for $31 million from the Arlen Realty and Development Corp. Mathieu had a reputation as a "mover" in Agache's headquarters, but Korvettes executives and store managers were turned off by his cold manner and French style of management. They were also shocked by the abrupt manner in which Leveque announced the new move. During the short intermission, Bob and his colleagues wondered if consumers could absorb still another image, and if they would be willing to readjust their attitudes toward the store after just having done so a year or so ago.

E. J. Korvettes was a pioneer firm in discount retailing and had a solid reputation as a low-priced hard-goods outlet. It was also a highly successful one with 50 stores in New York, New Jersey, Pennsylvania, Maryland, Virginia, Washington, D.C., and Detroit. Annual sales were about $600 million, but at the time it was acquired by Agache-Willot, it was operating far in the red. In 1978, the loss was $1.2 million; in the first quarter of 1979, the loss exploded to nearly $6 million, and suppliers were balking at extending further credit. It became clear that Korvettes was a distressed property and it was a helpless target against Agache, which had acquired and turned around several similar properties in Europe.

EARLY IMAGE STRATEGY

Bob Bernstein started in 1969 at one of the original, smaller Korvettes stores as sales clerk-manager of the small appliance department. He had just received his associate degree in retailing from a local community college, and was anxious to get experience in that type of business. His family owned a small chain of hardware stores in southern Maryland and he liked the retail business. He also thought his background in the hardware business would help him in a discount chain that specialized in hard goods. He worked hard, took odd-hour shifts that other employees balked at, and won several store awards for sales increases in his department. By 1972, he was transferred to assistant store manager at a larger store, and was given his own store in 1974.

By that time, other discount stores such as K-Mart, Zayre, and several large regional chains were well established and garnering increased shares of Korvettes's hard goods business. Korvettes's long-term strategy had been to offer national and other brands of appliances, household goods, and personal products at low prices, and in the early 1970s it added a line of standard, low-priced women's wear. It also offered periodic special-event discounts, such as a sale for senior citizens. Bob's store was able to hold its own, even though it was not in a prime location. It was situated as the only anchor in a medium-sized, older suburban shopping center in a large eastern metropolitan area.

THE "OTHER KORVETTES" STRATEGY

About two years after he took over his own store, Bob was faced with implementing a new company merchandising strategy. It was designed to enhance Korvettes's image and to place the stores in more direct competition with stores offering higher-priced fashion soft goods. The well-known Grey Advertising Agency promoted a new image that Korvettes's management hoped would replace its previous one of a hard-goods discounter. The

"Other Korvettes" theme highlighted fashion soft goods. It also pushed the idea that there was another new and enticing side to the conventional store— a side that offered better style and quality in men's, women's, and children's clothing. A new logo also appeared, with a clothes hanger suspended from the *o* in *Korvettes* (see Exhibit 7-1). The appeal and the prices were aimed somewhat above the store's regular customer base to attract a new market segment, but fashion rather than price was emphasized. Prices were fixed by the home office, and could not be changed locally to meet competition or to compensate for out-of-the-way locations. To support the campaign, $8 million was spent on spot TV advertising in 1978, and about half as much was spent in 1979.

Sales of the new soft-goods line started out well, with an initial spurt from the heavy promotional campaign, and for a short time it looked as though it would be successful in attracting new buyers. But soon Bob noticed a small but steady decline in monthly sales of the line, and he was puzzled by a 3 percent decline over six months in sales of conventional hard goods. It was the first drop he had experienced since he took over the store. He watched the local business periodicals to see if his competitors had similar drops, but most of them showed slight gains over similar periods in the past year.

Bob had a feeling that all was not well with the new merchandising image, but his regional manager tried to allay his fears, pointing out that new strategies always take a little time to catch on. He talked with other managers in his area and they were also concerned with the softening of sales, but none of them was able to get any specific information or data about sales of the entire 50 stores from the home office. Faced with this lack of information, Bob decided to attempt to determine on his own the attitudes of consumers to the new image. He talked to a friend on the business administration faculty of a local state university and arranged to have a modest survey taken. Together they developed a short questionnaire, which is shown in Exhibit 7-2. The questionnaire was administered the following week by marketing students to shoppers who were entering or leaving three area Korvettes stores. A simple tabulation of the results is shown in Exhibit 7-3. Bob had very little experience in market research and was not sure how to interpret the results himself, and he could not afford to have it done professionally. But the results were disquieting and seemed to indicate some problems with the way consumers perceived Korvettes and the way they were supposed to perceive it according to the new strategy. He sent copies of the data to his regional manager and to several executives at the home office, but heard nothing from them.

The first quarter of 1979 started out poorly and got progressively worse. The first month's overall sales were off 5 percent and the second month's were down 6.7 percent, compared to the same periods in 1978. By the end of the quarter, the overall drop was 6.9 percent—bringing the store the closest to a loss that it had been in its history. Rumors were rampant that the store would be closed, that there would be a new manager, that half the salespeople would be fired, and that the chain was up for sale.

THE AGACHE-WILLOT STRATEGY

By the following month, the word was official. Korvettes had been sold to Agache-Willot. After a short take-over period, during which Bob's store was visited several times by representatives of the new management, the meeting with Mathieu and Leveque was called.

After the intermission in the meeting, Mr. Schwartz, Korvettes's vice president for advertising, gave the details of the new strategy. He announced that Korvettes had split from Grey Advertising and was developing a new campaign, aimed at this target market:

1. Households with annual incomes of $15,000 to $30,000. Korvettes would compete for these customers against Sears and J. C. Penney Co.
2. Budget customers of regular department stores and the middle-to-upper-end customers of discounters.

While the company wanted to keep its excellent image in hard goods, it was anxious to develop a similar reputation in soft goods because the margins are higher. To do this, there would be an immediate reduction of 15 to 20 percent on the average item prices in the men's and children's wear departments. There would also be a similar reduction in hard goods. In addition, store managers were to have more flexibility in adjusting prices to meet local competition.

He went on to point out that the firm's experience of the past two years had taught them not to advertise fashion alone, but to emphasize both price and value in an uncluttered format that features a single item per merchandise group. For example, if velours are to be featured, ads will show a family group—parents and children—all wearing the garments.

The new program would also use family advertisements to capitalize on weekend business, with more emphasis placed on suburban print media than on the TV spots that were used in the past. The ads would try to create a sense of urgency that would pull customers into the stores on Friday evenings, Saturdays, and Sundays.

In conclusion, he announced the scheduled closing of 14 Korvettes stores, including some in New York, Pennsylvania, Maryland, New Jersey, and Virginia.

The room was silent as Mr. Leveque, Mr. Matthieu, and Mr. Schwartz left the stage without asking for questions or comments. As soon as they left the room, some of the managers gathered in small groups to discuss the new image. Those whose stores were being closed were called into a separate meeting, and left dejectedly. While Bob Bernstein's store had not been closed, he was quite sure it would be and he would be looking for another job. He knew that a retailing specialist with a good record was always in demand, so that aspect did not particularly concern him. But he wondered about the decisions and events that had caused a strong discounting pioneer such as Korvettes to find itself in its present precarious position.

Analysis Questions

1. What changes occurred in consumer attitudes that caused the decline in sales of Korvettes's hard goods?

2. What does the survey suggest in terms of attitude and image perception that consumers have of Korvettes?

3. In your opinion, will Agache-Willot's new strategy succeed? Why or why not?

E. J. KORVETTES

EXHIBIT 7-1

The New Korvettes Logo

E. J. KORVETTES

EXHIBIT 7-2

Bob Bernstein's Questionnaire

Interviewer instructions: You have been given procedures for selecting respondents. Once you have made your selection, smile and say, "Good *(appropriate time of day)*. We would like to ask you about your feelings toward Korvettes. Would you be kind enough to answer seven short questions? We don't ask your name and the information is kept strictly confidential."

Some respondents may not know or cannot articulate replies to questions. Please keep a count of these for each question.

1. (Hold up card listing seven department stores.)
Question: Which store (or stores) listed on this card would you say is closest, overall, to Korvettes?

Woodward & Lothrop (a mid-range local dept. chain)
Sears Roebuck and Co.
Garfinckels (an upper-range local dept. chain)
Zayre (a national lower-range discount chain)
Hecht Co. (a mid- to lower-mid-range regional dept. store)
K-Mart
J. C. Penney

2. (Hold up a copy of the new "Other Korvettes" logo.)
   Question: Here is a drawing of the new Korvettes logo. What does the clothes hanger on the "o" suggest to you?

3. (Hold up the card with four statements on it.)
   Question: Would you please select *one* of these statements that comes closest to the way you feel about Korvettes?
   a. It carries fashion merchandise.
   b. It is a standard discount department store.
   c. It carries mostly household goods and appliances.
   d. Its prices are about the lowest of any of the other stores.
   e. Don't know.

4. (Hold up card with nine occupations listed on it.)
   Question: Here are several well-known occupations. Who do you think would buy men's or women's clothing at Korvettes?

Office worker	School teacher	Mfg. plant manager
TV serviceman	Bank manager	Bus driver
Attorney	Small business owner	Stockbroker

5. (Hold up list of statements.)
   Question: Which *one* of these statements is closest to your feelings about the overall atmosphere at Korvettes?
   a. It is generally attractive and well arranged.
   b. It is about the way I'd expect a discount store to be.
   c. It is nicely decorated and a pleasant place to shop in.
   d. It is rather cold and "strictly business."

6. (Hold up list of statements.)
   Question: Which *one* of these statements comes closest to how you feel about buying male or female fashion clothes at Korvettes?
   a. They seem to be quality products, well worth the price.
   b. They are attractive, but overpriced for what you get.
   c. They are too expensive for my budget.
   d. I don't think of Korvettes as a fashion store.

7. (Hand the respondent the questionnaire sheet with these demographic questions and ask them to fill it out.)
   a. Are you: Male___ Female___ Married___ Single___ Other___
   b. How many children are there at home, under 18?_____
   c. Which age group are you in?
   18–24 ___ 25–34 ___ 35–44___
   45–54 ___ 55–64 ___ 65+___
   d. Which of the following best shows your household income?
Under $15,000 ___	$35–44,999 ___
$15–24,999 ___	$45–54,999 ___
$25–34,999 ___	Over $55,000 ___

EXHIBIT 7-3

Replies to Questionnaires
(n = 139)

1. Which store (or stores) is closest, overall, to Korvettes? (Multiple replies are permitted.)

a. Woodward & Lothrop	3	1.6%
b. Sears Roebuck and Co.	27	15.3%
c. Garfinckels	0	0
d. Zayre	63	35.6%
e. Hecht Co.	12	6.8%
f. K-Mart	54	30.5%
g. J. C. Penney	18	10.1%

2. What does the clothes hanger on the Korvettes logo suggest to you? (Placed in categories from open-ended replies.)

a. Korvettes sells clothes.	49	35.2%
b. Korvettes now has a larger women's clothing department.	17	12.2%
c. Korvettes sells fashion merchandise.	23	16.5%
d. Korvettes wants to attract attention to brand name.	27	19.4%
e. Don't know	14	10.1%
f. Other	4	2.9%

3. Which statement is closest to the way you feel about Korvettes?

a. It carries fashion merchandise.	21	15.1%
b. It is a standard discount department store.	63	45.3
c. It carries mostly household goods and appliances.	47	33.8%
d. Its prices are about the lowest of any of the other stores.	6	4.3%
e. Don't know	2	1.4%

4. Among these occupations, who would you say would buy men's or women's clothing at Korvettes? (Multiple replies are permitted.)

Office worker	72	22.9%	Small business owner	32	10.2%
TV serviceman	43	13.7%	Mfg. plant manager	15	4.8%
Attorney	8	2.5%	Bus driver	61	19.4%
School teacher	57	18.1%	Stockbroker	3	.9%
Bank manager	23	7.3%			

5. Which statement is closest to your feelings about the overall atmosphere at Korvettes?

a. Generally attractive and well arranged	12	8.6%
b. About the way I'd expect a discount store to be	86	61.9%
c. Nicely decorated and a pleasant place to shop in	11	7.9%
d. Rather cold and "strictly business"	27	19.4%
e. Don't know	3	2.1%

6. How do you feel about buying male or female fashion clothes at Korvettes?

a. They seem to be quality products, well worth the price.	31	22.3%
b. They are attractive, but overpriced for what you get.	19	13.7%
c. They are too expensive for my budget.	35	25.2
d. I don't think of Korvettes as a fashion store.	10	7.2%
e. Don't know, or haven't looked at clothes there.	44	31.6%

7. Demographic questions:

Sex:	Female	102	73.4%
	Male	37	26.6%
Age:	18–24	12	8.6%
	25–34	41	29.5
	35–44	50	36.0
	45–54	17	12.2
	55–64	9	6.5
	65+	7	5.0
	No reply	3	2.1
Income:	Under $15,000	22	15.8%
	$15–24,999	57	41.0
	$25–34,999	34	24.4
	$35–44,999	14	10.1
	$45–54,999	9	6.5
	$55,000+	3	2.1
Marital Status:	Married	87	62.5%
	Single	37	26.6
	Other	12	8.6
	No Reply	3	2.3
Children under 18:	Zero	61	43.9%
	One	43	30.9
	Two	26	18.7
	Three or more	9	6.5

Case 8

The Fairfax County Bottle Bill

"In one state during a recent presidential election, more people voted on the container legislation referendum than voted for president." So said the Glass Packaging Institute in an informational pamphlet about beverage container laws. While this was a single incident, feelings have run high on the seemingly unimportant issue of whether or not consumers should have the choice of buying their beverages in throw-away containers. Generally, this has been a question decided by individual states, although some counties and even municipalities have enacted their own container deposit laws.

One of these jurisdictions, Fairfax County, Virginia, a close-in suburb of Washington, D.C., passed such an ordinance. The subjective nature of this type of legislation is illustrated in the partial quotation as follows:

> In Section III-I-I Beverage Container Ordinance. A. There exists . . . a serious litter problem, costly to public funds, and it is the policy of the Commonwealth [of Virginia] to promote public convenience, enjoyment of public travel, protect public highways and enhance scenic beauty. That [the] use of certain non-reusable beverage containers is wasteful of resources and energy; and that the use of certain non-returnable beverage containers burdens the solid waste facilities of the County; and that unrestricted use of certain non-reusable beverage containers is detrimental to the health, safety and general welfare of the citizens of the County of Fairfax.

In enacting this ordinance, the county placed itself in the position of attempting to enforce it in a limited geographical area and without first consulting consumers within its jurisdiction. Later, it will be seen that these, and other problems, doomed the ordinance to an early demise.

BACKGROUND

Until about 1960, about 95 percent of the soft drinks and 50 percent of the beer came in returnable, refillable bottles on which was paid a small deposit. Today, we buy nearly 80 percent of our packaged beer and more than 60 percent of our soft drinks in disposable containers. As use of disposable containers has grown, so has opposition to their use. Concern about the litter and resource aspects of throw-away bottles and cans peaked in the late 1970s and early 1980s. This controversy pitted those concerned about the environment and resource conservation against a formidable array of container manufacturers, material producers, bottlers, and retailers in a pro-and-con battle over container deposit laws.

In this battle, both sides have engaged in a series of charges and countercharges consisting of oversimplified statements of factors that are rather complex when viewed objectively and in detail. Retailers and bottlers both incur substantial additional costs in handling and processing returnables. But there are ecological and resource considerations in the use of disposables. Generally, the advocates of deposit laws downplay the business costs and inflate resource savings, while those opposed do the opposite.

Supporters of these laws are concerned over the growing use of throw-aways, which has increased from under 25 percent of the soft-drink market in the 1960s to more than 60 percent today. They point out that, in a recent year, it took 1.6 million tons of steel, 575,000 tons of aluminum, and 6 million tons of glass to produce disposable containers, which, altogether, account for about 8 percent of municipal solid waste and 25 percent of all litter. Supporters within the states are joined by such organizations as the National Wildlife Federation, the National Audubon Society, and the League of Women Voters, all of whom express concern about the environment, quality of life, and wasteful depletion of natural resources.

Opponents point to what they see as the undesirable consequences of forced deposit legislation. They forecast a sizable loss of jobs in the container and basic materials industries, and predict that prices for beverages will increase as much as 50 percent because of higher costs. They argue that storage of used containers waiting to be collected is unsanitary, often attracting roaches and rodents. They state that when total recycling costs for aluminum cans are considered, the process is far from economical and that aluminum producers conduct recovery processes for public relations rather than for profit.

Opponents to these laws argue that while it is relatively easy for local plants to use refillable containers, it is quite expensive for larger firms, such as beer producers, who must collect, transport, and process reusable bottles. As to the question of litter, the industry position is that the ''bottle laws'' do not attack the total problem, since a study in Oregon showed total litter dropped only about 10 percent after passage of a container law. They suggest that the Washington State approach of taxing gross sales of groceries, newspapers, fast food, and other items, and using the proceeds for litter-reduction education and to fund litter pickup, is more realistic.

The potential loss of jobs is a major issue and has been credited with the defeat of deposit legislation in several states. However, proponents of bottle bills say this does not happen. Two business administration professors at Oregon State University studied the economic effects of that state's law and found it actually caused an increase in employment. Although manufacturing labor for producing containers decreased, there was a greater need for truck drivers and handlers for the empties. *Audubon* magazine claimed that the larger number of Oregon jobs netted the state $1.6 million in wages. Of course, what this suggests is a substitution of unskilled for skilled labor.

Forces on both sides of the issue believe that individual state and local laws create chaos in distribution since each law requires different procedures and types of deposits. Thus, only a national law would really work. Today, there are nine states with container deposit laws: Connecticut, Delaware, Iowa, Maine, Massachusetts, Michigan, New York, Oregon, and Vermont. Many smaller jurisdictions had container deposit ordinances during the 1970s, but most of them were repealed after public interest waned.

THE FAIRFAX COUNTY EXPERIMENT

The deceptive wording of the Fairfax County ordinance masks its major flaw. The phrase "certain non-reusable containers" has, in fact, a narrow application. It actually means that nonalcoholic, carbonated beverages can only be sold in nonreturnable containers if retailers agree to refund at least five cents to each consumer who returns an empty bottle or can. Beer, liquor, and noncarbonated beverages, such as iced tea, fruit punch, and chocolate drinks, are not included. Beer containers were left out because of a unique feature of Virginia law that gives the Alcoholic Beverage Commission jurisdiction over *all* aspects of alcoholic beverages, including details of how they are sold. Thus, the ordinance singles out only carbonated soft-drink containers as a source of litter that needs to be controlled.

Because Fairfax County is surrounded by jurisdictions that do not have bottle laws, there are problems of selected local enforcement. Retailers within the county wanted assurances that containers from these jurisdictions would not be presented for deposit return in county stores. So a special "deposit" sticker had to be affixed to each bottle sold in the county, identifying it as subject to deposit redemption.

Since the stated purpose of the ordinance was to reduce litter and to "beautify the highways and enhance scenic beauty," there were other difficulties as well:

1. Not only are beer cans and bottles excluded from the deposit requirement, but so are vending machines that dispense only noncarbonated beverages. So two major sources of bottle and can beverage litter remain within the county.
2. Exhibit 8-1 shows the geographical position of Fairfax County relative to adjacent jurisdictions, and suggests there will be heavy traffic between those jurisdictions and county points. So persons who live outside the county and consume beverages while traveling through it are likely to discard containers along county roads. Since the containers cannot be returned for deposit refund, they will not be scavenged.
3. After lying alongside the road, deposit stickers tend to wear or wash off, so the containers have no further value. Again, this problem discourages those who hope to profit by roadside scavenging, and a large part of the litter problem remains.

CONSUMER PRICES WITH
AND WITHOUT DEPOSIT ORDINANCES

Prodeposit advocates maintain that retail prices will be lower if deposits are required, while those against deposits say prices will be higher. Fairfax County is an ideal location to make consumer price comparisons because surrounding jurisdictions still sell beverages in one-way, no-deposit containers. Thus, advertising in metropolitan area media must show prices for each jurisdiction where there are differences. Exhibit 8-2 shows prices when the Fairfax ordinance had been in effect for about 18 months, and Exhibit 8-3 shows the information in tabular form. Pepsi prices were highest for one-way containers (21.5 cents) and lowest for refillables (16.125 cents). Coke's spread is smaller with 19.83 and 18.625 cents, respectively. Of course, these are sale prices, and store number 3 indicated in its ad that regular prices are 50 cents higher.

The exhibits suggest, however, that consumers do realize savings by buying returnable containers, and the industry's prediction of higher prices have not materialized, at least not in this situation. How consumers actually perceive the importance of these savings should be reflected in any changes they make in their shopping patterns.

RELATED COSTS

As suggested earlier, statistical cost benefit information from both sides is often difficult to verify or comprehend. Basic common sense and simple economics, however, indicate there are additional costs when retailers and bottlers change from deposit to returnable containers:

1. Two major food retail chains in the Washington area estimate nearly 50 weekly hours of labor per store are needed to affix stickers to each one-way bottle, make refunds, and sort the used containers. The store also has to allocate

storage space for them. Labor cost alone amounts to $350 (50 hrs @ $7) in county stores, plus $50 for space, for a total of $400. In the grocery business where profits are about 1.5 cents per sales dollar, each store must generate an additional $26,666 in sales to break even. It is difficult to see how retailers can absorb the additional costs so they must be passed on to consumers in overall higher grocery prices.

2. Bottlers who use refillables save the cost of a one-way bottle each time the reusables make a round trip, but there are offsetting costs. Used bottles have to be transported from retailers to bottling plants, and the additional time it takes to collect and load these bottles reduces the number of calls a driver can make. So there have to be more trucks and drivers to handle the same routes. Washing and sterilizing used bottles also means new equipment investment, increased operating costs, and higher insurance rates on the risk of foreign matter in the bottles. These expenses increase the number of round trips a bottler must get from refillables. The Environmental Protection Agency estimates it takes ten round trips, at a minimum, to break even.

SURVEY RESULTS

To determine whether or not consumers changed their shopping patterns because of Fairfax County's deposit ordinance, a survey was conducted by a local university. One hundred respondents were interviewed in four areas of the county that were geographically close to jurisdictions that had no bottle deposit requirement. Replies to selected questions in this survey are shown in Exhibit 8-4.

To fully appreciate the significance of the survey information, a unique feature of the Virginia sales tax system must be understood. The sales tax rate is 4 percent, of which 1 percent is returned to the locality where the retail sale occurred.

Exhibit 8-4 shows that nearly half (45 percent) of the respondents still buy beverages in throw-away containers, and six out of ten of these buyers make a trip outside the county to buy them. So for every dollar spent for soft drinks, the county loses one cent in sales tax revenue. But there may be another, more significant, loss because consumers are also likely to do their grocery shopping at the same stores where they buy their deposit-free soft drinks. If only two out of ten families that buy their soft drinks outside the county also buy their groceries there, the retail sales loss is over $35 million, with over $351,000 lost to the county from its share of sales tax revenues. This calculation used a county population of 600,000, an average household size of three, and an average weekly household grocery bill of $75.

THE ORDINANCE IN OPERATION

Any effort to reduce litter from beverage containers has to do more than single out one segment of the array of products that cause the problem. Since the Fairfax ordinance failed to do this, it was ineffective in achieving its purpose of litter control. Even if beer and other containers had been included in the law, the interjurisdictional mobility of people in this populated suburban area provides easy alternatives for those who object to the legislated inconvenience. But an important factor in terms of consumer behavior is that the product itself was changed. Consumers were accustomed to treating beverage packaging the same as other packaging. When the product was used or consumed, the package was discarded. By altering this aspect of "product," many consumers were apparently willing to go out of their way to obtain the product in its desired form. And since the ordinance was local, it was comparatively easy for consumers to circumvent it by buying elsewhere.

The usual reply to criticism of a bad law with good intentions is that it is better than no law at all. The Fairfax ordinance, however, does little more than substitute retailers and soft-drink distributors for the highway clean-up crew, and then for only a relatively small part of the total litter. By permitting one-way containers to be sold at all, the ordinance lulls environmentalists and consumers into believing they have solved the litter problem. They haven't.

In Fairfax County, the problems inherent in this largely ineffective and unpopular legislation were solved when the legislature of the Commonwealth of Virginia ruled the ordinance invalid.

Analysis Questions

1. What are the factors involved in "product" that caused some consumers to alter their buying habits? What, if anything, changed with regard to the physical product itself?

2. What learning theory is involved in this situation? What are the factors in the case that make this theory appropriate?

3. Can you calculate the expected loss to the county using data given in the case?

4. Considering the information in Exhibits 8-2 and 8-3, how do you account for the large proportion of respondents in the survey who thought the deposit law increased beverage prices?

FAIRFAX COUNTY BOTTLE BILL

EXHIBIT 8-1

County Map Showing Adjacent Jurisdictions

FAIRFAX COUNTY BOTTLE BILL

EXHIBIT 8-2

Not available in Fairfax county.

**save!
coca-cola or
tab**

reg. 1.21

88¢ (a)

92c in Montgomery county.
2 liter no return bottles.

Fairfax county only

**coca-cola,
tab or
fresca**

reg. 2.09

1 27
plus deposit

8 pack, 16 oz.
returnable bottles.

(C)
**RC COLA
OR
DIET RITE
COLA**

16 OZ. N.R. BOTTLES
6 PACK

$1 27

BONUS
BUY

SALE PRICE $1.39 IN MONTGOMERY COUNTY
DUE TO COUNTY SOFT DRINK TAX.
WITH THIS COUPON   EXPIRES 9-16-78-W
MINIMUM 60 CASES PER STORE

1.89 FAIRFAX & LOUDOUN COUNTIES
**RC COLA OR
DIET RITE COLA**
16 OZ. RETURNABLE BOTTLES
8 PACK

$1 29
PLUS
DEPOSIT

**FREE SGT. PEPPER POSTER
WITH PURCHASE OF DR. PEPPER**

(D)
● **DR. PEPPER**
● **SEVEN-UP**
● **DOUBLE COLA**

64 OZ.
N.R. BOTTLE

77¢

SALE PRICE 81c IN MONTGOMERY COUNTY
DUE TO COUNTY SOFT DRINK TAX.
WITH THIS COUPON   EXPIRES 10-28-78-C
MINIMUM 120 ASST. PER STORE

FAIRFAX COUNTY ONLY
● **DR. PEPPER** ● **SEVEN-UP**
● **DOUBLE COLA**   PLUS
64 OZ. N.R. BOTTLE   DEPOSIT **82¢**

**PEPSI or
DIET PEPSI**

6-pk.
16-oz.   **1.19**   Plus
nrb   Tax in
                      Mont. Co.

IN FAIRFAX COUNTY

16-oz.   **1.29**   Plus
8-pk.   Deposit

Limit 1 Case/4 - 6 pks.

FAIRFAX COUNTY BOTTLE BILL

EXHIBIT 8-3

Fairfax County and the Washington D.C. area Soft Drink Prices in Returnable and Nonreturnable Containers[a]

Store No.	Brand	# Bottles in Pkg.	# Ounces	Returnable Bottle Price	One-Way Bottle Price	Net Unit Price
1	Pepsi Cola	6	16		1.23	.205
1	Pepsi Cola	8	16	1.29		.16125
2	Coca Cola	6	16		1.19	.19833
2	Coca Cola	8	16	1.49		.18625
3	Pepsi Cola	6	16		1.29[b]	.215
3	Pepsi Cola	8	16	1.39[c]		.17375

[a] Prices do not include any bottle deposit.
[b] Advertisement indicates 50 cents saving, so normal price is $1.79 or .2983 per bottle.
[c] Advertisement indicates 48 cents saving, so normal price is $1.87 or .23375 per bottle.

FAIRFAX COUNTY BOTTLE BILL

EXHIBIT 8-4

**Replies to Selected Questions by 100 Randomly Chosen Fairfax County
Consumers in Four Locations
(Equal numbers were not selected from each location as shown below)**

Question	Total %	District or Town %			
		Annandale	McLean	Springfield	Vienna
Do you buy all or most of your groceries and soft drinks outside Fairfax County?					
Yes	61.0	47.4	80.0	50.0	65.0
No	39.0	52.6	20.0	50.0	35.0
Before the law, how did you buy soft drinks?					
Returnables only	15.0	15.7	16.0	10.5	15.0
Nonreturnables only	64.0	73.7	60.0	57.9	60.0
Both types	21.0	10.5	24.0	31.6	25.0
If you buy throw-aways, do you make a special trip to get them?					
Yes	57.0	37.5	54.5	66.6	60.0
No	43.0	62.5	45.5	33.3	40.0
Do you now buy soft drinks in throw-away containers?					
Yes	45.0	50.0	44.0	50.0	26.4
No	53.0	50.0	55.0	49.0	73.6
No reply	2.0	0	1.0	1.0	0
Do you think a law that bans throw-aways increases beverage prices to you?					
Yes	57.6	47.4	60.0	68.4	79.0
No	41.4	52.6	39.0	31.6	21.0
Don't know	1.0	0	1.0	0	0

Case 9

Which Coke Is It?

In 1886 John S. Pemberton, an Atlanta dentist, concocted the first batch of what he called "The Brain Tonic and Intellectual Beverage," which became Coca-Cola. Today, his "secret" formula known as "Merchandise 7X" is kept in the vault of an Atlanta bank, and its ingredients are known only to a few company executives. It has changed very little over the years. In 1903 a tiny trace of cocaine (.004 percent) was removed, but company officials say that the basic taste has never been altered.

The company itself is the world's largest producer and distributor of soft drink concentrates and syrups. Its principal products in early 1985 were Coca-Cola and caffeine-free Coca-Cola, Diet Coke and caffeine-free Diet Coke (low-calorie drinks), Cherry Coke, Fresca (a low-calorie citrus-based beverage), Sprite (a lemon-lime drink), TAB and caffeine-free TAB, Minute Maid orange soda, the Fanta line of eight flavors, and several other drinks. In 1984, about 68 percent of Coca-Cola syrup and concentrate was sold to approximately 500 bottlers, who prepare and sell the drink in individual territories; the rest was sold to approximately 4,000 authorized wholesalers, who resell the syrup to restaurants and other retailers. Operations outside the United States accounted for 38 percent of the total net operating revenues and nearly half of operating income in 1984. Coca-Cola's Columbia Pictures Industries, Inc., produces and distributes theatrical motion pictures and television series. The Foods Group of Coca-Cola makes and sells Minute Maid citrus juice products, Five Alive, Hi-C, and Bright and Early fruit beverages.

THE 1985 MEDIA HYPE

The spring of 1985 brought a number of important national and world events, but it is highly possible that none could compete with the ballyhoo that accompanied the changing of Dr. Pemberton's 99-year old formula—dubbed the "New Coke Event"—which was soon followed by the "Return to the Old Coke Event." Some marketing experts have suggested that the whole thing was orchestrated by Coca-Cola, which got millions of dollars worth of publicity for its brand. But tampering with the American public's favorite soft drink caused a consumer uproar, and possibly some brand-switching action as well. Despite Coke's public handwringing over problems with its new version, the company may well have received much more than the $4 million it spent in taste testing the new Coke, in free publicity. At the least, according to recent reports, its share of the overall U.S. soft-drink market has shown a significant increase since the two events.

THE PEPSI CHALLENGE

Pepsi-Cola had been challenging Coca-Cola with increasing aggressiveness for about ten years before the complacent soft drink giant began to stir in 1982. In that year, Coke's eroding position in the market triggered a change in the firm's business strategy, which was as sacrosanct as the original Coca-Cola formula. Its basis was simple: "Don't touch the recipe" and "Use individual, not family brands (Call them 'Tab')." The distribution system was also run by do and don't fiats: Don't compete with bottlers; Allow them a generous profitability, even the smallest and most inefficient ones; Don't meddle in your bottler's business. All of these rules worked extremely well for years.

But Pepsi had to fight for what it had. In the beginning, it used pure price differentiation, as shown in this 50-year-old jingle:

Pepsi-Cola hits the spot.
Twelve full ounces, that's a lot.
Twice as much for a nickel, too.
Pepsi-Cola is the drink for you.

It took a long time for Pepsi to start thinking that it might just be as good as Coca-Cola, if not better. But when it did, the direct challenge to Coke began with trade discounts to supermarkets and by using promotions rather than advertising. By 1979, Pepsi took the leadership away from Coca-Cola in take-home markets, although Coke has remained on top in fountain service and restaurants. It appears that, once introduced to Pepsi-Cola by price inducements, many consumers apparently agreed that it was just as good as Coca-Cola.

Michael Norkus, vice president of the Boston Consulting Group, suggests that Coca-Cola's prolonged period of success and production orientation may have done the firm more harm than its competitor did. He points out that "Pepsi's unrelenting aggressiveness may actually have helped its archrival to effect this massive change in its strategy by infusing it with enough anger and adrenalin to make the change. While the battle is far from over, Coca-Cola's change in belief—which prompted the change in taste—will have an impact far after the new Coke has stopped being news." In other words, Coca-Cola's move toward more of a consumer orientation may be more damaging to Pepsi in the long run.

ANNOUNCING THE NEW COKE

In 1984, regular Coca-Cola had a 21.8 percent share of the soft-drink market in the United States, a considerable drop from its 24.3 percent share in 1980. But the company's overall share moved up from 34.4 percent in 1980 to 36.4 percent in 1984, thanks to the introduction of other drink brands, along with diet and caffeine-free versions of Coke itself. Due largely to consumer life-style changes, Diet Coke has cannibalized its namesake somewhat, and was the third most popular soft drink in the United States. Regular Coke is still on top, though, with regular Pepsi in second place.

On April 23, 1985, the Coca-Cola company announced the first major change in the soft drink's formula since it was introduced 99 years earlier. The new taste had been first developed several years before while researchers were working on the formulation of Diet Coke, and the decision to make the change was the result of some of the most extensive market and consumer research in the history of the industry. The new Coke was to have a smoother, sweeter taste, but with only a few more calories. In a widespread, $4 million survey conducted for the company in secret, 55 percent of nearly 200,000 respondents said they liked the new version, while 45 percent preferred the old. With the brand showing, the preference was 61 to 39 percent for the new. When regular drinkers of Coke were tested, however, only 53 percent preferred the new version. Interestingly, over half (55 percent) of Pepsi drinkers chose the new Coke over Pepsi-Cola.

Coke also made some upscale changes to its can, adding gold tops and silver stripes to a redesigned red-and-white container, to give the perception of a different, but premium, product. Coke's chairman, Roberto Goizueta, announced the change at New York's Lincoln Center. He described the new product's taste as "smoother, rounder, yet bolder. It's a more harmonious flavor." And he added, "Thousands of consumers across the width and breadth of this country have told us this is the taste they prefer. The decision, in fact, was one of the easiest we have ever made." The company began producing the new formula on April 23, and expected to have the new

Coke on grocery shelves in two-thirds of the United States in three weeks. The nation would be covered by the end of May, with worldwide distribution by the end of 1985.

But the weeks following the announcement were not quiet ones. Egged on by the media, which characteristically turned up disgruntled consumers who did not like the new Coke and others who thought it tasted like Pepsi, consumers began to ally themselves into pro and con "new Coke" camps. Not one to hang back, Pepsi executive Roger Enrico said in full-page newspaper ads: "Coca-Cola is withdrawing their product from the market-place, and is reformulating brand Coke to be more like Pepsi. Too bad Ripley's not around. . . . He could have had a field day with this."

By the end of June, more than 40,000 consumers had phoned Coca-Cola on its 800-number hotline. Most were outraged "Cokaholics" who complained about the new formula's blandness, compared to the old product. The company mailed coupons for a free six-pack of new Coke to those who complained. Other consumers were shown on the media in the midst of their hoards of bottles and six-packs of the old Coke—some stocking up for use in the dark days ahead, and others preparing to sell at a profit when the supply finally dried up. In Seattle, a group called Old Coke Drinkers of America claimed to have 100,000 members. It was organized to exert pressure to bring back the old Coke, by sponsoring rallies and boycotts.

Coca-Cola, however, said that its shipments in May 1985, were 8 percent higher than the same month a year before. And reports from bottlers were that the new Coke was selling much better than expected. But the company had strong indications that at least some of the 47 percent of the old Coke drinkers in the research study who did not like the new Coke might move to other brands. And the further south the new Coke went, the more disappointing were the results. In the end, it was pressure from the bottlers that tipped the scale toward reintroducing the old formula. They were uneasy about the strength of the opposition to the new Coke. As one Alabama bottler put it: "Some consumers were mad. It was almost a psychological thing." And a consumer explained his problem even more clearly: "First it was the telephone company and now it's Coca-Cola. What's next?"

RETURN OF THE "CLASSIC"

Until July 1985, Coca-Cola had downplayed reports about the large number of unhappy Coke customers. It said its information indicated that only about 1 percent of the old Coke drinkers were switching brands, and that most of the complaints came from light users. But on July 10, 1985, the company announced that "thousands of dedicated customers have told us they still want the original taste as an option."

On July 11, in a surprise announcement, the company said it would reintroduce the regular brand as "Coke Classic" in the next several weeks. Chairman Goizueta explained: "Coca-Cola Classic—the new name for the original formula—will increase the share of the cola market (the six products that now bear the Coke name) as a megabrand." The company's reponse to consumer signals had been a rapid one, by industry standards. But it was also a fast turnaround for a company that thought it had its finger on the pulse of U.S. public opinion. Wall Street also thought the move was timely. Coca-Cola stock gained $2.35 a share on Wednesday, July 10, when the word first leaked out, and then added another $2.375 on Wednesday when the formal announcement was made. The stock closed on Wednesday at $74.75. The consolidated income statements for the quarters ending September 1984 and 1985 are shown in Exhibit 9-1. Net sales and net income for 1977 through 1984 are shown in Exhibit 9-2.

Some Coca-Cola executives suggest that an ideal situation would be for Coke Classic to maintain a "maturity" market share, without much advertising or promotion support, leaving the decisions to consumers as to which type they wanted. The new Coke would continue to be the company's flagship brand, and it will also be heavily supported in foreign markets. The new formulation may be even more important there than in the United States because Coke can use it in a fresh round of promotions. Also, there is no single major competitor challenging Coca-Cola overseas.

THE CONSUMER TASTE TEST

The chairman of Coca-Cola was quoted earlier as saying, "The decision [to change the formula] was one of the easiest we have ever made." In the taste test, well over half of the regular Coke drinkers liked the new version, and 47 percent did not. But what the research failed to measure was the psychological impact of changing a product that has been an American institution for a century, and few products could stir up as much emotion as Coke. Some psychologists suggest that the consumer uprising against the new Coke had less to do with the taste of the product itself than it did with the idea of changing an institution.

The company also gave more credence to the taste test than it deserved. While this type of test is important for a product like Coke, it is only one element of the marketing mix, which also includes price, packaging, advertising, and distribution. Many aspects of the test can introduce errors. For example, when a survey respondent walks up to a taste-test booth, the first sample often tastes better than the second, particularly on a hot day or if the respondent is thirsty. Also, respondents are more likely to choose a brand or a cup labeled 1 or A than they are 2 or B, and sip-tests may yield different results from a more leisurely test with full glasses of the product. Others criticize the two-choice taste test, pointing out that consumers have many more choices in a supermarket. They may choose new Coke over old in a taste test, but may actually prefer Pepsi or Royal Crown and buy them in the store.

Researchers try to minimize at least some of these "situational effects" by keeping test samples at the same temperature, serving only one sample from a container, and providing respondents with a cup of water or a cracker between samplings. But the sampling is mostly done in unnatural settings. Campbell Soup researchers say they often get vastly different results when respondents eat full bowls of soup or drink full glasses of juice at home, as opposed to results from sip- or small-cup tests in mail intercepts. One research executive says: "You have to be careful of the cumulative effect of a product. After extended use (drinking, say, a full glass), a product may suddenly seem too sweet or not really very thirst-quenching."

Scientists say that the sense of taste is a complex process that they do not fully understand. Flavor involves the interaction of taste buds, the sense of smell, color, and the trigeminal nerve, which responds to hot and cold or pain and irritation. So people's responses vary by time of day, whether or not they have eaten recently, and what they ate. As to color, market researchers say that 7-Up often beats colas in taste tests because people like its clear, light color and the green bottle. A Coca-Cola researcher says that only about half the population has taste buds sensitive enough to tell the difference between Coke and Pepsi. "If you remove the caramel color from Coke, a lot of people won't be able to tell it from one of the clear drinks, like Sprite," he points out.

THE AFTERMATH

June 1985 sales of the new Coke showed little improvement over sales a year earlier, and July was about the same. In early August, however, Coke's sugared sales (new and classic versus diet) were up 15 percent over the previous year. But some small part of that gain was due to the aggressive introduction of Cherry Coke. *Business Week* reported that extensive interviews with bottlers indicated that instead of the expected cannibalization of each other's sales, the two colas together have captured a larger share of the market than they would have separately.

Yet, sales of the Coke Classic have been greatest in Coke's traditional stronghold, the South and the Southwest. Its return was heralded from Texas to North Carolina, which was heartening news for Coca-Cola because imminent brand-switching in the southern states brought about the return of the regular formula. In the North, it is the other way around. Bottlers say new Coke is selling well.

Nevertheless, the company is still trying to make the new Coke its flagship brand, and it is pressuring bottlers to push it. But many bottlers are reluctant to, as one put it, "force the product down the consumer's throats." Their position is that the company was wrong in the first place to take regular Coke off the shelves and attempt to dictate what consumers would drink.

Another problem faced by all new soft-drink products sold in fountains and restaurants is the number of available dispensing spouts. Most fast-food chains are equipped to serve only one sugared cola so they must decide which of Coke's two brands to carry. This decision is crucial to Coca-Cola because one-third of Coke's U.S. sales are at fountains. If the decision moves away from the new Coke, there will be a serious problem in making it the flagship brand. And to make matters worse, Pepsi is moving aggressively toward the fountain business where it has historically been weak.

In the third quarter of 1985 ending in September, Coke Classic sales overtook the new formulation for the first time. By the end of the quarter, Classic had about a 70 percent share of the combined volume of the two sugared products. Its reintroduction in July is credited with increasing Coca-Cola's total domestic soft-drink sales in the third quarter by 8 percent over the same period in 1984. At the end of 1985, Coca-Cola's share of the U.S. soft-drink market had grown to 39 percent, an increase of 6 percent during the year. This was the largest share the company had achieved in decades. Pepsi-Cola's share grew 8 percent in 1984, to an overall 27 percent.

The company also announced that it pushed back the schedule for introducing the new Coke in the international market until the spring of 1986. It had originally planned the overseas introduction in the fall of 1985. While Coca-Cola can use the "new" designation on its overseas cans, it was forced to take it off the U.S. product in October 1985. Federal Trade Commission guidelines say that a product is no longer new after it has been on the market for six months.

In early 1986, Coca-Cola announced that it would market Coke Classic and new Coke separately. The Coke Classic theme would revert to the traditional classical conditioning one, depicting Coke has a part of the American landscape. It is likely that this perception was the underlying factor in the uprising of old Coke's brand-loyal customers in July 1985, which ultimately put the product back on the market. The new slogan, "Red, White, and You," calls attention to Coke's colors and fits nicely into that perception. Ads will use athletes and entertainers as well as ordinary people, with patriotic themes. The new Coke will compete directly with Pepsi Cola, and its ads will reflect more contemporary ideas, with high-tech visual effects. The new "Catch the Wave" slogan conveys a fast, modern tempo with a suggestion of sports and surfing.

Industry analysts say it will be a long time before they get a clear picture of the long-term effect of the new Coke product on sugared cola sales. But one thing is certain. The sleeping giant has awakened with renewed vigor and aggressiveness. Its new product maneuvers may have solidified its leadership in the soft drink industry after all.

Analysis Questions

    1. What do you think the underlying influences were that caused the consumer backlash against the new Coke? Do brand loyalty and operant (or instrumental) conditioning play a part?

    2. Why did Coca-Cola apparently put all its faith in its massive taste test? What else might they have done?

    3. Do you think that the Coke reformulation was simply a ploy devised by Coca-Cola to increase its market share by getting massive amounts of free publicity?

WHICH COKE IS IT?

EXHIBIT 9-1

Coca-Cola Company Abbreviated Consolidated Earning Statements (in millions)

	1984	1983	1982	1981	1980	1979
Net operating revenue	7,498	6,828	6,021	5,699	5,475	4,588
Cost of goods, services, selling, and admin exp.	5,986	5,836	5,141	4,913	4,738	3,899
Operating income	1,512	993	880	786	737	689
Interest and taxes net	563	435	377	346	333	295
Income-discont'd ops	—	1	9	42	19	26
NET INCOME	629	559	512	482	423	420

WHICH COKE IS IT?

EXHIBIT 9-2

Coca-Cola Company Operating Profit by Quarters, 1982–85 (three Quarters) (in millions)

Quarter	1982	1983	1984	1985
1	$102.2	$122.2	$138.0	$141.2
2	139.8	160.4	185.0	167.2
3	143.4	153.2	175.3	195.7
4	121.3	124.6	124.8	

Case 10

The Sport of Kings

In Shakopee, Minnesota, just outside of Minneapolis, the newest race track in the United States opened for business in late June 1985. It was only the second tract built in the nation in the past ten years, and cost some $70 million. It was odd enough that this track was built in Minnesota, a state not exactly teeming with industrial and other blue-collar workers. This group, together with minorities, have been the mainstay of most race tracks throughout the country. But even more puzzling, it comes at a time when horse racing is declining in popularity. Until 1984, horse racing was the best-attended spectator sport in the United States, but in that year it was edged out of its lead by baseball. Although major league baseball attendance is a little more than half of racing attendance, other leagues account for nearly an equal amount, and the total put racing in second place. Exhibit 10-1 shows the steady growth in the number of major league spectators since 1970 and the leveling off of racing attendance. The table also shows that football, both college and professional, is a poor third, with basketball, college and pro, fourth. Exhibit 10-2, however, shows that the net receipts from parimutuel betting have nearly doubled from 1970 to 1983. Parimutuel is a system of betting on races in which the winning bettors share the total amount bet, less a percentage for the track operators.

Canterbury Downs, the new Minnesota track, is supposed to contribute $150 million annually to the state's economy. But going to the races will be a new experience for many of its potential customers since only about half of those who live in the Minneapolis metropolitan area have ever been to a track. And only a tiny percentage of those who have can define such a common racing term as *exacta* accurately. The question is whether or not this unique location with its nonracing demographics can attract the estimated 10,000 daily customers who will spend an average of $120 each.

PROBLEMS AT OTHER TRACKS

Older tracks are having their own problems attracting customers, and the industry has been casting about for something that will rekindle the racing spirit. Noting the success of the Super Bowl and its phenomenal contribution to the coffers of professional football, the racing industry decided to stage a spectacular annual event called the Breeders' Cup. This extravaganza would feature about 100 horses, from which would be selected champions in a number of different horse-demographic races.

Winners of the top seven races would be awarded a total of $10 million in cash prizes, the most ever in the history of horse racing. The first Breeders' Cup was held on November 10, 1984 at the Hollywood Park track in California, which had been completely refurbished for the event. The television blitz and the four solid hours of racing with their accompanying commentary and pageantry were supposed to reach 7 percent of all U.S. television households. It actually attracted 5.1 percent, while the Kentucky Derby reached about 12 percent that same year. The second annual Breeders' Cup was run at Aqueduct Race Track in New York on November 2, 1985, with limited success. Thus far, the Breeders' Cup is not doing for racing what the Super Bowl does for football.

UNDERLYING PROBLEMS

Marketing observers say that the hype and hoopla of this kind of event will do little to solve the real problems of the racing business. It merely extends the futile approaches the industry has taken in the past, such as lobbying state legislatures for more racing days and trying to get permission to take more profitable bets. But neither showmanship nor modifications to the same old track fare are likely to change the attitudes of the younger market that racing so desperately needs.

Racing's sellers and buyers are a study in contrast. On the one side is a wealthy, cliquey, professional group of owners, trainers, and breeders. On the other are track customers: blue-collar workers, minorities, a few seedy touts, and some white-collar middle-class patrons. The former are beset by skyrocketing costs and the latter are upscale in age—the average age of a racing fan is 50. *Business Week* quotes a sports management consultant as saying, "The racing industry has not been innovative in marketing." One reason for this problem is that the sport is largely regional. Racing is closely regulated, usually by state racing commissions, which allocate an equal number of the available racing days to tracks in their jurisdiction. So when one track is running, the others may be closed. Another reason is that the sport itself is not too sure which market or markets it is competing against for fans. Are baseball, football, and basketball the main competition? Are off-track betting, state lotteries, and illegal gambling operations keeping customers away from the track? Are potential racing fans seeking other types of entertainment? Or is it all three? To some extent, they all compete for the customer's discretionary income.

CONSUMER ATTITUDES

New York tracks tried to change attitudes toward racing by luring younger potential fans to the races with attractions these customers were already favorable toward—concerts featuring big-name bands and entertainers. The gimmick brought these customers in, but they came to hear the music. Apparently their attitudes toward racing were unchanged since they bet very little. If attitudes and behavior are closely allied, as they are supposed to be, then attitudes of the younger population are negative toward horse racing.

Exhibit 10-3 shows results of a semantic differential scale measurement of attitudes and beliefs about horse racing, and Exhibit 10-4 depicts the perceived attractions of the four major spectator sports in the United States. The data in these exhibits were extracted from larger studies on spectator sports. Overall, the exhibits suggest largely unfavorable attitudes to racing and visiting the track.

Analysis Questions

1. Of the statements on the semantic differential image profile shown in Exhibit 10-4, which would you classify as overall attitudes (the affective component) and which are more related to beliefs (the cognitive component)?

2. What approach has the management of the Breeders' Cup event and the New York track concerts taken to attract younger customers? Why haven't either of these activities attracted more of the target group as active racing fans?

3. What approaches do you think the track owners might use to change attitudes or beliefs?

THE SPORT OF KINGS

EXHIBIT 10-1

Attendance for Spectator Sports, 1970–83
(000)

Sport	1970	1975	1978	1980	1982	1983
Baseball (majors)	29,191	30,373	41,402	43,746	45,415	46,269
Horseracing	69,704	78,662	75,324	74,690	76,858	75,693
Football[a]	39,537	42,457	47,728	49,633	45,043[b]	50,255
Basketball[a]	4,912[c]	7,591[c]	39,791	41,697	41,838	41,733

[a] Includes both college and professional attendance
[b] Season interrupted by professional strike
[c] Professional attendance only

THE SPORT OF KINGS

EXHIBIT 10-2

Net Receipts from Parimutuel Betting, 1970–83
(in millions)

1970	1975	1978	1980	1982	1983
$1,096	$1,568	$1,722	$1,859	$1,951	$1,974

THE SPORT OF KINGS

EXHIBIT 10-3

Race Track Image

Average Rating: Semantic Differential Scale

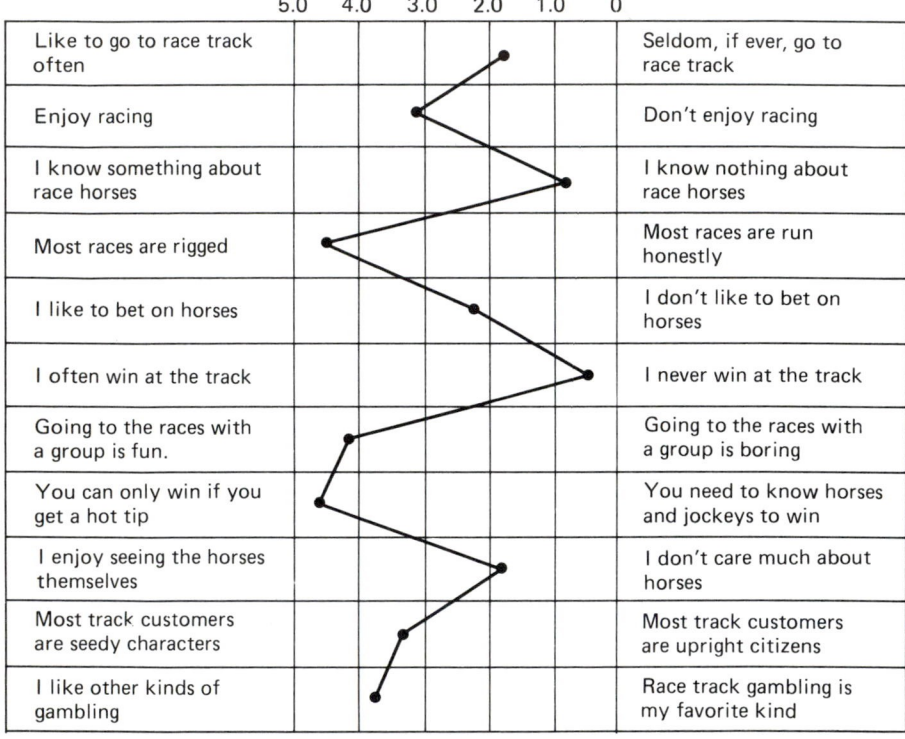

	5.0	4.0	3.0	2.0	1.0	0	
Like to go to race track often							Seldom, if ever, go to race track
Enjoy racing							Don't enjoy racing
I know something about race horses							I know nothing about race horses
Most races are rigged							Most races are run honestly
I like to bet on horses							I don't like to bet on horses
I often win at the track							I never win at the track
Going to the races with a group is fun.							Going to the races with a group is boring
You can only win if you get a hot tip							You need to know horses and jockeys to win
I enjoy seeing the horses themselves							I don't care much about horses
Most track customers are seedy characters							Most track customers are upright citizens
I like other kinds of gambling							Race track gambling is my favorite kind

THE SPORT OF KINGS

EXHIBIT 10-4

Perceived Attractions of Four Major Sports
(Rank Ordered)

Question: If you enjoy any of these sports, please list the reasons why you do.

Professional Football	Professional Basketball	Horse Racing	Major League Baseball
Action	Fast moving	Betting	Team play
Physical sport	Individual play	Know horses	Individual skills
Fast moving	Interesting to watch	Personal participation	Pennant race
Super Bowl	Strategy game	Know jockeys	
Colorful			

Case 11

Procter & Gamble— The Sign and the Symbol

Since it was founded in 1837 as a soap and candle-making firm, Procter & Gamble has been an American institution. Its Ivory soap, introduced in 1879, is probably the one product most people associate with the company, although it has a number of other noteworthy accomplishments to its credit. Procter & Gamble conducted its first market research in 1924 and, by acquiring an English soap firm, made its first overseas move in 1930. In 1932, P&G sponsored the first radio soap opera, called "The Puddle Family." Fourteen years later, in 1946, Tide was introduced, followed by Crest toothpaste in 1955, and Pampers in 1961. From 1980 through 1982 it embarked on a diversification program, acquiring Ben Hill Griffin Citrus and Norwich Eaton Pharmaceuticals.

Its 1924 expedition into market research marked the beginning of P&G's close relationship with its customers. This continuing dialogue between producer and consumer began, so the story goes, back in 1879 when a mixing vat worker forgot to turn off his machine when he went to lunch. When he came back, instead of the usual creamy substance ready to be molded into soap cakes, he found a frothy mixture that appeared to be useless. But he and his foreman decided the soap had not really been harmed and they were able to mold it well enough to sell. A few weeks later, P&G began getting pleas from storekeepers along the Ohio river for "more of that floating soap." Tracing back to the mistake, the firm found that air bubbles whipped into the liquid soap by the longer mixing process gave the soap a buoyancy that kept it afloat while its users were bathing or washing in the murky river.

This incident not only spawned Ivory soap, but it also gave life to a policy of being tuned-in to what consumers want. Today, P&G receives and replies to nearly half a million customer letters and telephone calls each year. One result of P&G's close attention to this overwhelming volume is that, in 1981, P&G products held six places out of the top ten household products, three of the top ten in health and beauty aids, and two of the top ten in food products. About one-half of the calls and letters are requests for information, one-third are complaints, and one-sixth are positive comments.

In addition to the contacts that are initiated by consumers themselves, P&G calls upon over 1.5 million people each year in research projects designed to find out what people think about its products, their packaging, effectiveness, and other characteristics. The research also includes inquiries into how people go about doing such household tasks as cleaning, preparing meals, and washing clothes. The firm's cautious entry into a toll-free telephone response program in 1974 helped with this research. The head of P&G's consumer services department describes results from the number on Duncan Hines brownie mix packages: "We learned that people in high altitudes needed special instructions for baking, and we added these to the package. We also found one of the box recipes was confusing and we changed that." Although consumers send in about 4,000 new product ideas a year, most of them do not usually amount to much. The real pay dirt comes from "basic" research where P&G asks the questions and observes people at their regular household chores.

P&G has also been a socially responsible firm. It reacted positively and rapidly to the discovery that its Rely brand tampons were related to toxic shock syndrome. Within about two weeks, they had removed this product from the shelves, although this action prematurely ended 20 years of research and a $75 million program. And they went even further, launching an educational campaign to inform women about the syndrome, the link between it and tampons, and the greater statistical link between it and the Rely brand. This positive and complete response was highly effective in preventing negative image connotations for the firm and its other products.

While the colorful legend of the birth of floating Ivory soap typifies P&G's diligent search for the views of those who contribute over 17 million purchase transactions each day for its products, another sinister and damaging legend has crept upon P&G more recently. Since 1976, the firm has been plagued by a spotty, nagging series of rumors that link Procter & Gamble with cults or religious subcultures. These rumors are all concerned with the trademark that the firm has used for over 100 years on all its products. This mark depicts a group of thirteen stars enclosed in a circle, in which is shown a bearded man-in-the-moon. According to P&G, this logo evolved from shipping practices along the Ohio and other midwestern rivers. Illiterate dock workers identified wooden crates of P&G's Star brand candles by placing crude plus marks on them so shippers would know whose product they were handling and where it should go. Later, when P&G began putting identifying stars on each box, artistic stevedores drew circles around them and added other decorations such as moon-faces—images that were popular at the time. P&G then made a stencil of the moon-man as a more elaborate crate-mark. But when someone erased the face on several boxes, a New Orleans wholesaler protested that he would only trust shipments that had the full Procter & Gamble seal on them. Exhibit 11-1 shows the evolution of the symbol.

Quick to recognize an eye-catching symbol, William Procter, the firm's cofounder, suggested using 13 stars to represent those in the original U.S. flag. In 1882, the revised seal was registered as a trademark under number 9,829, and has appeared on all P&G products ever since. Nearly 100 years later, in 1976, rumors linking the logo with cult symbolism began to appear with increasing strength and frequency. The *Wall Street Journal* reported a rampant rumor in southern Minnesota that "the Moonies have taken over Procter & Gamble!" No one could trace how it got started, but someone apparently connected the moon symbol with the Rev. Moon's Unification Church, and P&G reported several inquiries about the supposed takeover in 1979. Early in 1980, a nursing home newsletter in Gaylor, Minnesota, published a note by one of its employees saying that the "Moon Church" owned Procter & Gamble. A few days later, the Lafayette-Nicollet (Minnesota) *Ledger* heard about the article and nearly printed an editorial commenting favorably on a boycott of P&G products. Fortunately, someone contacted P&G before it was printed and the editorial that was actually published suggested that its readers check their sources before stirring up actions such as boycotts.

At the time, P&G thought the problem would go away, and took no overt action. For a while it did, but two years later it reappeared, this time in full force and apparently among Protestant fundamentalists. Now the rumor became more specific, charging that P&G's president, John Smale, appeared on national television (on the "Phil Donahue Show" or maybe it was "Merv Griffin"—no one seemed to be sure) and supposedly linked the firm's success with the devil, avowing his membership in the Church of Satan and stating that P&G tithed to that church. Professor Martin Marty of the University of Chicago cites the following excerpt from one of the tract flyers that were circulated at the time (see the enlarged logo, Exhibit 11-2):

Look for this emblem on all PROCTOR (sic) & GAMBLE PRODUCTS (a sorcerer's head & 13 stars). Which is a symbol of Satanism. One of the top officials of the PROCTOR AND GAMBLE COMPANY is an avowed Satanist. On national television recently, he gave all of the credit for the success of the company to SATAN. He said that they have placed their satanist symbol on all their products, so they can get SATAN into every home in America.

Thus, in 1982, when the seal's centennial should have been celebrated, P&G found itself coping with 300 calls a day to the toll-free numbers it lists on its packages; the calls peaked at about 15,000 for the month of June 1982. Nearly all the calls were related to the logo and P&G's supposed links to the Church of Satan. P&G countered with six lawsuits against rumor spreaders, including a popular Atlanta weatherman and four Amway products distributors. It also enlisted the help of such well-known clergymen as Jerry Falwell, Billy Graham, Archbishop Joseph Bernardin, and even Donald Wildmon, who had been a long-time objector to P&G's television programming. The company also used a media blitz explaining the trademark, and mailed thousands of letters to consumers citing the support of top religious leaders. By July, either because of these actions or because the rumors had run their course, the number of calls decreased and by the end of 1982, P&G quit keeping records on them and stopped worrying. During 1983 and early 1984 there were only about 35 calls a month.

But P&G's worries began anew in the fall of 1984 when Sister Domitilla Drobnsk, an elementary school principal in Clymer, Pa., found an unsigned leaflet in her mailbox. It told the story of how the president of Procter & Gamble appeared on the "Phil Donahue Show" to declare his company's support for the Church of Satan. It also showed the man-in-the-moon trademark, which was said to be the sign of Satan. Interpreting it as her duty to spread the word, the sister sent copies of the leaflet home with her students, together with a personal note urging a boycott of P&G products, such as Crest toothpaste, Tide, and Ivory soap. Sister Domitilla's efforts and those of others were quite productive. In October, piles of leaflets were reported in the Hairworks beauty salon on Clymer's main street and in the shower room at a nearby coal mine. A local supermarket refunded the price of a can of Folger's coffee to a customer who refused to drink the "devil's brew." Apparently other copies of the same or similar leaflets were distributed in western Pennsylvania near Clymer because in October 1984, P&G's calls skyrocketed to 5,000 a month with 1,600 of them from that area.

The other calls came from such places as Milwaukee, where Virginia Meves, editor of a weekly newspaper (circulation 6,000) that usually reports on such topics as abortion and government regulation, ran the Satanism story; and Stamford, Connecticut, where Sister Noel passed out leaflets to women of the Villa Maria retreat. Both of them, as well as Sister Domitilla, have retracted and repented their actions.

But there are still some people who are not ready to completely discount the rumors. Most troublesome to P&G are clergy, such as Father Trongo, pastor of St. Anthony's church in Clymer, Pa. "You can't rule out a connection [between the company and the Church of Satan]," he says, "P&G could be using the Satanism rumor as a tax write-off or a publicity gimmick. I wouldn't give a sermon [defending P&G]."

While the 1982 rumors centered mainly around Protestant fundamentalists, P&G attributed the 1984 sources to Roman Catholic nuns and priests, mostly in the Northeast. But calls also came in from certain regions in California, Wisconsin, western New York state (mostly around Buffalo), and Chicago, in addition to the areas already mentioned. The 1982 problem was national, but in 1984 it was more regional and was spread through flyers distributed in churches, schools, shopping malls, and workplaces. In 1984, a P&G representative said that the company knew of specific cases where "unauthorized persons connected with Catholic churches" in Buffalo and Nebraska had published false accusations in church bulletins. Catholic school children in Cleveland and Pittsburgh took home the same rumor.

Rumors of the type described here are passed through an informal yet efficient network by word-of-mouth, printed matter, and overheard conversation by people who really believe that P&G would put disguised symbols into their seal and tithe to a Satanic church. Although stars do show up in some Satanic systems, they appear in many other systems and symbols as well and have been universally used since primitive times. The "13" count has been associated with evil and bad luck. But it would take a dedicated symbol seeker to turn the seal upside down and look at it in a mirror to find the "666" that is supposed to be hidden in the curlicues of the beard of the man-in-the-moon. This number from the book of Revelations is a "mark of the beast" and an enemy of God. It is also a favorite occult emblem among superstitious Christians in America. But looking for such symbols and interpreting them in this way is excessive behavior, to say the least.

Examine any of the many Procter & Gamble products and the tiny seal will be found near the toll-free telephone number and patent numbers. Exhibit 11-3 shows reproductions of the seal from three consumer products. It is difficult to believe that it could be the center of so much rumor, controversy, and parental-like protection by P&G.

In mid-1984, Procter & Gamble appeared to be backing away from its coveted symbol. After considerable thought, the firm decided its moon-and-stars logos would not appear on its new twin-tower, 18-story office building in Cincinnati, although the original plans called for them. Eight of the seals had been made in bas-relief marble carvings. One P&G spokesman said they were dropped for "economy reasons," but the architect says P&G thought that they would further incite religious fundamentalists into more rumor spreading and boycotting.

In April 1985, the company announced it would remove the logo from its product packages in an attempt to squelch the Satanic association rumors. The symbol would be removed over the next several years as the packages were redesigned, but P&G would continue to use the seal on its letterhead and annual reports. On May 16, 1985, P&G filed suit against four individuals accusing them of spreading malicious and untrue statements linking the firm with Satanism. The company said it filed these suits against persons in Madison Heights, Va., Dunmore, Pa., and Wichita, Kansas.

More specifically, P&G accused them of libeling the firm's character by distributing literature that says P&G supported the church of Satan and that the P&G trademark is a symbol of Satanism. These individuals are also accused of encouraging others to stop buying Procter & Gamble products.

Analysis Questions

   1. What role do religious subcultures and subcultural symbolism play in the spread of the Satanism rumors? Does the symbol and what consumers see in it relate to their social environment?

   2. Do the people who spread the rumors really believe that P&G is in league with Satan and that the firm's president actually admitted it on a nationwide television program?

   3. P&G has been quite concerned about the rumors. What effect on the attitudes and beliefs of present and future buyers of P&G products might the rumors have?

   4. The symbol on P&G's products is so small that most people do not even notice it. Why did P&G take so long to decide to drop it?

Evolution of the Corporate Symbol

1. This crude cross, painted by a wharf hand on a wooden box of Star brand candles around 1851, was the beginning of the "Moon and Stars."

2. In time, the cross developed into this encircled star—still merely part of the rivermen's shipping "sign language."

3. The first standard trademark adopted by the Company was this roughly drawn crescent enclosing 13 stars.

4. The 1882 model "Moon and Stars" had been refined to this point, and registered in the U.S. Patent Office.

5. By 1902, our trademark, still basically the same, displayed some of the "gingerbread frills" typical of the turn-of-the-century.

6. Around 1920 the trademark became more simplistic—still, however, there was no fundamental change from the original design.

7. Finally, in 1930, a sculptor was commissioned by P&G to design today's authorized version of the famous "Moon and Stars."

Source: Used with permission of Procter & Gamble

PROCTER & GAMBLE

EXHIBIT 11-2

Present Corporate Symbol

Source: Used with permission of Procter & Gamble

PROCTER & GAMBLE

EXHIBIT 11-3

The Corporate Symbol on Several Products

If you have questions or comments about Charmin, please call us toll-free. In the continental U.S., call 1-800-543-0480 (Ohio residents call 1-800-582-0490). Made in U.S.A. by PROCTER & GAMBLE
Cincinnati, Ohio 45202 ©P&G
Made under one or more U.S. Patents: 3,994,771; and 4,191,609.

S

0

37000 60141

YELLOW

CONVENIENT JUMBO ROLL

IMPORTANT FOR MICROWAVE OWNERS—Use NEW, specially formulated BOUNTY MICROWAVE for your microwave tasks. It's a new Bounty made just for you.
Made under one or more U.S. Patents:
3,414,459; 3,905,863; 3,974,025; 4,191,609; and Des. 239,137.
IF YOU HAVE QUESTIONS OR COMMENTS ABOUT BOUNTY, please call us toll-free.
In the continental U.S., call 1-800-543-0480
(Ohio residents call 1-800-582-0490).
Made in U.S.A. by
PROCTER & GAMBLE  **M**
Cincinnati, Ohio 45202 ©P&G

0

37000 63361

Crest HAS AN ADVANCED FORMULA WITH FLUORISTAT* WHICH HAS BEEN CLINICALLY PROVEN TO FIGHT CAVITIES EVEN BETTER THAN ORIGINAL CREST.

"Crest has been shown to be an effective decay-preventive dentifrice that can be of significant value when used in a conscientiously applied program of oral hygiene and regular professional care."
Council on Dental Therapeutics–American Dental Association

INGREDIENTS: SODIUM FLUORIDE IN A DENTIFRICE BASE OF SORBITOL, WATER, HYDRATED SILICA, TRISODIUM PHOSPHATE, SODIUM LAURYL SULFATE, FLAVOR, SODIUM PHOSPHATE, XANTHAN GUM, CARBOMER-940, SODIUM SACCHARIN, TITANIUM DIOXIDE, AND FD&C BLUE NO. 1.

*Fluoristat is a trademark for a proven decay-preventive composition (active ingredient sodium fluoride)
If you have questions or comments about Crest, please call us toll-free.
In the continental U.S., call 1-800-543-7270 (Ohio residents call 1-800-582-1891).

Made in U.S.A. by PROCTER & GAMBLE,
Cincinnati, Ohio 45202 U.S. Pat. 4,254,101; 4,314,990

Case 12

Mary Kay Cosmetics

In late 1979, Martha Trescott was a housewife in Toledo, Ohio, with two small children in school. "In the beginning," Martha said, "I was just looking for something that would bring in a little extra money and would get me out of the house for a while." So she was delighted when she met her cousin Ellie from nearby Sandusky, Ohio, at the annual Trescott family picnic. Ellie had been with Mary Kay Cosmetics for several years and was now a sales director. "What she was doing fit right in with what I had in mind," Martha explained. "Ellie said all I had to do was give Mary Kay parties at my house a few times a month, and I enjoy doing things like that! She said she would teach me what I needed to know. I couldn't wait to get started."

Cousin Ellie explained in more detail what Martha had to do. The parties are usually held in the afternoon, but sometimes in the evening. They last about two hours and no more than five guests are invited. The hostess is the "beauty consultant" who gives a free facial to each guest and explains or demonstrates beauty tips at the same time. Afterward, she serves refreshments, then takes orders for the 45 products in the Mary Kay line. Ellie stressed that the guests need to be gently, but firmly, pushed into buying several of the products, not just one.

She went on to tell about the potential for moving up in the firm's sales group and about the chances for substantial earnings, and gave Martha a copy of the Mary Kay Marketing Plan (see Exhibit 12-1). She also stressed that each salesperson worked on commission and that the harder one worked, the higher the earnings would be, and she pointed out that each

Mary Kay consultant is an independent contractor, not an employee. The company simply acts as a wholesale house from which the consultant buys at wholesale prices and sells at retail to her clients.

Ellie, herself, had started as a Mary Kay beauty consultant in Sandusky about three years ago. "After a year or so giving parties," she said, "I began to find others just like you, Martha, who wanted to earn extra money. After I recruited a few, I was promoted to sales director, where I am now." In addition to her own sales commissions, Ellie gets an additional 4 percent for each new consultant she recruits, another commission for training them, and 3 percent of the sales that they make. She is also required to wear the sales director's uniform, which consists of a gray suit, Hanes quicksilver panty hose, and a pink, strawberry, or (preferred) amethyst blouse, when she is working. "Right now," she confided, "I'm trying to meet a higher sales quota so I can earn my pink Cadillac. And this is the best time to try for it because everybody will know Mary Kay after they feature her on '60 Minutes' later this month."

Ellie drew a chart showing that there were more rungs up the Mary Kay success ladder above sales director, including division manager and national sales director. Exhibit 12-2 shows this hierarchy.

MARY KAY'S COMPANY

Already a grandmother in 1963, Mary Katherine Ash bought the formula for her initial skin-care products for $500 from the granddaughter of a local Texas tanner. Then, with her son Richard, she began the company that is now among the top ten party-plan merchandisers in the United States. The firm started with only Mary Kay and her son as full-time employees, and used nine Dallas women who were willing to work on straight commission selling the products. The company's underlying philosophy finds its roots in the fundamentalist Christian beliefs of its founder: "God first, family second, and career third."

Initially, the company shrewdly positioned itself in the skin-care end of the cosmetics market—and this comparatively narrow niche is one of its strengths. A Mary Kay consultant has only about 50 items to show to a customer, while Avon representatives deliver catalogs with about 250 items out of 650 in the total line. Thus, Mary Kay consultants are able to carry inventory and deliver a customer's items immediately, while Avon representatives have to take orders and deliver the merchandise later.

Another strength is the way in which Mary Kay's sales force management is compensated and motivated. Its seven national sales managers earn well over $50,000 and 150 division managers earn over $40,000. Some members of the commission group do even better. The 31 national sales directors earn an average of $80,000, the 1,500 senior sales managers get fixed compensation plus 4 percent of the retail sales of their units, while the 4,000 sales directors earn an average salary of $25,000 plus 9 to 13 percent of retail sales, a 3 percent sales bonus, and a rental car. The strategy of this type of operation is the "pyramid," where incentives in the form of build-up commissions and exotic prizes entice "consultants" not only to sell heavily but, vital to the entire scheme, to recruit constantly.

Of Mary Kay's three children only the 41-year-old Richard is still with the firm, as its president. Mary Kay has been described as the "heart of Mary Kay cosmetics" but Richard is known as the "operational brains." Mary Kay has long since left the day-to-day affairs in Richard's hands. But she still works closely with the salespeople, who are vital to the firm's continued success, and is often found baking cookies for new management trainees or handing out rewards, such as pink Cadillacs, furs, jewels, and vacations at the company's annual inspirational sales meeting in Dallas.

She is also the "image" of the company, and the ideal, or envy, of other women who would like to mirror her success and life-style. She has taken her own passion for pink and parlayed it into a national symbol of her firm: the pink Cadillac. A typical photo of Mary Kay with the Cadillac is shown in Exhibit 12-3. She often wears a pink lace dress and lives in a 19,000 square foot pink mansion in Dallas. In the $5 million structure which has five bedrooms, eleven bathrooms, a library, game room, cabana, three kitchens, and an olympic-size swimming pool, she sees "just the right amount of room for a single woman who likes to entertain." On a recent shopping trip in France she bought enough antiques to fill an entire railroad boxcar; this went to furnish the pink mansion.

THE SUCCESS OF MARTHA TRESCOTT

"I just love Mary Kay," gushed cousin Ellie. "And I know you will too." Martha was a bit uneasy when Ellie told her she would have to buy her own "beauty showcase" kit of sample products, and probably a small inventory of popular items. "It helps to have the merchandise on hand," cautioned Ellie. "Otherwise you have to take an order and have the customer pay in advance. Some don't like to do that. Also, it means you have to deliver the order when it comes in." The basic showcase and inventory would cost about $750. The company suggests that new consultants start off with bank loans, since they do not usually have established credit. "The logic behind this," Ellie explained, "is that if consultants have to meet payments, they are forced to put the money back into the business, and won't spend it right away."

To get the cash for her initial investment, Martha borrowed $750 on a note from a bank, cosigned by her husband, and stocked her shelves. She spent the next several days learning how to give the facials, what kind of refreshments were best to serve, how to keep the conversation going, and how to sell, sell, sell. She was so anxious to begin that she stayed up late at night making lists of all her relatives and friends who might come to the parties themselves, and also bring others with them.

Soon she was hosting two parties a week. Her own enthusiasm for the products, and the expertise she acquired by constantly improving her technique for giving facials, seemed to motivate guests to spend lavishly. She was also rather surprised when several relatives, and other guests she did not know, asked about becoming Mary Kay consultants themselves. By the end of the following year, she had recruited almost enough novice consultants to qualify for her promotion to sales director. Her inventory had risen to over $1,500 and she had no problem getting credit. Also, her income had risen appreciably. She not only had income from her own sales but she got an additional percentage for training recruits, and a percentage of their sales. She kept in touch with what was happening in the company, and got new ideas for recruiting, training, and product promotion from the company "Newsline" publication, shown in Exhibit 12-4.

As a successful party-plan hostess, she also assumed the role of an opinion leader in her specialty area. Martha had worked hard to become an expert in giving facials and probably something of an actress as well. At the same time, she satisfied some needs of her own—to interest the guests in her product line and to make a profit by selling it. Since she is known either first- or second-hand to her customers, and since the brand she sells has a good reputation, the two act together as risk reducers. She also fulfills a social function by providing a party occasion as well as a buying opportunity.

In 1983, her income matched that of her husband. "If anyone asks why I've been so successful," Martha remarked, "it's because I wanted to make it. Just dangle a mink coat in front of me!"

By late 1983, she had over 150 consultants working for her and was driving a pink Cadillac. But sales were becoming a little harder to make and recruiting was also more difficult. Martha knew that nearly half of those she recruited would only last a few months, and would have to be replaced. But she was concerned that a few of her more steady and faithful salespeople were leaving, mostly to take full-time jobs. She knew that the success of her operation lay in constantly replenishing the sales force. The new recruits are enthusiastic at first, and their initial sales are high. This source accounted for nearly two-thirds of Martha's, as well as the company's, income. And the novices also bring in other recruits, bolstering the base of the pyramid. If recruiting slows, the new blood is lost and sales stagnate.

Another problem that was brought up by consultants with increasing frequency during 1984 was attendance at the parties. "I have to invite eight or ten now, and hope that four or five will show up. Sometimes, only one or two will come and even they don't buy." Others reported that sales were as brisk as ever. But Martha knew that a number of factors were involved in the party-plan business. First, of course, working women could not come to parties during the day and did not want to give up precious time in the evenings or on weekends. Second, these same working women are the pool from which new recruits came and they are now opting for the security of full-time salaried jobs. Third, many women are now earning comfortable incomes and prefer to shop for more expensive beauty products at department stores and salons. And because they have less time, they may buy their makeup where they do the rest of their shopping—at the supermarket. She also read in a "Newsline" that the direct-selling approach that Mary Kay and others were using depended upon networks of relationships—women selling to their extended family, family, friends, and neighbors. This type of selling does best in ordinary neighborhoods, small towns, and in urban, working-class, or ethnic areas.

In spite of these problems, Martha's group was performing reasonably well but sales were just about holding their own. She had also seen data showing that door-to-door (including party-plan) sales were about 11 percent of total retail makeup sales in 1984—the same percentage as in 1980. Exhibit 12-5 shows the retail sales breakdown.

But recruiting spurted in late 1984 and early 1985, expanding the base and bringing in new orders. In mid-1985, Martha began using direct-mail advertising to attract customers who were reluctant to attend parties. These circulars advertised free "color consulting" by appointment, listed sale-priced Mary Kay products, and solicited applications for positions as beauty consultants. By the fall of 1985, she had earned her second pink Cadillac.

THE FUTURE OF MARY KAY

Although many sales directors like Martha continue to do well, some experts wonder if Mary Kay, as a party-plan retailer, has any place to go. If social trends and the economy continue in their present direction, the firm will eventually run out of recruits. As recently as two years ago, nearly 120,000 Mary Kay salespeople were either fired from the company or left for other reasons. Of those remaining, only about 60,000 were really productive.

In an attempt to revitalize the recruiting effort in 1984, Mary Kay devoted all of its advertising and promotion to recruiting and more than quadrupled the budget for it. And, in 1984, financial rewards for salespeople who bring in new recruits were also increased substantially, while all hiring at the corporate level was frozen.

In addition to expanding the product line somewhat, Richard has moved the firm's products into markets in Canada, Australia, Argentina, and Guatemala, but thus far some of these have been less than successful.

Mary Kay's earnings peaked in the first quarter of 1983 at $12 million, but dropped to less than half of that by the third quarter. Since then there has been a steady decline. In 1979, its common shares sold for about $5, but in May 1981 they peaked at $66, and Rogers announced a two-for-one split. Since then they have sold for $13, with a low of $8. See Exhibit 12-6 for earnings since 1980.

Skin-care products have accounted for nearly half of the firm's earnings, with makeup the next largest at 25 percent. Mary Kay, herself, is enthusiastic about plans to further expand the line. "We have only 4 percent of the total retail cosmetics market," she says. "The way I see it, 96 percent of the people in the U.S. are using the wrong product."

Analysis Questions

1. How are "situational factors" involved in the party-plan concept, and the recruiting process?

2. What do Exhibits 12-5 and 12-6 suggest to you about Mary Kay's lower sales and earnings in recent years?

3. What shifts in life-styles or social patterns have made "party selling" more difficult today than it was in the past?

4. Mary Kay depends upon the party-plan and a constant influx of new recruits to communicate product information and to sell. Can you think of methods the firm can use to communicate to working women?

MARY KAY COSMETICS

EXHIBIT 12-1

The Mary Kay Marketing Plan

When Mary Kay and Richard Rogers founded the Company, they developed a special marketing plan, including the best features and avoiding the mistakes which Mary Kay has seen in her twenty years with direct sales companies. They made sure that every salesperson's opportunity is as big as her ambition and her ability.

Beauty Consultants are the wholesale purchasers of Mary Kay products and, operating independently of corporate management, derive their profits from retail sales of Mary Kay products to the ultimate consumers. Beauty Consultants may consult with Sales Directors concerning their Mary Kay businesses.

Each Sales Director began as a Beauty Consultant, and gained the title of Sales Director in the Mary Kay independent sales organization by demonstrating her ability to sell and to build a successful sales unit of her own. A Sales Director makes available: meetings, training, motivation and suggestions for Beauty Consultants within her sales units who wish to share the benefits of her experience. She receives additional incentive compensation from the Company for her sales leadership activities in the form of a percentage of her total unit sales.

Marketing Built on Retail Sales. The entire marketing structure is based upon and intended to foster retail sales to ultimate consumers, with commissions being earned only on products sold at retail.

All Products Are Purchased Directly from the Company. All products are purchased by everyone (Sales Directors and Beauty Consultants) directly from the Company based on the *same* discount schedule. There is only *one* wholesale sale (from Company to Consultant) and *one* retail sale (from Consultant to customer). Our products do not pass through several levels of distributors. Every Consultant is recruited to sell her own products at retail, rather than to others at wholesale.

Mary Kay Does Not Sell Franchises or Distributorships. You Decide to Advance Yourself on the Basis of Proven Ability. In some companies there are several levels of distributors and a "distributorship" at any level can be purchased by buying a required amount of product, or by paying prescribed fees. "Managers" can thus buy their way in, whether or not they know anything about the product, or how to manage a business. In Mary Kay, you know your Sales Director first proved her abilities as a Consultant. She is your "business

EXHIBIT 12-1 (*Cont'd.*)

consultant," has been in your place, and knows what to do to help you. And you can decide to become a Sales Director, too, by proving your own ability.

There are No Territories to Limit Where You May Sell or Recruit. Many companies sell franchise rights within a limited geographic area and many assign territories. Mary Kay feels this is unnecessary. You can recruit and sell merchandise in any of the 50 states, U.S. Territories, or Puerto Rico—on trips or when you visit relatives.

This means that you may hold beauty shows (which we also call skin care classes) and take orders wherever you happen to be. Because your business is your own, your hours are yours also.

Your Beauty Showcase Is the Beginning of a Rewarding Career. Beginning your Mary Kay career starts with a beauty showcase and does not require the purchase of any additional amount of product. Many new Consultants find it both convenient and profitable to order a modest inventory of merchandise at the outset of their careers. This enables them to obtain the most favorable discount and to better serve their initial retail customers.

From time to time, Mary Kay Cosmetics offers special incentives to new Consultants in connection with initial orders of merchandise. These offers may result in special discounts and may even enable new Consultants to earn their showcases. This inventory purchase is entirely at the discretion of the individual Consultant. No compensation is earned by anyone on a new Consultant's beauty showcase purchase, i.e., "for introducing a new Beauty Consultant." Advancement cannot be "bought" by an "investment"; it must be earned. Original and unused products are repurchased by the Company from terminating Beauty Consultants and destroyed.

Avenues of Income on the Mary Kay Ladder of Success

The Mary Kay marketing plan provides substantial earning opportunities and benefits for each Beauty Consultant through the following avenues of income.

Beauty Shows. When Beauty Consultants teach skin care to five or six guests in someone's home, they receive a generous profit for the products they sell. Beauty shows provide a continuous source of profit for their business.

Facials. Consultants also provide individualized skin care classes for their customers. Complimentary facials provide another opportunity to introduce Mary Kay products and earn a profit while doing so.

Reorders. Beauty Consultants provide their customers with dependable, personalized service. This gives them a solid base of recorder customers and a continuous source of profit.

Recruiting Commissions and "VIP Car". As they share their Mary Kay opportunity with others, Consultants develop their careers and build their businesses. When they provide their new recruits with career guidance, they receive 4%, 8% or 12% recruiting commissions from the Company on all wholesale orders placed by these recruits. The amount of the check depends upon the number of active recruits and the amount of their monthly purchases. Recruiting commissions can become a sizeable contribution to their income as well as lead to use of a "VIP Car."

Dovetailing. Occasionally, Consultants are unable to hold a previously booked beauty show. When they ask another Consultant to hold or dovetail it, they are still able to earn a percentage of the profit from sales made at that show.

Advancement to Sales Directorship. Proven leadership, recruiting and sales ability lead to advancement as a Mary Kay Sales Director. Mary Kay Directors not only receive income from the above-mentioned sources, but an additional Director's commission from the Company for educating, motivating and inspiring their unit members to success by providing them with the necessary training. They also share their business knowledge and experience. Mary Kay Sales Directors may also receive unit and recruiting bonuses, additional Company-sponsored insurance benefits and Seminar awards including the popular pink Cadillacs and Regals.

Company Promotions and Unit Contests. When Consultants achieve certain sales and recruiting goals, they earn valuable contest prizes from the Company and their sales unit.

Self-Employment Benefits Program. Mary Kay Consultants who are active with the Company are able to enjoy self-employment benefits programs designed to aid them in meeting their Health, Dental/Optional Group Life and Product Replacement Insurance needs.

The Ultimate Achievements in Mary Kay. The climb up the Mary Kay ladder of success to Senior, Future National and National Sales Directorship represents significant management, leadership and teaching experience. These top Directors enjoy even more income earning opportunities, Company-sponsored benefits and a special sense of accomplishment in having helped so many others to achieve success in their Mary Kay careers.

Each year, hundreds of Sales Directors earn over $30,000 in commissions, and we have more women earning over $50,000 a year than any other company. Our National Sales Directors average approximately $150,000 a year.

Special Help in Developing Self-Confidence. The typical first reaction to a recruiting proposal to become a Mary Kay Consultant is: "Me in sales? Oh, I've never sold anything in my life!"

While this remark is made frequently, Beauty Consultants consistently prove that it's a false fear particularly since they begin learning *how to teach skin care* almost immediately.

Mary Kay Cosmetics is eager to contribute to their career growth and reminds them that they're "in business for themselves, but not by themselves," with these supplementary aids:

- Good, reliable products
- Proven market acceptance
- Advertising and public relations support
- Publications
- Career-building aids
- Training materials
- Incentives for productivity
- Inspirational and motivational resources

Thus, the Mary Kay career opportunity is only limited to the ambitions, determination and willingness to work which each Consultant demonstrates. Consistent efforts, positive attitude and the desire to help others succeed, are the keys to a profitable and rewarding career as a Mary Kay Beauty Consultant.

Source: Reproduced by courtesy of Mary Kay Cosmetics, Inc.

MARY KAY COSMETICS

EXHIBIT 12-2

Sales Hierarchy

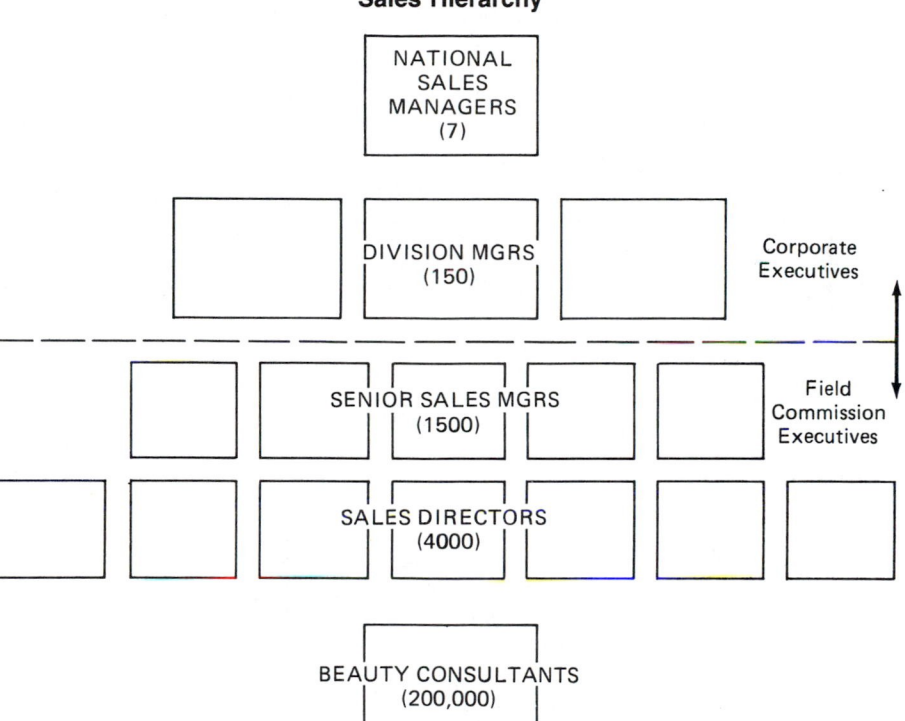

MARY KAY COSMETICS

EXHIBIT 12-3

Source: Reproduced by courtesy of Mary Kay Cosmetics, Inc.

MARY KAY COSMETICS, INC.

newsline

- ● Advertising and P.R. Notes, pages 4 & 5
- ● Mary Kay Milestones, page 6
- ● Business Briefings, pages 7 & 8

Growing Profits Cast a Glow on Mary Kay Cosmetics, Inc.

"Industry analysts say the biggest problem they have with Mary Kay Cosmetics is that they can't find much bad to say about the company." **Dallas Morning News,** February 13, 1983

For The Incomparable Mary Kay, Skin Is Not To Be Treated Lightly.

"Scientific rather than commercial, "Skin Deep" (at the Museum of Science & Industry in Chicago) is a guide to how the human skin functions and how to care for it."

"Her (Mary Kay's) company has bankrolled 1,500 square feet of museum space because she thinks the public needs information about skin, the human body's largest organ." *Chicago Sun Times, December 21, 1982*

The Industry's Hottest Segment ...

at the moment is skin-care products, with Dallas-based Mary Kay Cosmetics, Inc. the growth leader. **TIME, October 11, 1982**

New Vogue: Company Culture

"Management thinkers now acknowledge that organizations have distinct identities and tones, often acquired from their chief executive — Mary Kay Cosmetics' cheerful nurturing of employees ... are repeatedly assured by the founder, Mary Kay Ash, that 'you can do it.'"
The New York Times, January 7, 1983

Study Shows Mary Kay Ranks Tops Among Career Women

In a recent survey conducted by *SELF* magazine, Mary Kay was shown to have the greatest rate of increase in customer loyalty in all product categories; placed number one in customer loyalty in the facial foundation category and placed second in customer brand loyalty in both the facial moisturizer and brush-on blushers categories.
SELF magazine survey, 1983

newsline

is published by **Mary Kay Cosmetics, Inc.** for use by its independent **Beauty Consultants** and Sales Directors. **Betheny L. Reid, Editor and Coordinator of Public Relations.**

Source: Reproduced by courtesy of Mary Kay Cosmetics, Inc.

MARY KAY COSMETICS

EXHIBIT 12-5

Retail Sales Breakdown by Sales Source 1980–84
(in billions)

Sales Source	Amount	Percent
Drug and Department Stores	1980 $1.8	72%
	1984 $2.38	66%
Mass Merchandisers and Food Stores	1980 $ .42	17%
	1984 $ .828	23%
Door-to-Door	1980 $ .275	11%
	1984 $ .396	11%
Total sales	1980 $2.5	
	1984 $3.6	

MARY KAY COSMETICS

EXHIBIT 12-6

Selected Sales and Income Data, 1980–84
(000)

	1980	1981	1982	1983	1984
Net Sales	$166,938	$235,196	$304,275	$323,758	$277,500
Cost of Sales	52,484	71,100	87,807	88,960	79,867
Selling, G&A Exp.	86,998	120,880	154,104	168,757	156,202
Operating Income	27,456	43,316	62,364	66,041	41,431
Net Income	15,135	24,155	35,372	36,654	41,431

Case 13

The Pearl Travel Service

It was after closing time on a dark winter afternoon. In the small office at the rear of her store-front travel agency, Pearl Kaufman was pondering an article she had just read in the *Wall Street Journal*:

> Most travel agents see strength in both vacation and business travel, especially the latter. In Boston, Corporate bookings are 20% stronger than they were a year ago, while vacation bookings are 10% stronger. . . . But travelers are bargain conscious, forcing agents to work harder than usual. "It's much more competitive and dog-eat-dog out there," says a travel spokesman in San Francisco. "Many corporate clients insist on discount fares," notes a Portland, Maine agent. A Chicago booker says that more business travelers achieve savings by arranging trips well in advance—40 days to 2 months. To keep business, more agents are forced to split commissions with corporate clients.

She thought back over the four years since she started the business and the hopes she had for quick success and expansion. She also wondered why some of the record numbers of travelers managed to avoid using her firm's services. While the agency had been moderately profitable, business had levelled off, and for the past two years the increase in earnings had hardly exceeded the inflation rate. "Maybe I should just go back to Freedom Travel, where I can work regular hours and make a better living than I do now," she mused. Idly, she picked up her four-year income statement and glanced over it, although she knew every figure by heart (see Exhibit 13-1).

HISTORY OF THE AGENCY

After graduating from an Illinois community college, Pearl was hired as a trainee by Freedom Travel, a midwest chain with over 75 offices in major and some smaller cities. After an intensive three-month training program, she was assigned as an assistant to tour directors on several U.S. and foreign tours. There she learned the practical side of the business: how to make the dozens of arrangements needed for tours, how to assure that accommodations and services were satisfactory, and how to handle the sometimes difficult personalities in the tour group. After several of these tours, she settled into one of Freedom's offices in a medium-sized Indiana city.

Pearl was intelligent and hard working, and in two years when the manager was transferred to a larger office, she moved into that job. But she never lost sight of her long-term objective—to have her own agency. About a year after her promotion, Freedom decided to close the office and consolidate it with one in a nearby city. Although she was offered the assistant manager's job in the larger agency, Pearl saw this as the chance she had been waiting for. Quickly, she arranged to sublet the location, bought the furniture and equipment from Freedom at a sacrifice price, and hired the two assistants who had worked for her. It was business as usual when the sign Pearl Travel Service replaced Freedom's above the store window.

THE EARLY YEARS

During the first year, Pearl's net income increased 10 percent over the amount she had received from Freedom, and she was able to give her employees small raises. But commissions, her main source of income, had not increased much. Expecting that most of her business would come from regular customers telling others about her services, Pearl used only token, reminder advertising in local newspapers. But in the second year she began running weekend ads on special tours in the travel section of the Sunday paper. Bookings increased and so did commission income, which was up 30 percent over the previous year. The third year was disappointing, with commission income rising less than one-fourth of the increase of the previous year. Last year, Pearl noted sadly, it was up only 7 percent, about equal to the increase of year 3 over year 2.

TODAY'S PROBLEMS

Pearl wondered, as she looked over the income statements, what she might do to increase her customer base. Her main competitor was a regional chain with an office in the downtown area, while hers was in a large suburban shopping center. Also, the chain could buy discount tickets in bulk, which added appreciably to its profitability. It also offered rides to the airport and free gifts based on the amount of bookings during the year. But the chain tended to be rather inflexible and some of Pearl's customers who had tried it returned to her, complaining they did not get much personal attention.

Pearl also noted that increases in advertising of $3000 in year 3 and over $4000 in year 4 were not bringing in much more business. In her third year, she had continued to advertise the same number of tours, but offered a different mixture from earlier years, using the format shown in Exhibit 13-2. Most of the $3000 increase in advertising expenditures, however, went into ads and radio commercials aimed at people who were not aware that travel agents normally did not charge commissions to make travel or hotel reservations. She still used this theme, but was not sure how effective the ads were in attracting new business. She also wondered if these ads were helping her competitors as much as they did her. The ads were similar to those shown in Exhibit 13-3.

She knew that most of her commission income came from domestic travel reservations (with a commission rate of about 10%), overseas travel (8% commission), hotel reservations (10% commission), and tours (10% commission). The breakdown of customer type was:

a. Corporate travel and hotel reservations (33%)
b. Individual travel and hotel reservations (30%)
c. Tour reservations (26%)
d. Miscellaneous other (11%)

This customer mix had stayed about the same since Pearl took over the agency, although the percentage of tour reservations had risen 10 percent since she began advertising. Tours were more work, but they were also more expensive than individual reservations so commissions were higher.

She was concerned particularly about the corporate part of the business. Because only travel agents could get commissions, it was industry practice for agencies to set up "branches" in the offices of their corporate customers. These branches were actually the company's travel department and they handled reservations, ticketing, and other arrangements. The travel agency then refunded part of its commission, usually 3 percent, to the client firm to help defray the salaries and operating expenses of the "branch." Pearl refunded 5 percent because Freedom had allowed that amount before she took over.

COMMUNICATION AND ADVERTISING

Pearl was concerned about how she could identify and reach those in her area who were likely to be consumers of travel services. She knew that her present clients were older—age 55 or more. They used both tours and individual reservations and were a steady year-round business. But in the last year or so more younger customers seemed to be travelling in off seasons, as well as in the busy summer months. She had heard that her competitors—the chain and two other independents—seemed to be doing well. She also knew that once clients used her services they were satisfied and likely to come back. They recommended her to their friends, but that method was not generating enough new business. Something else had to be done, and some new type of advertising was probably the answer.

She remembered from her experience with the Freedom agency that some type of celebrity might be useful in attracting attention to ads. But she also recalled that the source used in the ad, celebrity or not, had to have credibility in the mind of consumers. The problem was that most celebrities in the area would charge a heavy fee for permission to use their photograph in an advertisement. Many of them would not associate themselves with advertising at all. About a year ago, though, her advertising agency had suggested a well-known and well-liked TV weather reporter whose photo could be used in an ad for $1,500, but she wasn't sure this was the right type of person—one who might simulate an opinion leader.

Almost all the other businesses in her shopping mall used the yellow pages extensively, with separate, freestanding advertisements or at least a bold-face type listing. The Freedom agency, however, had always used a plain single line, and a district manager once told her that people did not use yellow pages much to find travel agencies.

Pearl was still not sure whether she should continue to advertise both individual tours and the advantages of using travel agents. If she could decide on a single goal, she could allocate a large part of her rather meager budget to it.

Analysis Questions

1. What type of advertising was Pearl's ad that told consumers they paid no commission for travel agency services? What is the problem with this kind of ad? Should Pearl continue to use it?

2. Why didn't the Freedom management use yellow page advertising?

3. Do you think the weather reporter would be enough of a celebrity for consumers to notice the ad? Would he be a credible source?

4. How should Pearl redesign her advertising/communication plan?

PEARL TRAVEL SERVICE

EXHIBIT 13-1

Income Statements, Years One through Four

	Year 1	Year 2	Year 3	Year 4
Commission Income	$157,810	$201,880	$217,770	$233,100
Less Expenses:				
Corporate refunds	22,010	36,204	37,155	39,112
Salaries	54,352	65,191	72,751	77,565
Rent & utilities	37,341	41,753	46,200	50,123
Advertising	5,666	9,430	12,414	16,751
Administration & tax	6,349	9,017	11,653	15,307
Total Expenses	125,718	161,595	180,173	198,858
Net Income	32,092	40,285	37,597	34,242

PUT YOURSELF IN THIS PICTURE...

With PEARL TRAVEL SAFARIS

Visit exotic Kenya with four game parks and majestic Kilimanjaro Mountain! See animals in their natural habitat! Explore the contrasts of Nairobi! 10 glorious days, $2350 - 3195 including airfare from Chicago. Experienced leaders, small groups.

Safaris leave Jan. 15, Feb. 10, and Feb. 25. For information and free brochure: CALL PEARL!

PEARL TRAVEL SERVICE
202 West Friel St.

375-2349

Train, Plane, Boat, Hotel, Theme Park...

Let your LOCAL TRAVEL AGENT make reservations for you . . FREE.

There is no extra cost to you when Pearl Travel makes normal reservations for you! And we can find times to fit your schedule, special fares to fit your budget, and hotels to fit your style!

We can book individual travel, fly-drive tours, all inclusive plans for groups, and special tours for senior citizens.

Call PEARL TRAVEL SERVICE Today!

PEARL TRAVEL SERVICE 202 West Friel Street 375-2349

YOUR LOCALLY OWNED TRAVEL AGENT

Case 14

The Soviet Central Department Store

"A toaster is a simple device, great for day-old bread, but it is an unfamiliar amenity for the average Soviet citizen." So said the Soviet weekly magazine *Nedelya*. This was a response to a letter to the editor, quoted by United Press, from Yuri Makarov of Kiev. He wrote:

> There exists a relatively simple and cheap device, called a toaster, thanks to which all the bread in the household will be eaten, down to the last crumb. All one has to do is heat it up a bit and brown it, spread butter, jam, honey or whatever you have on top and believe me, it's tasty! But toasters are made in this country only at the V. I. Lenin factory in Beltsy (Moldavian SSR). Why are there no toasters for sale?

Nedelya sent a representative to look around Moscow, to discover what this "toaster" was, but could not find a single one at any store. Looking further into the situation, a reporter discovered that there really was only one factory making toasters and it produced less than 10,000 a year. In a country of 270 million people, the factory can provide one toaster per year for each 30,000 people!

AVERAGE CONSUMERS

Antanas and Silva Benkis live in Kaunas, an industrial city in about the center of the Lithuanian Socialist Soviet Republic. He works as a foreman in a state machine tool factory, earning about 200 rubles a month, and she earns 170 rubles a month as the supervisor of a state day-care center in the apartment complex where they live. At an exchange rate of about $1.29 (U.S.) per ruble, their comparative incomes are about $258 and $219. But these figures are not directly comparable since the Benkises pay only about 10 rubles a month for housing, plus utilities. They pay practically no income tax, no social security tax, and medical and dental care are provided without cost. But the basic income amount still does not tell the whole story. Antanas received two substantial bonuses last year, one for "hard work" and the other because his plant exceeded its quota. Silva got one too, for working in party-related activities during her free time.

Since there were few luxury items, interesting clothes, or household goods to be had in Kaunas, Antanas and Silva took a four-day shopping holiday in Vilnius, the capital city. It is about 75 miles east of Kaunas and close to the border of the Soviet Byelorussian Republic.

POLITICAL HISTORY

The Lithuanian Socialist Soviet Republic (SSR), whose western border is the chilly Baltic Sea, is bordered on the north by the Latvian SSR, and on the east by the Soviet Union. It has an area of 26,175 square miles and a population of about 3.4 million, about the same as the Washington, D.C. metropolitan area. Lithuania has had a turbulent history. In the early fourteenth century, its ruler, Gedemin, and his successors extended the country's borders and elevated it to a major European power. By the end of the century, close ties were developed with Poland, and this influence extended over the Lithuanian upper classes so that their culture became almost entirely Polish. This influence continued until the eighteenth century when Poland was partitioned and Lithuania became part of the Russian empire.

From the end of World War I until 1940, when it was occupied by Soviet troops, Lithuania was an independent republic. But the German–Soviet Pact of 1939 secretly assigned it to the Soviet sphere of influence. Nevertheless, the Germans occupied the country until 1944 when they were driven out by Russian troops, and the Lithuanian Socialist Soviet Republic was established soon afterward. By 1949, most agriculture had been organized into collective and state farms. Industry was also nationalized and production was oriented toward Soviet markets.

The Lithuanian economy has been mainly agricultural, producing potatoes, sugar beets, cattle, hogs, and dairy products. More recently, however, the Soviet Union has emphasized industrialization, including ship building, machinery manufacture, and the manufacturing of forest products, such as furniture, building materials, and paper. Clothing and other textile products have taken on increasing importance in the late 1970s and 1980s.

CONSUMERS IN THE SOVIET ECONOMY

The Soviet retail system ranges from the huge GUM department store in Moscow's Red Square and department stores in other large cities to a tiny Berkakit grocery in Siberia. (This store often has coffee or other goods not available in Moscow because of hitches in the distribution system.) Retail outlets are small and specialized; a butcher, a baker, a bookstore—nearly all of them are drab and bare. But there is a chain of special shops for VIPs that sells quality foods and other goods seldom seen in regular stores.

The Benkises took their short September vacation in Vilnius to attend part of the ten-day back-to-school celebration sponsored by the Central Department Store. While their shopping list was not extensive, they planned to stay three or four days and do little else but shop. They knew that just getting items on their list, if they were in stock, would take considerable time. Then, too, there was always the lucky chance that other things would show up in the stores, as well.

Their first stop was in the square outside the Central Department Store. It was a mass of color, with crowds milling through the multihued tents where merchandise from the various store departments was set up for sale. Parents and children bought school bags, pencil boxes, paint sets, and clothing. A man under a big blue umbrella sold mugs of kvass, a popular drink, drawn from an orange tank. Sylva and Antanas bought two glasses at the odd price of 38 kopeks each. Although his pockets seemed to be bulging with change, the vendor claimed to have none for the 80 kopeks Sylva offered so she told him to keep the change.

Other children watched a puppet theater perform the Three Little Pigs while Antanas queued up in one line for a winter jacket and Sylva joined another for a pair of shoes. In the line she chatted with a wide-eyed visitor from Moscow, who said she had never seen anything like this there. She also whispered that there was a rumor that a new shipment of winter coats would be in stock the next day.

The fair is really a "sales promotion," but such capitalist terms are not considered in good communist taste so it is simply called a "fair." In the Soviet Union, this type of selling is quite unusual, to say the least. The Central Department Store has two other fairs during the year, but its manager has no say in pricing sale markdowns. Instead, the store calls in a group of government specialists to decide on prices for slow-moving merchandise. Usually the experts lower them. Regular prices are also set by the government and are about the same throughout the USSR.

Clutching their purchases from the outside fair, the Benkises ventured into the store. They had not visited Vilnius since the store was built, in the late 1970s. It is a large structure that in many ways resembles Sears Roebuck or J. C. Penney. Its four floors display every kind of goods, from busts of Lenin to bottles of cologne, and from diving suits to dishes. But there are few choices in brands. Sylva Benkis can select only between the china with the lilies or the one with pine boughs.

The store is modern and well kept by any standard and it is similar in construction to stores the Russians have been building in their larger cities. It is situated on the Neris River near the downtown section of Vilnius. Modern escalators whisk customers between floors, and an attendant on each landing helps Sylva and others who are unsure how to get off. More than 600 salespeople deal with the 50,000 to 60,000 customers who pack the store every day. But even that many clerks are not enough to prevent long queues in nearly every department. More than 40 women are lined up at the fabric counter, and almost twice as many in the women's fashion section. Loudspeakers constantly blare K-Mart-like "blue light specials" to customers who cannot leave their place in line to take advantage of them.

Sylva is about number 23 in the line for fashion dresses. It moves slowly because each customer makes her selection and may try a garment on, while others wait. Finally, it is Sylva's turn and she selects one dress and a wool two-piece suit, for a total of 250 rubles. Now, she must go to the area cash register line where she buys a 250-ruble chit, and returns to the end of the fashion line. Finally, she surrenders her chit and receives the merchandise. At the same time, Antanas was in line buying a suit, on another floor. On his way back to meet Sylva, he saw a line in the kitchenware department and got into it immediately, although he had no idea what could be bought at the counter. But he did know if the line was this long, it must be something useful. Eventually, he found it was food choppers. The Benkises already had one, but food choppers were scarce and he could sell it at a fat profit.

Professor Leo Hecht, a Soviet expert, suggests that this cumbersome procedure has the effect of dampening consumer demand since there is a finite amount of time for consumers to spend in lines. It also reduces the resources devoted to consumer goods production, yet permits the Soviets to say that virtually all types of products are "available" in the USSR.

COMMUNICATION AND CONSUMER BEHAVIOR

Sylva Benkis came to Vilnius because she had heard from her supervisor that Central expected a shipment of new fashion dresses from the Lelia clothing factory during the fair, and that good shoes would also be available. In Vilnius, the Benkises stayed with Antanas's aunt and uncle, who passed on the rumor that heaters and a new type of food chopper might be in stock at Central or other stores in the city.

This type of interpersonal communication is vitally important to consumers since advertising is tightly restricted throughout the Soviet Union. But the Central Department Store does such things as sending notices announcing new receipts or promoting other goods to a Government Central Advertising Bureau. If this bureau finds the notices to have "social value," it may send them on to newspapers, radio, or television. The notices are informational rather than persuasive, but that is all there is. And stores must be careful because announcing goods that may not arrive, or publicizing high-demand but scarce items, may cause consumers to panic.

Thus, the "grapevine" and these notices are the only ways consumers are informed about the availability of goods. The first day of their visit, Sylva was overjoyed to hear that stockings could be had at Central since they were not available in Kaunas. Instead of buying the three pair she really needed, she bought 15. As one Soviet newspaper put it: "When goods are scarce and lines are long, hoarding is a natural and justifiable reaction."

DETERMINING CONSUMER NEEDS AND DESIRES

A team of 20 specialists is assigned to analyze consumer tastes and advise on buying. But their analysis often consists of determining what items are likely to be available, then which of those items consumers are likely to buy. This is not a difficult task in an economy where shortages are commonplace, and demand constantly exceeds supply. Thus, inefficient merchandising is the rule, and the Central Department Store tries to be the exception. It points proudly to its inventory turn: approximately once a month—"The highest rate in the Soviet Union," says the store's deputy director, V. Stanevicius.

Many of the salesclerks still do their calculating on an abacus, although the store has two computers. These spew out detailed reports on business in each of the store's 40 departments, every morning at 9 A.M. Everything is done by plan, and if a section lags behind its quota, it must do something to meet it—maybe ask the factory for extra fast-moving, popular goods.

PRODUCING CONSUMER GOODS

The Central Department Store does most of its buying from six wholesalers and ten factories in Lithuania. One of these is the Lelia clothing factory, located on a shady street in the southwest section of Vilnius. Its 2,000 employees produce over 125 items and up to 600 styles each year of suits, coats, dresses, and slacks. While much of the factory output goes to stores in the Lithuanian Socialist Soviet Republic, the rest is sold to the other SSRs, who send their own trucks to pick up the merchandise.

But like Central itself, Lelia's production is closely controlled by the government. In this case, decisions are made by Gosplan, a sprawling state planning organization in Moscow, and a bevy of other related agencies. The factory deals with one government unit to get wool, another when it wants to sell its dress output, another when it wants to set prices, another to do the buying for it, and still another if new equipment is needed.

FASHION DESIGN

The design of Sylva Benkis's clothing purchases, for example, began over 18 months earlier at the Vilnius House of Fashion, a subsidiary of the Ministry of Light Industry. The House of Fashion is supposed to keep in touch with the latest in fashion and "looks" so it checks with the ministry, local factories, and retailers such as Central. Out of all this evolves a line of clothing to be made in Lithuania, which eventually terminates in fashion drawings and a production plan for the Lelia factory.

By May of each year, the factory and Lelia have agreed on the next year's plan. By December, the details are worked out and production begins in January. A typical plan requires a certain number of women's winter coats in a given style at a specified price. The factory has to work out the number of sizes and other details with its customers. There is no provision for consumer input to the research process, so occasionally buyers reject some items even in the face of shortages. One item, a loose-fitting women's coat knit in wool, bombed in Lithuania so Lelia shipped it to another part of the USSR where it sold almost overnight.

Women's fashion dresses sell for about 100 rubles, coats for 150, and shoes for about 40. Since these are both expensive and scarce, there are many dry cleaning shops throughout the USSR that try to maintain clothing in usable form for as long as possible. But because of the generally poor quality of clothes, almost all women sew most of their own and even some of their husband's clothing.

BACK TO KAUNAS

After four full days of queuing in lines, Sylva and Antanas boarded the bus for Kaunas, along with other merchandise-laden passengers. Sylva's purchases included a warm fur-trimmed coat, two dresses, stockings, a wool jacket (wrong color), two pair of slacks for work, several blouses, and underwear. Antanas carried a new two-piece suit (choice of blue or brown), three shirts, a wool sweater, a fur hat, socks, and underwear. They also had a food chopper, a fan-driven electric heater, and a shopping bag full of candy and other delicacies. They smiled happily at each other as the bus started to move.

They spent the equivalent of two month's wages, plus extras, for both of them, but few of the items they were bringing back could be bought at home. And money was not that much of a problem. Soviet consumers know that they must buy legitimately by standing in interminable lines or use other, more expensive sources. So they try to supplement their income and both the Benkises have engaged in several common and widespread activities for doing this. Antanas does mechanical and carpentry repairs for cash for his friends and neighbors. He also brings home a few tools or supplies from the factory and sells them at high prices. Sylva also sells a few items from her day-care center, and does after-hours baby sitting. It appears that practically everyone in the Soviet Union is both a consumer and a seller, involved in some illegal enterprise. The kvass vendor at the Vilnius fair probably doubled his income by setting his price at an odd figure and "keeping the change." Dr. Hecht observes: "Soviet citizens like the system because they have developed a million ways to circumvent it. They dread the possibility of change, which would impose complete adherence to legality, since this would cut their living standards radically. By the same token, the state is well apprised of these transgressions and does little to counteract them."

PROMISES OF MORE GOODS

In late 1985, the Soviet government announced a program that would nearly double the amount of consumer goods available in stores during the next 15 years. The plan, which the ruling politboro approved in September, promises an increase in nonfood commodities such as shoes, household appliances, and television sets equal to 1.8 or 1.9 times the 1985 production, by the year 2000. The plan also calls for a similar rise in services, including restaurants and repairs. This announcement very likely is a response to continuing complaints by Soviet citizens about slow and inefficient restaurants, repair work, and deliveries. They are also becoming less tolerant of shoddy and poorly made products and shortages of everything from winter boots to construction materials. But some Western analysts say that the artificially induced growth rates would very likely lead to products of even lower quality than those made today.

Analysis Questions

1. Without print or electronic media advertising, do consumers seem able to get the information they need? What communication system do they use? How does it seem to work?

2. American society has a set of traditional cultural or "core" values. Based on this case, which three of these contrast most sharply with the apparent values of Soviet consumers? Explain.

3. The shopping process the Benkises went through seems overly cumbersome and time consuming. Yet, they seem to accept it calmly. How do you account for that?

Case 15

Bridge-O-Matic, Inc.

Bob Lambert stuck a label on the last package and tossed it into the nearly full mail bag nearby. He glanced at the clock. It was 11:30 P.M. and he had to be up at 5:30 to catch the 7:02 commuter train to Boston. About an hour ago, Christine, his wife, had finished typing labels and made up the bank deposit slip for the day's mail-order receipts. Now, she was upstairs correcting papers for her fifth-grade class. They were more than a little tired and somewhat discouraged tonight. Bob's full-time job with an insurance firm in Boston was a good one, his promotion prospects were bright, and Chris enjoyed teaching. But to run a mail-order business at home took almost all their time. And to make matters worse, Bob was not really sure that this "moonlighting" enterprise was as profitable as they hoped it would be.

The Lamberts' mail-order product was a hand-held, hand-operated device for teaching the card game of contract bridge. Working with an engineer who lived in the same neighborhood, who was also an avid bridge player, they had developed the product about three years ago. While the device was unique in itself, there were several mechanical, electrical, and electronic-based bridge teaching methods on the market. But because of their product's simple design, portability, and programmed learning features, they thought their method and device were the easiest way to learn the game.

THE GAME OF BRIDGE

The game of bridge was an outgrowth of *whist*, which, itself, evolved from many other card games. The name *whist* was first used in England in the latter part of the seventeenth century and the game was played with some modifications until the 1890s. In 1894, a new game called bridge-whist was developed in London, and the name was soon shortened to bridge. Its basic difference from whist was that the dealer named the trump suit and the privilege could be "bridged" to the dealer's partner. The partner's hand, or the "dummy," is exposed and played by the dealer. Until about 1904, bridge-whist was the most popular member of the whist family of card games. It was introduced to New York in 1894 and almost immediately supplanted whist in the card rooms of men's clubs.

Bridge was itself rapidly supplanted by auction bridge, in which each player had the option of bidding for the trump suit. The original game became obsolete about 1910. Late in the 1920s, contract bridge suddenly gained widespread popularity in the United States, despite strong opposition from established card clubs. Contract differs from auction bridge mainly in the scoring process.

The founder of contract bridge is generally considered to be an American, Howard S. Vanderbilt, who developed the game with a group of friends while on a Caribbean cruise. His method of scoring, with only some minor changes, is still in use. By 1928, contract had replaced auction bridge among leading players in the United States and was also popular in British clubs. Nevertheless, the majority of players still preferred auction.

Ely Culbertson, an American authority on contract bridge, founded the magazine *Bridge World*. He also engaged in a controversy with Sidney Lenz, a leading proponent of auction bridge, that ended in a world-famous match between the two and their partners. The Culbertson side won the 150-rubber match by 8,090 points, and the publicity from the battle made contract bridge a fad in the United States, Europe, and South America. A sizable market was created by this widespread interest, spurring demand for card tables, chairs, and other equipment, and rental fees for meeting places for the large number of clubs. Newspapers had bridge correspondents and ran daily bridge articles by a nationally known authority on the game.

By 1935, however, the passion had cooled and the public lost interest in media discussions of the game and its fine points. Nonetheless, the game continued to attract players and there are about 40 million bridge players in the United States alone. New books on contract bridge appear frequently, written for both seasoned players and novices. Several bridge periodicals are published in the United States, with wide circulations. The American Contract Bridge League, with more than 200,000 members, is the official governing body for the game and it sponsors annual tournaments which include special divisions for teenagers and old-timers.

The most interesting marketing-related factor in this situation was the early realization by the media and authors of books or articles that consumers were so varied in their degree of skill that no single presentation would appeal to even a majority of them. In other words, there was no basis on which the market could be segmented, and there was no appeal that would attract a mass market.

BACKGROUND

Bob and Christine Lambert live in Stonewall, a town of about 15,000 on the north coast of Massachusetts, 15 miles from Boston. It is a rather quiet town since a large part of its working population commutes to Boston and is glad to get back to the fishing village atmosphere of Stonewall at the end of the day. There are several tourist type seafood restaurants in town, and a few rather seedy bars, both of which are avoided by the middle-middle-class group that makes up most of Stonewall's population. By and large, the townspeople live quietly and do most of their entertaining at home. So it is not remarkable that bridge is the most popular game and playing it the most important social occasion in town. The quarterly tournament and the annual bridge dinner dance at the small country club are occasions no one in the "bridge group" would miss.

The Lamberts are avid players, and are at the forefront of the most important bridge group in town. Chris is a born organizer and has been president of this group for seven years. She also ran the quarterly tournaments and worked tirelessly for the annual dance—all in addition to playing bridge at least once a week. Bob has also been active in the group and conducted classes to help newcomers learn the game and to give advanced instruction to those who wanted to play better. He has always been alert for new ideas and methods to use in his classes, and has tried several mechanical teaching devices but without much success. One of these was called Autobridge, a simulated game where bids and hands for the four players were displayed on a card that was inserted into the playing device. Small slotted windows covered the card and were uncovered in proper sequence, illustrating the proper method of bidding, playing, and scoring. He also tried a complex and expensive electronic "teacher" but found it to be too simple for seasoned players and too complicated for novices. He kept on looking and thinking about a method or a device that would serve both "markets."

THE NEW PRODUCT IDEA

One evening on the way to a bridge game, Chris told him about a new method of computerized learning that was being tried out at her school. It was really a version of the old flash cards or programmed-learning workbooks, but the computer made it more interesting. A question or situation was shown on the screen, such as how to spell a word, correct the incorrect part of a sentence, solve this equation, etc. Complex problems could be broken into a series of simpler ones leading to the final solution. After the student made a try, a message appeared indicating whether or not the answer was correct. If not, the message suggested a second trial, and eventually provided the correct solution. Bob was fascinated with the process, and could easily visualize how it would work with both simple and complex bridge situations. The next day, at lunch in the employees' cafeteria, he explained his idea to a friend, another bridge enthusiast. Together they sketched out the first few "frames" of a basic bridge lesson, and discussed the potential of bridge software, and how easy it would be to produce it with ever-increasing complexity so that each of the many groups of players could begin at their point of expertise.

Although neither of them voiced concerns about it, they both recognized the basic problem: each potential consumer needed a computer to run the software. And there would have to be software versions for each of the major computer brands and models. The probability that even a minor part of the market would buy a computer to learn bridge was likely to be very low. Also, Bob conceded, it was like learning to play a piano. The pupil had to be seated at the keyboard to do it. There had to be another way!

Several months went by. Bob and Chris had just about given up trying to design a product that could provide several levels of learning and still be portable and inexpensive. While some of their ideas seemed to be quite simple, when they consulted with a computer expert in the bridge club, the designs had a way of becoming rapidly complicated.

One rainy Saturday the Lamberts were cleaning out closets and cupboards when Chris held up an old-fashioned camera with roll-up film. "Do we want to save this relic?" she asked. But as she uttered the words she realized she held the solution to their problem in her hand. "Bob!" she shouted, "we can put the lessons on a roll, just like film. One frame can be facts that have to be learned. The next frame can be a situation or example where the student uses those facts. The answer will be printed on the reverse side of the roll and it can be seen by simply turning the device over." Excited, they dropped everything and began trying to design a camera-type holder and a prototype for the lesson rolls. After a number of tries, Bob said, "We don't seem to be getting anywhere by ourselves. Maybe its time we talked to an expert." Fortunaely, the bridge club had members with a wide variety of expertise. Charlie Reynolds, who lived just down the street, was a design engineer and agreed to "Take a quick look" at the problem.

As the Lamberts breathlessly explained what they were trying to do, Charlie was caught up in their enthusiasm and began to sketch out several ideas. "It has to be plastic," he said, "otherwise it will be heavy, harder to make, and more expensive. It has to come apart easily so the rolls can be inserted, but hold together solidly if it is going to be carried about. There has to be enough tension on the turning mechanism so that the rolls will stay tightly wound—and a few other things have to be worked out. But it isn't complicated and should be easy to manufacture." Bob and Chris were heartened by Charlie's comments and he suggested that they talk with Ron Wells, another club member, who had experience in the development and marketing of several new products. He could advise them on how to proceed.

The following Tuesday, the Lamberts met with Ron Wells, who was interested in their product idea, but somewhat less enthusiastic than Charlie Reynolds. "You have two problems," he cautioned. "First, you have to decide if there really is a market for your device, how large the market is likely to be, and how you plan to reach it. Second, you then must decide if you want to go ahead with the product, and that decision will require spending a considerable amount of money that you put up yourselves or raise by setting up a corporation and selling stock. To begin, you can either hire a research firm to look at the market or you can try to do it yourselves by gathering as much information as you can, then trying to estimate the market size and what share of it you might be able to get. Just keep in mind that there are thousands of new products battling for recognition in the marketplace. A few succeed but most do not. When your research is done, let's get together again to discuss the next step."

THE FIRST STEPS

Subdued, the Lamberts discussed Ron Well's candid advice, and the following day Bob asked several Boston market research firms for cost estimates on gathering information for the bridge device. The lowest "rough" estimate was $7,500, but Roger Ames, vice president of one of the firms, happened to be an ardent bridge player and he suggested Bob contact one of the national bridge associations to get information on the size of the market, and to try questionnaires or focus groups in bridge clubs in several Boston suburbs. Results of the local research could be applied to the national data to get a "quick and dirty" estimate of market potential. For example, if there are about 5 million new bridge learners each year, and local research suggests 10 percent of the respondent-learners would be interested in the new device, market potential is 500,000. If the Lamberts think they can get 10 percent of that potential for their product, they should sell up to 50,000 units per year.

Over the next several months Bob and Chris, with Charlie Reynold's help, had two working models of the device made from wood at a cost of $400 each. See Exhibits 15-1 and 15-2 for descriptions of the model and how it works. They also found a plastics manufacturer who quoted $2.76 each for 5,000 and $2.09 for 10,000 or more, and a printer who would supply lesson rolls and instructional booklets. They devoted almost all their spare time to gathering market information, demonstrating the models, and distributing short questionnaires at bridge clubs in several Boston suburbs. They decided against focus groups after Mr. Ames suggested they would have to hire qualified group leaders. The results of their research are summarized in Exhibit 15-3.

Using this information, they met again with Ron Wells. While the data seemed to indicate a rather high sales potential for the new device, Ron was still cautious. With his help, the Lamberts decided upon a retail price of $9.95, postpaid for direct orders with 40 percent off for trade business. They prepared a pro forma income statement for the first year which is shown in Exhibit 15-4. Although they had not included much on this point in their questionnaire, Bob and Chris thought that bridge magazines would be the best way to reach both novices and advanced players who wanted to improve their games. They also thought there would be a sizable market through gift stores and gift sections of department or discount stores. Since they planned to conduct their business entirely by mail, they chose one bridge periodical and one gift trade journal for their advertising program.

THE DECISION TO GO AHEAD

Although they had not made a formal decision to go ahead with the venture, the Lamberts had clearly decided to do so. With a personal loan of $15,000 from a local bank and their rather substantial personal savings, they were ready to begin. They ordered 2,500 devices, basic instructional rolls, booklets, and cards that purchasers could use to order additional sets. Fortunately, they were able to get the plastic device for $2.09, after some negotiating with the manufacturer, and an agreement to buy at least 5000 in the next 12 months. They placed one-sixth page ads in the gift trade magazine for September and in *Bridge World* (a magazine for serious bridge players) for November, hoping for Christmas gift business. They planned to use their spacious basement for processing orders and making shipments, and to hire neighborhood teenagers if the workload got heavy.

The merchandise arrived in late August and the Lamberts worked nights and weekends to assemble all the parts. They they sat back and waited for orders to pour in. By the end of September, they received six orders from small retail stores for a total of 140 units. A few more came in during October, and by early November they stopped altogether. Disappointed, Bob and Chris hoped for heavy Christmas orders from individual buyers to arrive during the next month or so. But by mid-December, they shipped only 83 units, of which 35 went to a retirement home in California.

After a rather dismal Christmas, they were almost ready to give up the product and take their losses. "I don't understand it," grumbled Bob, "people we talked with were interested in the product, price doesn't seem to be a problem, and there are plenty of bridge learners. But no sales!" They began to appreciate Ron Wells's caution, and decided to see if he would arrange for them to meet with someone in the mail-order business who could advise them whether to try again or abandon the product. The following week Ron Wells introduced them to Myrna Webster, a small catalog retailer in Portsmouth, N.H., and to Ave Bregman, who had written a beginner's bridge book several years before, and whom the Lamberts knew slightly.

Mrs. Webster had some useful suggestions. She thought the product would not be a good gift item, but individuals might buy it for themselves. She suggested it might be attractive to other mail-order houses for display in their catalogs, if it were drop-shipped and the margin was high enough. "If you do this," she cautioned, "you must set up a separate name for your own mail-order firm so other sellers won't think the producer is competing with them." She also thought advertising might be more productive in home and garden magazines, *Apartment Living*, or regional magazines such as *Yankee* or *Southern Living*. "You will want to keep in mind," she said, "that while there are many prospective bridge players under 20 today, most people take up the game in their late twenties or early thirties. This is the market you will have to reach."

But the most interesting comments came from Mr. Bregman. "We have to recognize," he said, "that bridge is different from most other card games. It isn't recreation, like hearts or canasta; people play to win. It takes skill, concentration, and the use of strategy and tactics. In a way, it's a status game like tennis and players are highly competitive. There are different levels of playing qualification, similar to colored belts in karate, and each of these is a kind of aspiration group for those below it. While bridge group meetings may be social occasions, the players are not necessarily social, nor do they necessarily socialize, except to verbally replay a hand or the game. Beginners need to master the basic rules from a book or some kind of device, but they learn the real game from someone else, and by actually playing. As I found when trying to promote my book, the market is very limited and it has so many parts that it is both expensive and difficult to reach. I think you have a very interesting product. It breaks the theory into small sections then puts them together in examples. It can be used anywhere, it's light, and easy to carry. Most of all, it's cheap."

"I agree with Myrna about advertising," he continued, "but use smaller, inexpensive ads. If people are looking for this kind of thing, they'll see the ad. If not, a bigger one won't help. Also, the Contract Bridge Association finds that most of its new members sign up from October through February, and if that is an indication of the peak interest in bridge, it might be the best time to advertise.'' He also gave the Lamberts some data describing typical bridge members of the Contract Bridge Association. ''Keep in mind,'' he cautioned, ''that all this information won't be useful to you, but parts of it suggest the overall interests of bridge players. Maybe you can combine it with some data about your customers later on to get some kind of a profile.''

THE SECOND TRIAL

After several days of thinking about and discussing this advice, which they should have sought earlier, Bob and Chris decided they had come this far and should make a second try for success. They needed to work fast to enter the winter mail-order market, so they selected three magazines, one in each group recommended by Myrna Webster:

Southern Living (regional magazine)	1/12 page in January	$ 750.00
Better Homes	1/12 page in February	1,900.00
Apartment Life	1/12 page in February	1,250.00
		$ 3,900.00

They also sent out direct-mail literature to 30 selected mail-order houses. Three of them responded and agreed to advertise the item locally. The address in the ads the Lamberts used was coded so the effectiveness of each magazine could be determined.

By mid-February, orders began trickling in, but by early March, the Lamberts had to hire helpers to package orders and take them to the post office. On March 1, Chris ordered 2,500 more devices and these were half gone by mid-April, when orders began to decline little by little. On May 1, they totalled to orders up to that time:

Source of Orders	Number	Unit Price	Total Amt.
Gift & Novelty Trade Journal[a]	140	$5.97	$ 835.80
Bridge World	83	9.95	825.85
Southern Living	1,707	9.95	17,004.55
Better Homes	981	9.95	9,760.95
Apartment Life	422	9.95	4,198.90
Yankee Novelties[a]	95	5.97	567.15
Clifton Crafts[a]	129	5.97	770.13
Alice's of Atlanta[a]	205	5.97	1,223.85
Totals	3,762		$35,187.18

[a] Trade sales

By June, orders were coming in at about 75 per week, but by July they had dropped to less than 50. At the end of the month, total sales revenue since the enterprise began came to $43,678, with 4,899 units sold. The product was a success! But was it? The income statement Bob and Chris prepared for the ten months they had been in business showed a net profit of only $8,514 (see Exhibit 15-4).

It was at this point that Bob was wondering what they should do about their marketing venture. They had made some mistakes, yet they had realized an actual profit that was close to the prediction in their pro forma statement, but with less than half the sales volume. And their profit might have been greater if they had looked more carefully into the consumer behavior characteristics of the market that Mr. Bregman pointed out. Still, the profit seemed small compared to the time they had put into planning and operating the business. There were several questions they still needed answers to, and decisions that had to be made if they were to continue in business.

He went upstairs and talked it over with Christine. He wondered how they might get more information about the consumers who actually ordered the product. They had saved all the orders, and these would be a valuable source of information. By sorting a batch of the orders into categories, they were able to prepare a rough consumer profile, as Mr. Bregman had suggested earlier. The profile is shown in Exhibit 15-5.

From this small sample, they seemed to have a better "feel" for their market than they had before, and planned to look at more of the past orders the next day. If a larger sample confirmed what they knew now, it would certainly help in selecting media that should give the greatest profit per dollar spent in advertising. They both agreed that the little research project they just finished was a milestone in their education in the entrepreneurial business world. They were becoming more self-confident and began to feel rather pleased with the progress they had made, mostly through their own efforts. At this point, there was no question that they would continue the business.

Analysis Questions

1. Why do you think the response was so poor from the bridge magazine ads? What should the Lamberts have done instead?

2. Why isn't Bridge-O-Matic a saleable gift item? In what departments or sections might it be sold in retail stores?

3. What did the consumer profile tell the Lamberts about their target market? What did this information suggest they should do about advertising? What types of magazines should they use?

4. Should they continue mail ordering the product?

BRIDGE-O-MATIC, INC.

EXHIBIT 15-1

The beginner is encouraged to read the first three lessons of the bridge booklet. These lessons discuss the mechanics of the game and scoring. After reviewing these lessons, begin the series "Introduction to Bidding" and continue with the series "Introduction to Play." (Introduction to Bidding 1 comes loaded and ready to play.) Use lessons 4 to 10 of the bridge booklet as a reference while playing the "Introduction to Bidding" series.

Each roll contains 30 frames. Begin each frame by reading the bridge situation and question on front side. Then turn the machine over to the reverse side to read answers and further discussion. Turn the machine back to the front side and advance to the next frame.

To advance the paper to the next frame, move the upper wheels forward, or away from you. As the paper advances from one frame to the next, a series of red dots will appear in the East hand opening. Continue advancing the paper *until the red dots disappear and the next frame number appears in the lower right corner of the East hand opening.* To reverse the direction of the paper and correct for alignment, move the lower wheels toward you. (See Fig. 1).

After the completion of each roll, open the case, remove both spools, and rewind the played roll. After rewinding, remove the wheels from the rewound roll and place a rubber band around the roll.

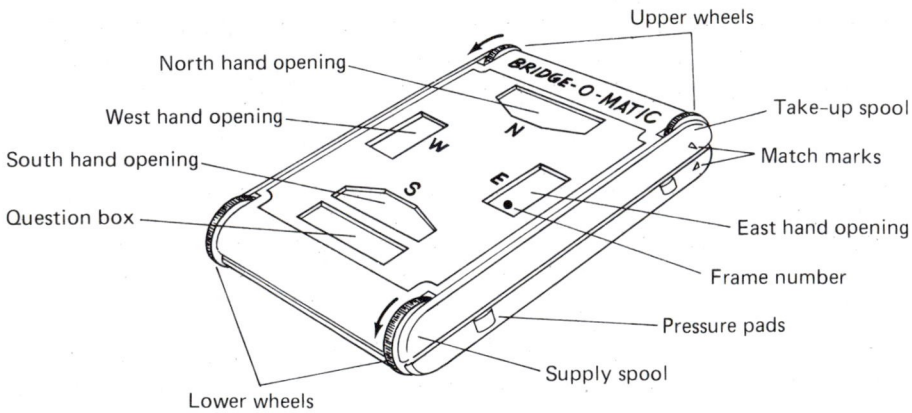

BRIDGE-O-MATIC, INC.

EXHIBIT 15-3

Questionnaire and Research Results

Before passing out questionnaires, the Bridge-O-Matic model is demonstrated. The questions are shown below together with replies by three categories of self-designated players. n = 62

Question	Percent of Replies From		
	Learner	Average Player	Advanced Player
1. In general, what level of bridge player do you consider yourself to be?	12%	57%	31%
2. About how often do you play?			
Weekly or more often	22%	55%	74%
Once or twice a month	40	27	21
Once every 2–3 months	29	14	4
Less often than once in 2–3 months	9	4	1
3. How did you originally learn to play? (You may answer more than one method)			
Help from others while playing	77%	72%	67%
Reading a bridge book	31	41	37
Using some kind of teaching device	24	29	17
4. *For Learning Players Only*: Would you recommend the Bridge-O-Matic device to other learners to help learn bridge?			
Yes, it should help a lot!	39%		
I think it might be useful	40		
It wouldn't help too much	21		
5. *For Average or Advanced Players Only*: With advanced lessons, would you use Bridge-O-Matic to help you improve your game?			
Yes		32%	8%
No		68	92
6. What features do you particularly like about the Bridge-O-Matic device?			
Can use it anywhere—portable	53%	36%	55%
Easy, excellent way to learn	61	22	14
Helps learn or improve game	43	28	21
Reasonably priced	39	45	28

BRIDGE-O-MATIC

EXHIBIT 15-4

Twelve-Month Pro Forma and Ten-Month Actual Income Statements

	Pro Forma 9/30		Actual 7/31
Sales 5,000 @ $9.95	$49,750	3,776 @ $9.95	$37,571
5,000 @ $5.97	29,850	1,023 @ $5.97	6,107
10,000	79,600	4,899	43,678
Cost of Device @ $2.09	20,900		10,239
Sales of Rolls and Inst. @ $1.26	12,600		6,172
	33,500		16,411
Gross	46,100		27,267
Operating Expenses			
Advertising	17,100		9,300
Packing and Shipping @ $1.23	12,230		6,025
Administration and Office	4,850		2,180
Interest Expense	1,500		1,250
	35,680		18,755
Net Income	10,420		8,512

BRIDGE-O-MATIC, INC.

EXHIBIT 15-5

Profile for Bridge Device Prospective Customers

1. Information from the Contract Bridge Association (Mr. Bregman):

Sex distribution:	Female	60.0%
	Male	40.0
Age of members:	Under 34	19.0%
	35–44	15.0
	45–54	24.8
	55–64	21.9
	65+	19.3
Income level:	Under $25,000	29.4%
	$25–50,000	32.0
	Over $50,000	38.6
Occupation:	Professional	48.0%
	Work in home	14.0
	Other	21.0
	Retired	17.0
Marital Status:	Married	75.0%
Educational level:	Below college	17.8%
	Some college	33.6
	College or grad.	48.6
Geographical distribution:	Middle and South Atlantic	32.0%
	Pacific	21.5
	E. North Central	14.3
	All other areas	32.2
Non-bridge activities:	Golf	30.0%
(Multiple answers permitted)	Fine arts	19.0
	Reading	18.0
	Hiking, outdoor	18.0
	Tennis	16.5
	Other	37.0

2. Information from Customer Orders:

More buyers come from small cities and towns in the Southeast, Midwest, and West. About two-thirds of those who placed orders are female and seemed to be upscale in income and social class (checking accounts, printed stationery, some affluent suburbs). A large proportion (60–70%) are married (from address, letterhead). About half or more appear to be upscale in age (handwriting, writing style, or from senior homes). Not much interest from younger groups (low response from *Apartment Life* magazine).

Case 16

The Old Spaghetti Mill

The scene is a suburban home on a Friday evening. It is a little after 5:00 p.m. Jane, age eight, and Jim, age ten, are sprawled in front of the television set in the family room. They hear Mom's car in the driveway and a moment later she walks in. "What a day! I must have shown this woman a dozen houses and she wants to see a dozen more tomorrow. Let's eat out." "Yeah," the kids shout simultaneously, "McDonalds!" "I don't care where," said Mom, "as long as it isn't here. Let's see where Dad wants to go when he gets home." A little while later, Dad walks in. "We're going out to McDonalds!" cries Jim. "OK with me," says Dad, "but how about trying the Spaghetti Mill over in Appledale? Jim Johnson told me about it the other day. He and Joanne should know; they go to a lot of restaurants, and they said lots of people take their kids there."

BACKGROUND

The Old Spaghetti Mill is a large, limited-menu restaurant with table service and a bar. It is located along a well-traveled state road about eight miles from the downtown section of a large eastern city. Although this road is the most direct route from a freeway exit to the city's northwestern suburbs, it is also the most congested, passing through business districts and shopping areas of varying sizes and densities. The restaurant is near a crossroad where several other east-west and north-south roads converge in what had been a small country center known as Appledale some 20 years before. While its country nature disappeared, the name remained and now Appledale contains a number of stores, restaurants, and service businesses. It also hosts a large neighborhood shopping center with 40 stores, anchored by a major super-market and a K-Mart. While Appledale cannot be called run-down, neither can it be considered a modern or well-kept area. Nevertheless, since it forms a hub to several access roads leading to northern and eastern suburbs, it is a busy commercial area.

The Spaghetti Mill is owned by Tri-State Restaurants, Inc., which, in turn, is controlled by Ray Osborne and several members of his family. The corporation owns 12 restaurants in this and two adjacent states, but there is no pattern or theme to them. There are three in a large seacoast city: a pancake house, a seafood "grotto," and a standard "sit-down" featuring American specialties. In addition to the Spaghetti Mill, another pancake house, a steak-roast beef restaurant, and a Mexican "Hacienda" are located in the metropolitan area surrounding Appledale. The other five are in larger cities in the two nearby states.

The "Mill," as it is known locally, is a large, one-story building that had once housed a W. T. Grant store. There is a spacious parking lot in front, with easy access to Appledale Road. Inside, there is a medium-sized lobby with coat racks, rest rooms, and a hostess station. Off the lobby is an open section, with a service bar in the rear and a small "family" area with a few tables. Since the Mill does not take reservations, patrons could wait in the bar on busy nights until their names were called. An intimate disco-theque can also be accessed from the right side of the lobby. A plan of the complex is shown in Exhibit 16-1.

The large dining room seats 280 at a total of 74 tables, whose sizes are distributed as follows:

2 person	20
4 person	42
6 person	12

There is little demand for large parties at the Mill, but when they are scheduled, tables are set up at the far end of the dining room and are isolated by a movable partition that extends from floor to ceiling. The Mill's menu is shown in Exhibit 16-2.

TARGET MARKET

The Spaghetti Mill's initial strategy was to attract younger consumers, roughly in the 21–34 age group who would eat a late dinner and then move on to the discotheque for the rest of the evening. Thus, most of the dinner business is parties of two or four. Often, couples who came for dinner and dancing became acquainted with each other at the discotheque and made up parties of four and even six when they next came to the Mill. The hostess has come to know many of these "regulars" and estimates that most of them come in about once every two or three weeks.

It was a little after 6:00 P.M. when Mom, Dad, and the kids got to the Spaghetti Mill. The lobby was a little crowded, but the hostess promised them a table in about ten minutes. They noticed the calls for other patrons came rather quickly, and it seemed they waited no time at all until they were called and seated. Dad was a little surprised at the rather limited menu, but was very pleased with the prices. When he asked the kids what they wanted, Jane cried, "Spaghetti and meatballs." "I want hamburger steak," said Jim. "Would you kids like a soda or something while we're waiting?" asked Dad. "Okay, two Cokes and two dry martinis," he ordered from the waiter. "And we'll have a large carafe of red wine with dinner."

During the past several months, the manager noticed that the early dinner period, between about 5:00 and 6:30 P.M., was attracting more and more customers. Until about eight or ten months ago, there were seldom more than eight or ten parties seated during that time. She also noticed that there seemed to be more children—as many as one-third of all the diners, and that the number of three- and four-person groups had risen considerably. After about 7:00 P.M., though, the customers were more likely to be younger couples, older married couples, and groups of four or more adults.

The manager, Maggie Thurston, discussed this change in the mix of customers with Ray Osborne, Tri-State's president and CEO, when he dropped in for lunch one day. He visited about once a week since his offices were only a quarter of a mile down the road. "And another thing," she said, "liquor, wine, and beer sales have nearly doubled in the past six months, and most of it seems to be in the dining room. Disco sales are up only a little." She showed Mr. Osborne the data in Exhibit 16-3, which she had tabulated from the dinner checks for the past week. Both food and liquor were included, with the latter broken down into three time periods: 5:00 to 6:30, 6:30 to 8:30, and after 8:30. He was quite interested in her figures and they discussed the situation for a while. They wondered why this new group of customers suddenly materialized. Because of its relatively low prices, the Mill had done little advertising. Except for the large sign on Appledale Road, the only advertising had been periodic "50 cents off" coupons in local suburban newspapers to stimulate weekday sales. But this promotion had not been very successful, and the new customers were coming in on weekends when the coupons were not valid.

A NEW MARKET SEGMENT?

Before he left, Mr. Osborne asked Ms. Thurston for a few additional numbers, then took all the data back to his office. There he made some additional calculations, which are shown in Exhibits 16-4 and 16-5. He was somewhat surprised to note that Ms. Thurston's tabulations showed that cocktails and mixed drinks far surpassed sales of wine and beer, and he noted the relatively high number of drinks per person in the 5:00 to 7:00 P.M. period. He was also amazed to see the large number of diners served during that time and the high proportion of low-priced pasta dishes that were sold in comparison to the relatively stable sales of steak, even on weekends. Even the inexpensive chopped steak dinner was a comparatively slow seller.

Mr. Osborne was quite pleased with the performance of the Mill, since it had been his idea from the beginning. He found the location and designed both the exterior and interior himself, the latter with some help from his sister-in-law who was a commercial decorator. In the short space of three years—not long for a restaurant—the Mill was a financial success, and most of it had come in the past year.

But there was more involved in his recent detailed interest in the Mill's sales and its customer mix. After all, the company had analysts and accountants on its staff to do that. For some time he had been considering revising Tri-State's hodgepodge pattern of restaurants and concentrating on a single theme that offered something unique and that could be used in other geographical areas—perhaps even franchised! Tri-State was prepared to open another restaurant somewhere in its territory, but had not yet decided what type it would be. So the Mill's recent success made it a likely prototype for a group of future restaurants.

But Mr. Osborne was a little uneasy about going ahead on the basis of the operational and financial data he now had, favorable though they were. The Mill had moved from sluggish, plodding improvement to an overnight success. It was clear that there had been a major change in the demographic makeup of the Mill's customers, but it was not clear why this change had occurred. He wanted more information on this before he went any further with his plans.

Mr. Osborne was no stranger to marketing research. He had used it several times in the past when he needed to know what type of restaurant would be most likely to succeed in a particular area or location. What he needed to know now he would probably find out by using focus groups rather than by conducting personal interview surveys, mainly because the information he needed would probably have to be extracted from consumers. Before he contacted the market research consultants, he got together with Maggie Thurston and Tri-State's marketing vice president. After explaining the situation to them, he asked them to help in making a list of things they needed to know. They came up with a list of five topics to be explored in the focus interviews:

1. How did the new customers find out about the Mill? Did they ask an opinion leader? Did it just come up in conversations? Did they see the sign or the ads?
2. Which member of the household made the suggestion or decision to go out to dinner? Which member suggested the Spaghetti Mill?
3. What motivated that family member to suggest the Mill? Why did they want to go there?
4. What features of the Mill did family members enjoy most, or think were most important (e.g., informality, price, selection, quantity, service, parking, location, etc.)?
5. Where does the family usually go out to dinner together? Why do they like it?

SELECTION OF GROUPS

He contacted Tri-State's research firm and set up a meeting for the following day. In it, they confirmed that focus groups were the way to go and they began the process of planning for them, whom they would include, and how they would be selected. Obviously they would need to be members of the new customer group who had actually dined at the Mill. The research director suggested that two groups be set up. One would include individual adults from different family groups. It would enable discussion to be conducted without interaction from other family members. The second would be made up of the members of three or four families who ate at the Mill, including any children over the age of ten. This group would provide interaction within the family group, and discussion with other familes as well. There would be two sets of each group.

People leaving the restaurant would be offered the opportunity to be a member of the groups, which would meet twice at a nearby location for one and a half hours each time. For each meeting, individuals would receive a $15 dinner certificate, and a free carafe of wine. Families would receive a $30 certificate. The panel members were lined up during the following week, and the focus groups were conducted by experienced group leaders the next two weeks after that. Mr. Osborne and several of his executives watched the first two groups through one-way mirrors.

RESEARCH FINDINGS

While the final report from the marketing research organization was a lengthy one, and included a detailed analysis of the discussions, the findings were consolidated as follows:

Individual Adults

In the two individual sessions, there was a total of 12 males and 14 females, all within the ages of 26–38; median 34, mode 33. All lived in households with one or more children. The males got information about the Mill from friends or office-mates, in about even proportions by asking for recommendations from someone they considered might have the knowledge, or the Mill came up in conversations about where to take the kids. While females also got information from similar sources, more of them said they heard about it on radio or saw an ad on TV. In the discussion, two even described the ad (the one they described was from an Italian restaurant on the other side of the city). About half of the group said they passed by the Mill about twice a week or more. Most females believed the Mill was suggested by the male adult, but many of the males thought it came from the children or the female. But the initial suggestion, or plan, to go out to dinner apparently came equally from the male and female. During the discussion, it was brought out that mostly, the decision was on the spur of the moment, after one or the other (or both) had had a hard day. There was a good deal of give-and-take in the discussion about motivating factors for choosing this restaurant. Initially, the consensus was because the atmosphere was informal—a good place to take the kids (socially acceptable), then it changed to a cheap place with average food, the helpings were large, and it filled the kids up. Later, sparked by an off-chance remark, there was general agreement (after a somewhat heated discussion between the males and females) that it was one of the few restaurants where the entire family could have a sit-down, served dinner, where the parents could get a drink, as well.

After this, it was easier to discuss the Mill's most important attributes. With some minor disagreement, they ended up as: (1) you can get a drink there, (2) it's cheap and reasonably good, and (3) it's informal enough to take the kids.

While the group mentioned a number of different restaurants where they normally went with the family, many of these were rather formal and expensive (socially acceptable). The concept here is that people often first bring out socially acceptable points (there may be more than one) then move on to the real points or motives. After some members questioned these choices, it became apparent that most families went to fast-food outlets, with McDonalds, Pizza Hut, and Roy Rogers leading the list. These, they said, were where the kids wanted to go, but they could eat at the Spaghetti Mill for about the same price (for food) as at the fast-food outlets.

Family Groups

There were two groups. The first consisted of three families. Two of these were male-female, two children each. The third was male, two children. The second group was three male-female, each with one child. Thus, the two groups were composed of 6 adult males, 5 adult females, 5 female children, 4 male children. The two groups reacted very similarly to the suggestions of the leader. Five of the males and four of the females (all of whom were employed outside the home) said they got information by asking at work, in conversations at work, or at social occasions, and three said they also noticed the restaurant and its sign while driving by. The last female said she heard about the Mill during social conversations, and saw an ad. In the discussion, several males and females said they saw TV ads, but the children were sure *they* had never seen such an ad, even late at night. Those children who had heard of the Mill did so from friends at school or in the neighborhood. Less than half of them had heard of it before they went there. As with the other group, all but two of the males thought the Mill was suggested by the female or one of the children, while the children thought it had come from the adult male. The decision to go out for a family dinner was initiated by the male most of the time if it was planned in advance. Mostly, if the decision was made after the working adult(s) got home, or before any cooking was begun, it was initiated by the adult female. This is the way almost all decisions to go to the Mill were made. Motivation did not emerge as clearly with this group as with the other, but the kids maintained that they most often wanted to go to one of the regular fast-food outlets for hamburgers or pizza. They explained: "Mom or Dad always wants to go to the Spaghetti Mill. Sometimes one does, and the other doesn't, but we seem to end up there anyway." Another said: "When we all go out together, it's always the Mill. I get tired of it. We get better spaghetti at home." The parents rationalized, "We don't have to dress up, they have big servings, it's cheap, and you can get a drink if you want one."

While the group didn't actually rank the attributes, they emerged somewhat in this order: (1) the food is good and reasonably priced, (2) they let you take your time, no rushing, and (3) it's close to home, no parking hassle, and they don't seem to mind the kids. The families also went to the standard fast-food restaurants, but the kids felt that most of those visits were when either one or the other parent had to work late or was out of town. There was much more discussion of schedules by children in families where both parents, or the single parent, worked than there was in the adult group, even though the proportion of working parents was about the same.

The time is 7:25 P.M.. Mom, Dad, and the kids are leaving the Mill. The kids are full; Mom and Dad are relaxed. "And all of this for four people for a little over $30. Hard to believe!" chuckled Dad. "We'll have to come back here."

Analysis Questions

1. When the decision to go out to eat is made on the "spur of the moment," is it autonomic? Syncratic? Dominated by the male or female adult? Children? What part did opinion leaders play in the decision?

2. What factors did the focus groups bring out that might be difficult to get from questionnaires? Were the two groups consistent?

3. It is clear from this case that a great deal of the information about the Spaghetti Mill is diffused by interpersonal communication, or word of mouth. What does this case suggest that the Mill might do in terms of product and promotion to help this information-sharing process along?

THE OLD SPAGHETTI MILL

EXHIBIT 16-1

Restaurant Floor Plan

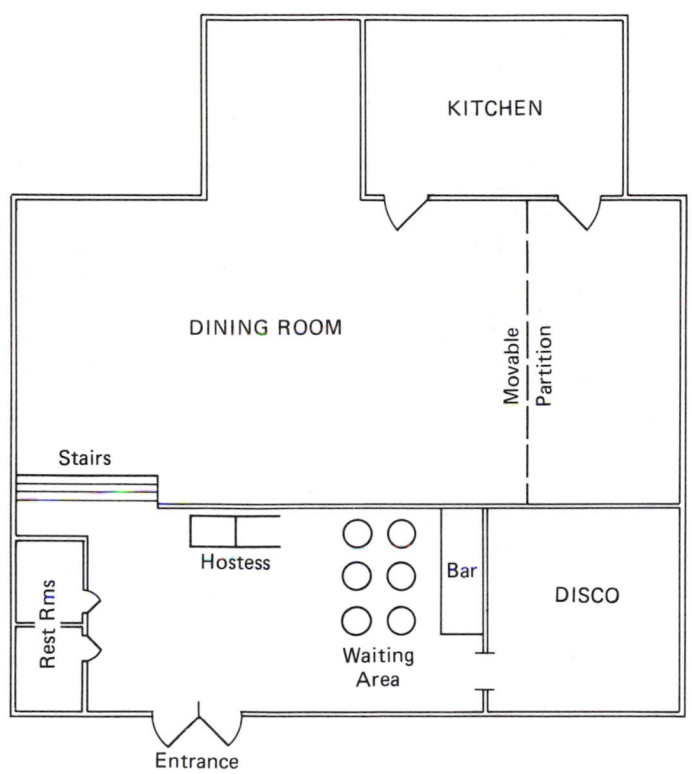

PARKING LOT

THE OLD SPAGHETTI MILL

EXHIBIT 16-2

Dinner Menu

Appetizers	Antipasto (for 2)		$3.50
	Shrimp Cocktail		5.00
	Soup du Jour	Bowl .95	Cup .70
Dinners	*Pasta*		
	Spaghetti with Sauce (1)		$3.95
	Meat Sauce		
	Meatballs		
	Clam Sauce		
	Mushroom Sauce		
	Onion & Garlic Sauce		
	Extra Sauce $1.00		
	Ravioli		4.25
	Canneloni		4.95
	Fettucini Alfredo		4.95
	Children's portion $1.00 less		
	Beef		
	Sizzling 12 oz. Prime T-Bone		9.95
	Sizzling 10 oz. Sirloin		7.95
	Chopped Steak w/mushroom sauce		5.95
	All dinners served with salad bar, bread and butter. Steak main dishes also include potato or spaghetti.		
	Salad Bar only		2.95
Desserts	Ice Cream		$1.50
	French Pastry Tray		2.00
	Tortelloni or Spumoni		2.50
Beverages	Coffee Tea Milk Soft Drinks		
	House vintage wine Carafe:		
	Small $4.50 Large $7.50		
	Beer: Domestic		$1.50
	Imported		$3.00
	Cocktails Mixed Drinks		

NO SUBSTITUTIONS PLEASE

THE OLD SPAGHETTI MILL

EXHIBIT 16-3

**Number of Menu Items Sold in Six-Day Period (Closed Mondays)
(From Tabulation of Dinner Dining Room Checks)**

Description	Tues.	Wed.	Thurs.	Fri.	Sat.	Sun.
No. Customers	178	204	246	489	513	326
Pasta Items						
($3.95–$4.95)	129	147	169	371	378	235
Beef Items						
T-Bone ($9.95)	20	29	28	43	46	35
Sirloin ($7.95)	15	10	24	45	51	27
Chopped Steak	11	14	19	20	16	20
Total	46	53	71	108	113	82
Salad Bar Only	3	4	6	10	22	9
Beverages[a] servings						
Beer	46	37	46	89	133	74
Wine	14	41	33	85	152	71
Cocktails or Mixed Drinks	51	63	78	151	194	86
Total	111	141	157	325	479	231

[a] Beer is counted by the bottle or glass. Wine is sold by the glass or carafe, but is counted only by the glass; carafes are converted to glass equivalents.

THE OLD SPAGHETTI MILL

EXHIBIT 16-4

Number of Adults Served Beverages by Time Period for Six Days—Dinner Only

Description	Tues.	Wed.	Thurs.	Fri.	Sat.	Sun.
No. of Adults Served	86	121	145	277	345	196
Time Periods						
5 to 7 P.M.	24	35	59	137	165	64
7 to 9 P.M.	32	51	55	84	107	77
After 9 P.M.	30	35	31	56	73	55

THE OLD SPAGHETTI MILL

EXHIBIT 16-5

Types of Beverages Served by Time Period for Six Days—Dinner Only

Time Periods	Tues.			Wed.			Thurs.			Fri.			Sat.			Sun.		
	M	W	B	M	W	B	M	W	B	M	W	B	M	W	B	M	W	B
5–7 P.M.	8	6	10	4	17	14	18	23	18	61	27	49	52	67	46	17	34	13
7–9 P.M.	20	3	9	24	17	10	29	12	14	38	22	24	31	54	22	26	20	31
9 P.M.+	15	4	11	23	1	11	17	5	9	30	18	8	27	19	27	19	11	25

B = Beer
W = Wine
M = Cocktails or Mixed Drinks

Case 17

Riverside Savings Bank

In March 1984, John Fraser, chairman of the board of directors of the Riverside Savings Bank, was discussing the future of the bank with its board members. "It appears that we at the bank have some problems. Even though we are on the edge of a fast-growing metropolitan area and we still rank number five among similar institutions, we have had some decline in the growth of savings deposits. Rather than wait any longer for a trend to show clearly, I wonder if we shouldn't take a closer look at our market. Perhaps we need to serve it in different ways."

Actually, in response to the growing population in Seneca County, Riverside had already made a number of major changes in the past five years. While the main office was located in an older section of Seneca City, the county seat, three branch offices had opened since 1978. The nearest branch, a walk-in facility, was established in the Seneca Shopping Center, which opened in 1979. The other two branches were both walk-in and drive-in and were located in relatively new (1980 and 1981) shopping centers on access roads that run from a nearby thruway to the towns of Harrison and Woodford-Toland. Exhibit 17-1 shows the location of the main bank and of the three branch offices. This expansion reflected the expanding population and changing character of the hitherto rural farming area.

EARLY HISTORY

The Riverside was established as a savings and loan association in 1926 by several Seneca City businessmen and attorneys to provide a source of long-term loans for farmers and home buyers, as well as a repository for their savings. As differentiated from a "commercial" bank, Riverside could accept savings deposits, make home mortgage and certain other loans, but could not offer checking accounts or services that were the exclusive prerogative of the commercial banks. Nonetheless, it prospered over the years. By 1975, over 4,000 loans were outstanding for a total of over $100 million, and the total of the savings accounts was $65 million. See Exhibits 17-2 and 17-3 for a balance sheet and recent operating statements.

In 1970 the bank constructed a large, substantial building in the downtown area of Seneca City. Riverside's lobby was a comfortable, shabby-genteel kind of place where customers liked to stop by and chat for a while after attending to bank business, or just when they went by. Until the mid- to late 1970s, most of these customers were Seneca County farmers, businessmen from Seneca City and its neighboring towns, and local people, mostly blue-collar workers in several small manufacturing and service businesses. Others were white-collar salespeople in local stores, as well as office and clerical county employees. The bank officers often came out of their offices and spent a few minutes discussing the weather, crops, and business conditions with these visitors.

Riverside had spent very little on advertising or sales promotion. There was some reminder advertising in the Seneca City newspaper, which served all towns and rural areas in the county, together with a few spot announcements on the local radio station. Most of the advertising stressed the virtues of saving and called attention to the interest rate paid by savings and loan associations (which was one-quarter point higher than that offered by commercial banks). In the spring of each year, the bank offered a choice of small electrical appliances to each new customer who deposited over $200 in a savings account.

CHANGING CONDITIONS

Several new conditions challenged Riverside to rethink its approach. During 1982, changes in the banking laws brought about a turning point in Riverside's somewhat market-oriented but generally conservative strategy. For the first time, savings and loan associations were permitted to offer NOW checking accounts, business loans, auto loans, and a number of other services that placed them in direct competition with commercial banks. One of Riverside's first moves was to assure that its new position was firmly established in the minds of consumers by changing its name to the Riverside Savings Bank.

Except for the three towns shown in Exhibit 17-1, the county was still largely rural, but shopping areas, fast-food franchises, and service businesses were proliferating along the access roads that led to the interstate thruways. One of these, Biggers Avenue, was a commercial "strip" from the thruway to the Seneca City town line. Several large housing developments had grown up behind the strip, on both sides. The houses, both the single-detached dwelling and the town-house variety, were designed mainly for medium- to lower-income families who were unable to find adequate housing in the state capital of Jefferson City, about 20 miles away. So, although the latest population figures showed Seneca City to have about 100,000 inhabitants, practically all the recent growth was in the newer housing areas near the thruway. The downtown sections of Seneca City, Harrison, and Woodford-Toland were all but deserted.

THE NEW MARKET

When asking about the market, Mr. Fraser was referring directly to this new, large group of "bedroom" residents. Most of this group worked in Jefferson City and commuted the 20 miles each way on the thruway. By living this rather long commuting distance away from the city, people were able to buy a single-family home or town-house for from $20,000 to $30,000 less than they would pay for a comparable dwelling in or near Jefferson City. These commuters were state employees, clerical or lower-level managerial workers, or owners-managers of small businesses, primarily in the lower-middle class. A second, smaller group of new residents was composed of employees of a rapidly expanding plant near Seneca that made electronic controls for the automobile industry. The bank had received most of this market information from builders, real estate agents, and from the few mortgage loans Riverside had made to new residents. Most of these residents, however, had obtained their loans from Jefferson City banks. From discussions with local businessmen, Mr. Fraser found that many of the new residents still kept their checking accounts in the city.

As the discussion continued in the board room, Roger Chapman, the bank's president, commented on plans announced the previous week by the Central Bank and Trust Co. Central was a full-service commercial bank with its main office in Jefferson City. It was planning to build a large, multistory office building almost directly across the access road from Riverside's Seneca Shopping Center branch. "Most of the traffic in and out of this immediate area uses that road," Chapman said, "I understand that Central is putting one of their branches on the main floor and placing three, large, illuminated signs on the top floor. With that kind of exposure, they sure have the potential of hurting us in the long run."

Both Chapman and Fraser were local men in their early sixties. While they devoted a considerable amount of time to the bank's activities, they also ran a law practice and a Chevrolet agency, respectively. As is usually the case in this type of financial institution, the bank officers are investors, and a full-time executive vice president or chief operating officer is hired to run the organization. Frank Lindstrom was Riverside's executive vice president. He joined the bank as an assistant cashier in 1969 after receiving his bachelors degree in business administration from a local university. Five years later, he earned an MBA through evening courses, majoring in finance and marketing. With inate intelligence and hard work, he moved up rapidly and, three years ago, was selected to be Riverside's third chief operating executive.

PLANNING DISCUSSION

"It seems to me," said Mr. Lindstrom, "that we need to develop an overall strategy for the next five years. The Jefferson City PMSA (Primary Metropolitan Statistical Area) is crawling steadily toward us and soon we'll be just another suburban town. Two things are very clear. First, we have a market that is vastly different from the one we have served since we opened in 1926. Our newer residents have different life-styles, they are in different social classes, and they participate in different kinds of activities. Second, we are not attracting that market. Maybe the reason we aren't is that we have an old-fashioned image, or because we haven't told them enough about us. The point is, we don't know, and we need to find out more about these potential customers: who they are, what their needs are, and why they continue to bank away from what is now their home. We also need to know who does the banking and who makes the decision about where to bank. We need to be more aggressive in making mortgage loans to this market. Now that we are a full-service bank, we can offer everything the commercials do, and if customers have their mortgage with us, they will use our other services as well. Third, we want to be sure we don't make so many changes to get this new market that we alienate our old one. But before we do anything, I think we should form a committee to get the basic information together and to make suggestions as to what we should do."

After some further discussion, the board elected Mr. Lindstrom, George Kulak (the comptroller), and Flo LaFrance, manager of the Woodford-Toland branch, to serve as a three-person committee. They were instructed to make recommendations to the board by August 1.

The group met several times in the following months, and gathered a considerable amount of information about the Seneca County area, including the most logical direction of expansion, new road plans, plans for new shopping centers, firm and tentative plans for home building, prospective industrial locations, and area zoning. Their findings indicated that most of the shopping and residential expansion in Harrison and Woodford Toland would take place along the Route 95 freeway, in the semiopen area between the two towns. In Seneca City itself, expansion would be mostly to the north and northwest since the land east and northeast was somewhat wet and undesirable for building. The automotive electronic components plant (See

Exhibit 17-1) on the north side of route 295 was scheduled for expansion in 1986, to more than double its present size. The total work force would increase from 800 to 1,500 at that time. There were also plans underway by a group from Jefferson City to build a shopping center on the road between the plant and Seneca City.

When it came to discussions about customers and their characteristics, the committee gathered some general demographic data for the new residents from county records. They were able to compare these data with those of Riverside's present customers from bank files (see Exhibit 17-4). They were also able to extract information on the various ways both groups saved from mortgage applications, but there were only 177 of these from new residents. Mr. Lindstrom also did some research in recent marketing journals and college-level texts. He thought the following statistics might have some bearing on Riverside's strategic planning:

Recently, women have played more influential roles in male-dominated areas, such as financial services.

There is more joint decision making in middle-class families than in upper- or lower-class ones. Wives who are working, and those having more liberated views, are more active in family financial decisions.

Families look to peers in the same social class for purchase information on goods and services.

Families in life cycle stage 3 are not as financially secure as those in the "newlywed" stage, mainly because they may be buying a home. In stage 4, however, their salaries are rising. They begin saving for children's education, and start making financial plans.

Before reporting to the board, the committee thought it should review the information it had collected, together with what it knew about potential competition.

Analysis Questions

1. What are the major differences in personal and social characteristics between Riverside's present customers and the new residents? How might these differences influence saving and banking habits, including why newcomers still bank in Jefferson City?

2. Are there any factors other than those mentioned in the case (e.g., life cycle stages) that that might influence banking habits?

3. What do you think has caused the problems Riverside has today? What strategies should it pursue to attract the new market? Will this market be profitable in the near future?

4. What advertising and promotion appeals should Riverside use to reach the new market?

RIVERSIDE SAVINGS BANK

EXHIBIT 17-1

Seneca County

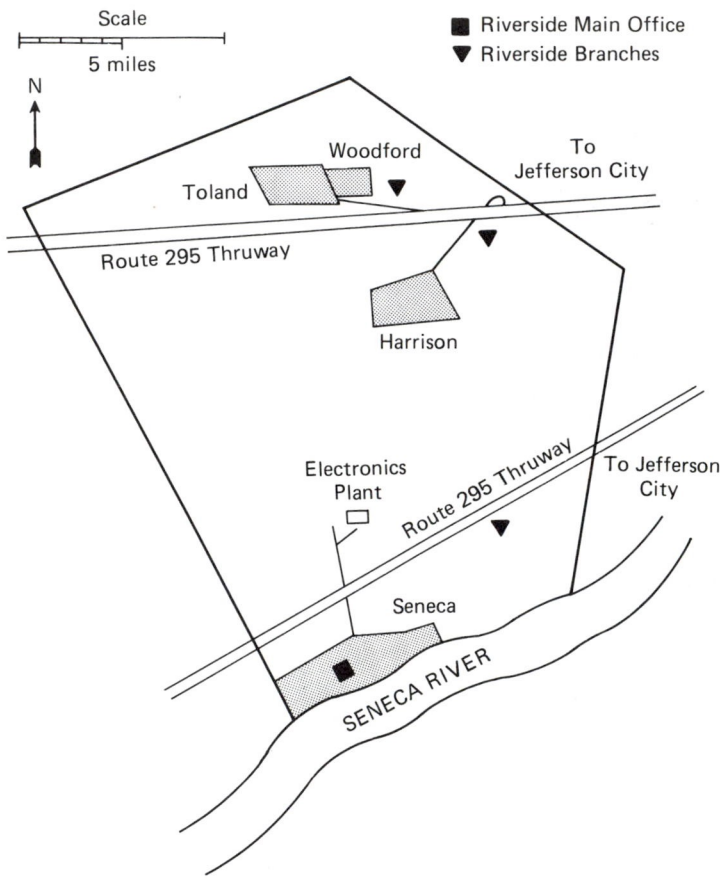

RIVERSIDE SAVINGS BANK

EXHIBIT 17-2

Balance Sheet Assets, December 31, 1985

Assets	
Mortgage Loans Outstanding	$120,558
Insured Mortgages and MB Securities	15,757
Home Improvement Loans	1,383
Loans on Savings Accounts	1,008
Loans on Mobile Homes	821
Other Consumer Loans	1,923
Cash and Investments—liquid	17,544
Other Investments	3,647
Federal Home Loan Bank Stock	1,475
Investment in Service Corporations	1,401
Other Assets	8,397
Total	$176,511

RIVERSIDE SAVINGS BANK

EXHIBIT 17-3

Operating Statements 1983, 1984 and 1985

	1983	*1984*	*1985*
Operating Income	$14,297	$16,613	$18,319
Operating Expenses	2,017	2,287	2,619
Net Operating Income	12,280	14,324	15,700
Interest on Savings Deposits	10,601	13,788	15,000
Interest on Borrowed Funds	1,477	2,347	2,983
Net Income Before Taxes	304	(1,568)	(1,502)
Net Income After Taxes	199	(1,181)	(1,066)

RIVERSIDE SAVINGS BANK

EXHIBIT 17-4

Demographic Data: Present Customers and New Residents

Category	Present Customers	New Residents
Savings Method		
Savings Accounts	79.4%	61.2%
Money Market Funds	21.3	14.4
Savings Certificates	39.0	19.8
Common Stocks	8.3	21.7
Mutual Funds	15.9	3.8
U.S. Treasury Bills/Bonds	5.3	6.6
Corporate/Tax-Exempt Bonds	4.9	3.2
Age		
18–25	4.3	14.7
26–34	10.1	30.1
35–44	22.5	37.3
45–54	29.6	11.5
55–64	16.3	4.0
65+	17.2	2.4
Education		
High School or Less	39.2	21.5
2 years of College	28.4	27.3
College Graduate	21.7	35.8
Graduate Degree	10.7	15.4
Income		
Under $15,000	10.7	10.3
$15–24,000	16.0	24.6
$25–34,000	23.5	21.4
$35–44,000	24.1	15.2
$45–54,000	10.3	16.9
Over $54,000	15.4	11.6
Occupation		
Artisan/Technical/Service	18.3	10.1
Clerical/Retail Sales	12.7	27.3
Manufacturing	27.1	12.2
Gov't/Managerial	12.5	28.6
Home	15.4	4.2
Retired	9.8	1.1
Other	4.2	16.5
Female Adult Members Employed	23.7	41.3

Case 18

Hatton and Mayer Gentlemen's Wear

Ernest Hatton and his partner, Sid Mayer, turned out the lights, then tried the lock as they closed the front door to their store. Just as they walked out into the mall, an older man rushed up. It appeared as though he wore a dinner jacket over an undershirt. "Are you closed?" he panted. "Just turned out the lights," Sid replied. "Open in the morning. 9:30." "But I've just got to get a dress shirt. I ripped mine down the front putting it on," the man exclaimed, "and I've got to make a speech at nine o'clock!" "We'll fix you up," said Sid, unlocking the door. "You go ahead, Ernest. See you tomorrow. What size?" he asked, turning to the customer. "15, 35, for studs, if you have one," the older man replied.

While Sid was getting the shirt, the customer introduced himself. "I'm Jeff Henderson," he said. "I certainly appreciate your taking the time to help me out; I should have looked at that old shirt earlier." He went on to explain that he was president of the area council of senior citizen's clubs, and that he was the speaker at the annual banquet downtown at the Copley Plaza Hotel that evening. As he walked with Sid to the cash register, he went on to say, "I used to own Henderson Wholesalers down in Quincy before I retired three years ago. I've been in here once or twice before, and I sure won't forget your helping me out in a pinch." He paid and rushed out.

BACKGROUND

Hatton and Mayer was not really founded, but sort of materialized over the years in Boston's north end. Sid's father Sam had started a tailoring business in 1921, and because he was active in local politics, he was soon fitting many of Boston's officials. But his high quality and workmanship brought him more business than he could handle. The number of garments he could make by hand was limited, and thus, so was his income. He had hired several helpers, but their work was never up to his standards and they didn't last long.

"I guess I'll never be anything but a poor tailor," he confided to his friend Byron Hatton, who owned the dry goods store next door. "I sell my suits and coats for good prices, but I just can't make enough of them."

"Maybe you should put in a good line of clothes for customers who would be satisfied with a well-tailored, ready-made suit, and with your alterations it would be the next best thing to hand-made," Byron suggested in a half-joking manner. But Sam was thoughtful. "I could do that," he said slowly, "but there isn't enough room in my store for a tailoring room and a retail showroom. I'd have to move." Byron was becoming a little excited. "We could put our stores together, go into partnership!" he shouted.

This was the beginning, in 1930, of Hatton and Mayer, Men's Clothiers. Even in the depression years, the business prospered and after World War II, it moved to a prestige location on Boylston street not far from the Boston Common. It became "the" place where boys were outfitted for prep school and college, and where business and professional men "on their way up" bought their clothes. As the movement of the middle classes to the suburbs became apparent, H & M opened a branch in a new suburban shopping center in the early 1950s.

The oldest sons of the two families had been schoolmates through high school and were close friends. Both worked in the store Saturdays and during summer vactions. But they went to separate colleges and when they graduated, Sid got a job at City Hall and Ernest worked for an industrial abrasives firm in Worcester, about 40 miles east. They saw each other from time to time, but it appeared to the families as though they were drifting apart. So no one could have been more surprised than Byron and Sam when they both appeared for Sunday dinner at the Mayers and announced they wanted to go into the business.

Byron retired in 1963 and Sam in 1965. By 1972, the "boys" had closed the downtown store, since the area was declining, and established their main store in a prestige suburban shopping mall. They also had two branches in similar malls, and one in Portland, Maine. Their market remained essentially the same as it had been in the 1930s, but their (unwritten) objective was: "To be an alternative to Brooks Brothers since it had become a regional chain." (Brooks Brothers was an upscale, status men's and women's clothing store in the eastern United States.) If it was the real objective, it had been a successful one since Hatton and Mayer became a well-known status brand, respected for quality and personal attention to detail. The business was also quite profitable. Although H & M followed the slight changes that characterized men's fashions, such as wide versus narrow lapels and double- or single-breasted suits, they avoided being blatantly trendy.

BREAD UPON THE WATERS

Sid had forgotten about the dress-shirt incident when, about ten days later, a well-dressed older couple came into the store during the mid-afternoon slack period. The man wanted to look at raincoats and, since most of their salespeople took a break at this time, Sid waited on him. "Jeff Henderson sent me here," the man said as he tried on an expensive coat. "He told me one of your people helped him out the other evening, and that you had some good-looking clothes. We usually go to Holloways [a department store]," He tried on another coat. "It looks like Jeff was right about your merchandise," he said, as he called his wife, to get her approval. When she looked it over and nodded, he ordered, "Wrap it up."

Some of the salespeople began to drift back as the couple was leaving. One of them mentioned to Sid, "Seems to me I've seen a few more older customers than usual the last couple of weeks." Thinking it over, Sid thought so too, although he hadn't really noticed it at the time, so he asked Ernest. "Yes, there do seem to be a few more than usual," Ernest said, "and some of them must be new because I don't recognize them." While the older customers did not exactly stand out, most of H & M's clientele were young to middle-aged business and professional men, most of whom were from the baby-boom generation. They could be described as "achievers" who were moving up in their occupations, and often asked Sid's or Ernest's advice about clothes. The partners, who were in their fifties, joked about being a "father figure" for many men in that group.

A NEW MARKET SEGMENT?

There were, of course, a number of older men who had bought at H & M since their younger days, and Ernest and Sid knew almost all of them by name. But this abrupt change in the mix of their customers alerted the partners that a little investigation might be in order. They had not thought much about the potential of catering to an older clientele, although they had read some articles about the increasing affluence of that group. But as they discussed it over lunch the next day, they had a number of questions about whether or not they should actively go after the segment.

Sid suggested that since Jeff Henderson was indirectly responsible for their problem, it might be a good idea to contact him to see if he could provide answers to some of their questions. As the head of what seemed to be a large and influential organization, he should have some idea of what the general needs and desires of its members were.

Mr. Henderson seemed delighted to receive a luncheon invitation and, after they had finished the meal, listened carefully to Ernest as he explained what they were looking for:

> I have to admit that I'm quite surprised at how comprehensive your questions are, but I wonder if you shouldn't try to delve a little deeper into the motives these consumers might have to buy your kind of clothing. Apparently the market you cater to now is looking for status, mildly trendy, business and professional clothing that says 'I have arrived.' I suspect that many of your new 'older' customers are retired and may be interested in clothes that are more personally flattering, that make them look younger. Also, you said more older couples are coming in. Do you notice that women are more influential in these situations, while your present customers tend to make their own choices? I can give you some rather simple answers to some or all the questions, but the kind of decision you need to make will take more than that.

He went on to suggest that the best way to proceed would be to gather population and income trend information. "The Census Bureau makes projections on these, by age, geographic area, and many other break-downs," he pointed out. He also suggested that there was a wealth of additional data and other information to be found in academic research literature. "Our organization doesn't keep this on file," he said, "but we go to the library whenever we need to get anything specific. You can find most of the articles in the Business Periodicals Index there. But suppose I do this—I'm going to the library tomorrow on another matter. I'll collect some basic data for you, and give you a list of some characteristics of this market that have been researched. If you need more information, you can take it from there. But you will have to make a few observations yourself about how these newer customers behave and what motivates them."

MR. HENDERSON'S INFORMATION

True to his word, Mr. Henderson breezed into the store abut three o'clock the following Friday. He was armed with a bundle of papers and a sheaf of his own handwritten notes. As he, Ernest, and Sid settled down in a small conference room, he said, "I'll start out by talking about people over fifty, since it is considered 'mid-life' and most companies selling consumer goods aren't interested in anyone over that age." He went on to point out that the U.S. government defines "senior citizens" as those over 65 years of age, although the medical profession fixes 75 as the age when we start becoming increasingly frail. A New York advertising agency survey also identified a group called "extended middle-age" from 60 to 75. This group no longer has the work responsibilities of the fifties middle-age, and does not yet have the infirmities of old age. Ninety percent of them show no decline in mental powers, and only 17 percent of those over 65 are unable to carry on major activities because of ill health. This should be a new demographic market for those who have ignored all buyers over 50.

AGE AND MARKET SIZE AND INCOME

"This whole market segment is growing rapidly," Mr. Henderson said, and brought out a chart, Exhibit 18-1. He explained that the real growth in the over-55 population will begin in 1990, increasing about 1 percent by 2000. But in the next ten years the growth will be 6.2 percent, and 4.7 percent in the following ten, bringing this segment to nearly one-third of the U.S. population by 2020.

He went on to explain that only recently has the poverty rate of the elderly dipped below that of the general population (Exhibit 18-2). In 1983, both per capita household income and financial assets were considerably greater for over 50 households than for younger ones (see Exhibits 18-3 and 18-4). Also, from 1985 to 2000, total income of the 50+ group will increase by about 55 percent, and the proportion of households with incomes over $25,000 will jump 58 percent (Exhibit 18-5).

Mr. Henderson said that while many of the members of the senior citizen clubs in his council were not affluent, they were not living in poverty either. "Most of them are comfortable. They live in their own homes or apartments and drive cars. I guess about ten to 15 percent of our membership might be considered affluent." He held up Exhibit 18-6, showing the income of one generation beginning in stage 2 of the family life cycle in 1940 and ending in stage 5. Although income drops at age 65, the 55–65 years have the highest income of any stage in the cycle, by far.

BETTER EDUCATED

Mr. Henderson suggested that each succeeding generation of the older segment has a higher level of education, which, in turn, brings increasing affluence and more market potential. For households headed by persons in the 30–35 age group today, about 30 percent have college degrees but for those 65 to 70, the proportion is only 12 percent. Most of those, however, are in the higher income segment of the older population. As more educated consumers enter the over 50, or over 65 group, they are likely to demand more products, services, and attention than do the mid-lifers or the elderly of today.

INDIVIDUAL CHARACTERISTICS

"I jotted down some findings of several academic studies that might have some bearing on your questions. These are life-style and personality characteristics that might help with your decision," Mr. Henderson said. He briefly described them, cautioning Sid and Ernest that these results apply to the majority in the studies and not necessarily to all other consumers:

> The elderly are less likely to complain to the management of stores and companies from which they have received poor goods or services.
>
> They generally do not feel old and do not like to be reminded they are old. Many, even those in their early seventies, look and act younger. They are also very active in the market.
>
> They have a considerable amount of leisure time, and many of them devote at least some of it to politics. They are a major force in several states and areas, and apply continuing pressure for increased benefits.
>
> They "learn" and react to advertising messages in the same way as other age groups, but at not quite the same pace. Newspaper ads get better results than fast-moving television ones.
>
> They replace fewer household appliances than do younger consumers, but they spend more on travel and clothing.
>
> A large proportion (60%) of the retired population started drawing benefits before the age of 65, and about one-third of married women stopped work about three years before starting to draw social security benefits.
>
> Many firms offer discounts to the elderly. While many take advantage of the lower prices, others resent being asked if they are eligible for them. Mr. Henderson noted that in some areas the telephone company places a special symbol in the yellow pages for firms that offer senior-citizen discounts. He also had a summary (Exhibit 18-7) of special discounts and services offered by airlines and by Sears Roebuck's new "Mature Outlook" organization.

ANSWERING THE QUESTIONS

"I hope this is enough information to lead you to the right decision about the market potential of older consumers. I noticed in some of the articles I read that we are called a "subculture" because many of us are no longer in the mainstream. But I think you will find there is more of a market than most businessmen think there is, and it is bound to increase steadily in the next ten to 20 years. I suspect that the people I sent to your store have started you thinking about it. Good luck."

With this last statement, he waved and left the store. Sid and Ernest looked at each other thoughtfully, picked up the papers Mr. Henderson had left, and began trying to answer the questions that the three of them raised. "What we are talking about is formulating a strategy that will let us serve two markets, yet will not alienate either one," said Ernest, "and that may not be very easy to do."

Analysis Questions

1. Are there enough affluent older customers in this market today? What is its future potential? Will it increase in size? What factors are important here?

2. Are the tastes of this market, in general, similar or different from H & M's

present market segment? Do they need separate lines? Do they need to employ older salespeople for this market?

3. Should H & M open a separate store for "seniors" (or whatever term would be acceptable)? Or should they simply add them to the segment already served by the present stores? What would be the problems associated with these proposals, if any?

HATTON AND MAYER

EXHIBIT 18-1

U.S. Aged Distribution, 1980–2020

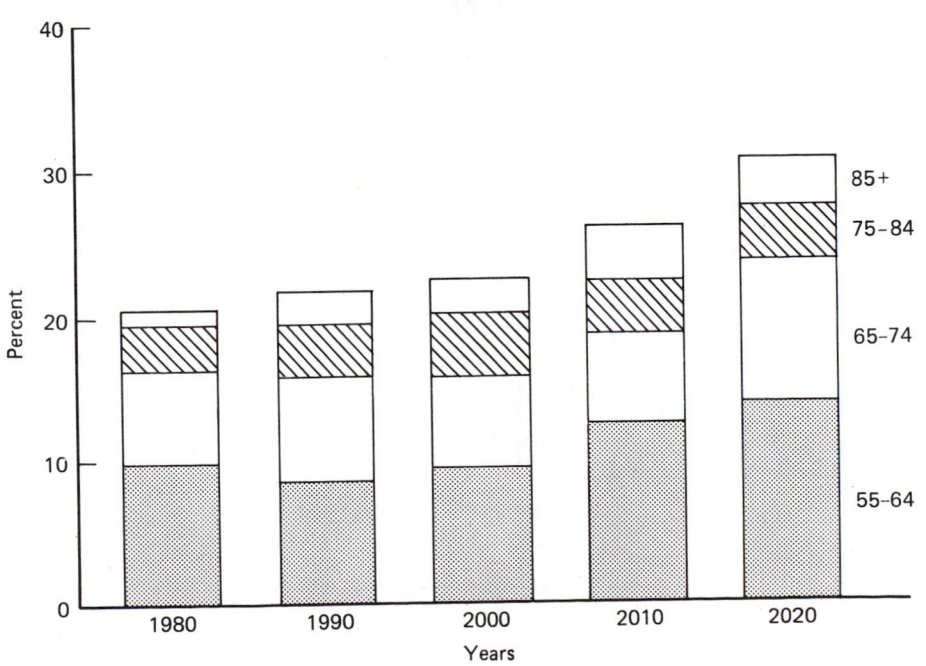

Poverty Rates in the United States, 1966–84

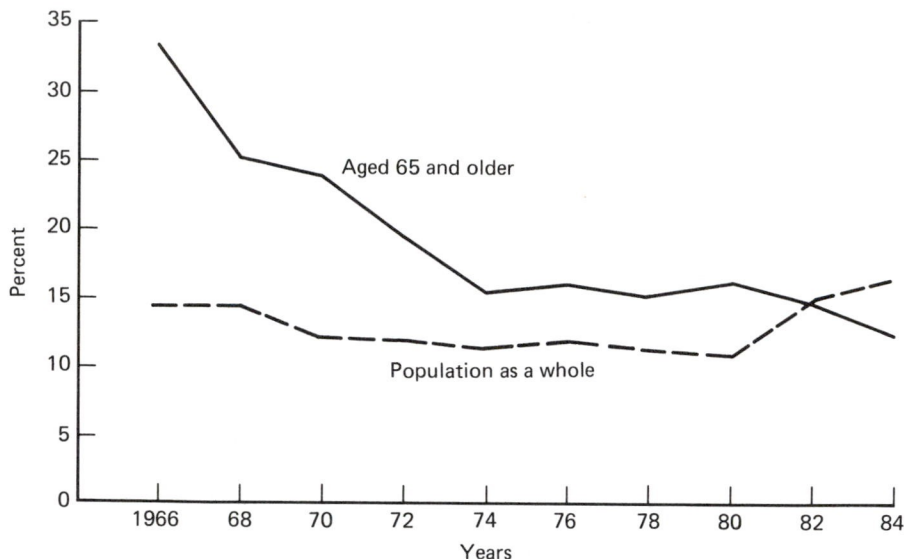

Household Income Per Person, Over 50 Population, 1983

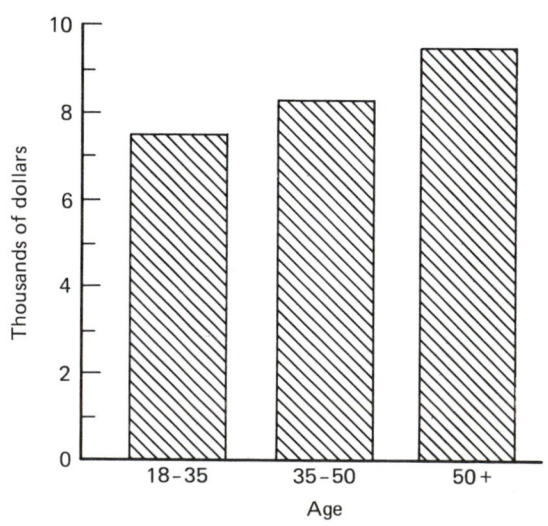

Financial Assets of Head of Household by Age, 1983

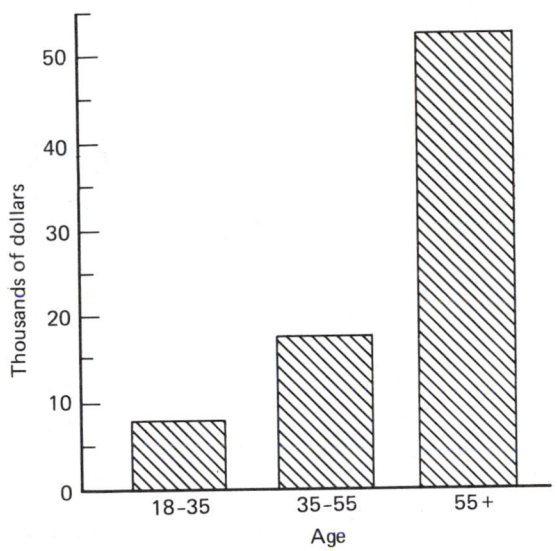

HATTON AND MAYER

EXHIBIT 18-5

Household and Income Growth, Over 50 Population, 1985–2000

Household or Income	Percent Growth
Total number of Households	+23%
Total Household Income	+55%
Mean Annual Household Income	+27%
Households with Incomes Over $25,000	+58%

Income of One Generation Through the Life Cycle

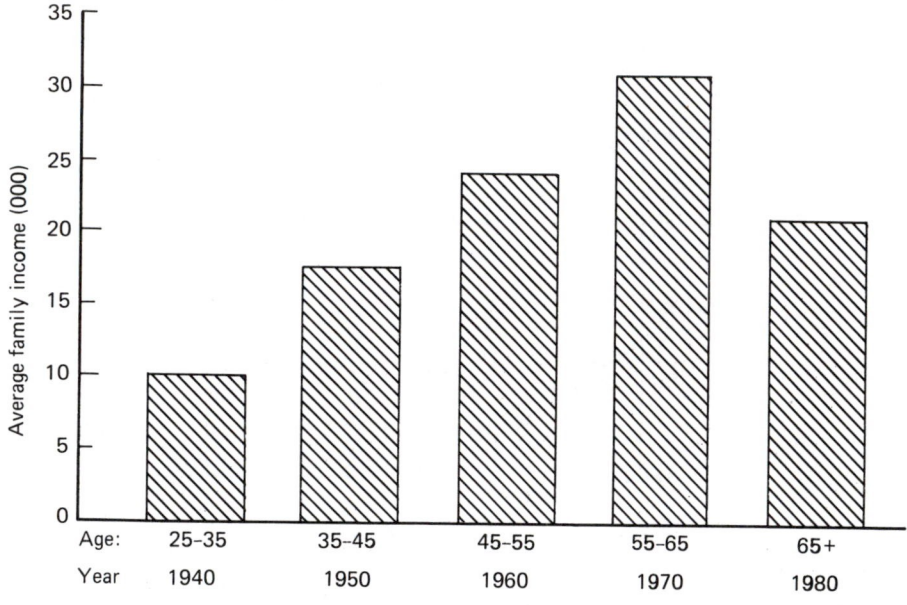

Recent Benefit Offerings to Older Consumers

Sears Roebuck and Co. recently started the Mature Outlook Membership organization for people over 50. For an annual membership fee of $7.50, the organization offers a combination of benefits, information, and discounts especially tailored to the needs of older persons. Some of the benefits are:

Mail-order pharmacy service, same-day service at "lowest possible prices," and same-day processing.

Coupon savers book for up to 30 percent discounts on some Sears items.

Auto service coupons worth $42 at Sears Automotive Centers.

Savings on vacation tours, bus travel, and groceries.

American Airlines and TWA announced additional discounts for older travelers:

American will offer a 10 percent discount to people 65 and over who pay a one-time $25 fee.

TWA has made a similar offer of a 10 percent discount for unrestricted travel to TWA's domestic cities and some foreign routes. A unique feature of TWA's program is a rebate system of from 5 to 50 percent on the purchase of consumer goods, with proof of previous travel on TWA.

Minneapolis-based Republic Airlines is introducing similar discounts in March 1986, in addition to discounts at Holiday Inn Hotels.

Case 19

The Profit Cemetery

There are about 10,000 active cemeteries in the United States today, not counting national and military ones. Approximately 60 percent of them, or about 5,700, are privately owned, and 50 percent are profit-making enterprises. Most of the for-profit cemeteries are located in the South or west of the Mississippi River. The remaining 40 percent are publicly owned by state or local governments, are affiliated with churches or synagogues, or are owned by nonprofit associations such as fraternal orders or cooperatives. In the United States today, about one new cemetery is opened each year, compared to several dozen in the 1940s and 1950s.

EARLY HISTORY AND DEVELOPMENT

In the United States during the eighteenth and early nineteenth centuries, numerous small family cemetery plots were set aside on farms when there were no established towns nearby with cemeteries and no undertaking facilities. Many of these still exist today, particularly in New England and in the South, and some of them have expanded into large, organized nonprofit family enterprises. Other cemeteries were generally located in town centers, especially adjacent to churches. As the towns grew, authorities recognized that use of in-town land for this purpose was both a health hazard and an impractical use of valuable land. Thus, plots were set aside on the outskirts of towns and growing cities. Generally they were maintained by church sextons, with costs often shared by the church and the municipalities.

There are two basic types of cemeteries: the traditional and the so-called memorial park or garden. The former is the type we visualize when we think of cemeteries: upright marking stones and a variety of structures, including above-ground buildings and stone encasements. Here, the families may choose their own individual monument or grave marker.

Around 1910, the memorial park concept was introduced. In these cemeteries, only certain styles and materials may be used for grave markers, and the markers must be set flush with the ground. Two strategies are involved. First, the area is designed to resemble a large park with rolling lawns, trees, flower gardens, and fountains, offering a more pleasant and cheerful atmosphere than the traditional somber, compartmented graveyard. Second, the use of flush markers reduces maintenance costs substantially since the area may be mowed like a golf course instead of hand trimmed. Because of this factor, many of the traditional cemeteries have moved to the "garden" concept as they expanded.

AVAILABLE FACILITIES

When we visualize a cemetery, we also think of underground burial plots. These are either standard size—at least eight by three feet—or as small as four by three feet for younger children. No part of the casket can be less than four feet from normal ground level, but cremated remains (cremains) may be buried in a much smaller plot. Some cemeteries also provide lawn crypts, usually precast concrete storage vaults for caskets, which are installed just below ground level and covered with a layer of sod. When underground plots are used, the casket must be enclosed in a vault, or grave liner, because caskets eventually collapse and cause depressions in the cemetery ground that complicate maintenance and give the grounds an unsightly appearance. The vault may be a concrete or metal container or, more recently, reinforced plastic. It may vary from a simple shoe-box structure to an ornate sarcophagus. A grave liner, on the other hand, is a bottom slab—two end and two side pieces that are notched and held together with metal bands and a top. Because of this construction, liners are usually much cheaper than vaults.

Above ground, there are mausoleums, which are usually stone buildings where one or more caskets may be stored, and columbariums for cremains. Often the two may be combined in the same structure. The mausoleum may be a completely closed building, usually with an entry door of heavy material, or a "garden" variety where the crypt openings are exposed to the outdoors, faced by an area of plants or shrubs. The individual or family mausoleum is seldom built today, but community ones housing up to several thousand interments are becoming more common, particularly in urban areas where land values are high.

Other cemetery services include perpetual care for the cemetery area itself, including maintenance of walkways, roads, fences, landscaping, and protection from vandalism. These services are paid for out of income from endowment funds. Most states require that such funds be established by dedicating a percentage of the price of gravesites. Massachusetts requires 30 percent while Virginia requires only 10 percent. Today many full-service cemeteries will have a chapel, a crematory, a florist shop, and production shops for making grave markers, vaults, and liners.

WOODLAWN

The largest mausoleum so far is the Woodlawn Cemetery in Nashville, Tenn. Woodlawn has no spacious lawns or imposing grave stones. Instead, it is a 20-story building with room for 258,000 "graves." Named by some the "Death Hilton," it will accommodate in its seven acres the number of casket interments that would normally use 192 acres. Even though the building costs are included in the consumer's burial costs, prices are reasonable since there is no grave to open and close, and no marker, grave liner, or vault. The casket is standard size, made of steel, inexpensive, and designed to slide easily into the crypt.

The overall concept is an interesting one. In its literature, Woodlawn says it provides a "warm, dry, protected" resting place instead of a "dark, damp hole in the ground." There is also a Garden of Jesus on the grounds, complete with a replica of the tomb of Christ built with "actual stones from Jerusalem."

PRICES

At Woodlawn, prices vary inversely by location, although the reasoning behind this is obscure. The lower floors cost more than the upper ones (which are closer to heaven). However, the price of locations within a tier of crypts is more logical. "Heaven Level" upper and "Heart Level" middle levels are more expensive than "Prayer Level" at floor or kneeling height.

Normally, prices for conventional cemetery space include the cost of the lot itself plus a deposit in a perpetual care endowment fund. The cost of a marker, vault, or liner, their installation, opening and closing the site, and interment/recording fees are all extra. The fee is analogous to a title search in other real estate transactions. The cost for all these items varies from $1,000 to $3,000, with an average of about $1,200. But the cost varies considerably by location and by the type of facilities purchased. At Woodlawn Cemetery in the Bronx, N.Y. (not the one we discussed earlier), a family-sized, top-of-the-line mausoleum room in a prime location costs about $80,000. On the other hand, an ocean-view lot overlooking the famous

Diamond Head, just outside of Honolulu, Hawaii, can be had for around $1,750. In Dallas, a lot near waterfalls and the Dallas Live Oaks is $1,300, and in the well-known Forest Lawn of Glendale, Calif., 35 square feet is about $2,500.

SERVICE CORPORATION INTERNATIONAL

Generally, the $5 billion a year funeral parlor and cemetery businesses are local "mom-and-pop" operations. But the Houston-based Service Corporation International (SCI) is a small giant in this industry, with sales of well over $250 million. It would be hard to tell that its 280 funeral parlors (out of 22,000 in the United States) are owned by a corporation since SCI keeps them looking like all other neighborhood or small town ones. With this strategy, SCI retains the strong loyalty people have for their local funeral homes, and few notice that there has been a change in management when the original owners are bought out.

But one of SCI's big moneymakers is its land holdings. In 1983, its cemetery division earned $8.9 million, up from only $3.3 million in 1981. SCI has about 4,200 acres of cemetery land, most of which came along with its funeral home acquisitions over the years. It is carried on the books at about $10,000 an acre, or $42 million, but is worth many times that today, even though only half has been developed. Included in part of these holdings are some 51 cemeteries in 27 states, the District of Columbia, and five Canadian provinces. The strategy of the cemetery division is to sell land in small parcels over time. At the same time, it is busy buying new cemeteries, mostly those in "combination" locations where the funeral home is inside cemetery grounds. It plans to buy about six cemeteries a year for the next several years in such demographically suited locations as Florida, Texas, California, and Colorado. In these locations, population is growing, church cemeteries are not a factor, and few choose cremation.

THE PREPLANNING ALTERNATIVE

Following the social and family relationships in the United States closely, SCI was apparently convinced that there were increasing numbers of nuclear families or singles who had no one to make funeral arrangements for them, or who wanted to relieve survivors of the task. So in 1977, the firm began selling its products, including burial plots, in advance of need. Using television personalities in ads, radio, direct mail and personal selling, they have pushed the idea of prearranged and prepaid funeral services and prepurchased cemetery lots. Buyers are usually people over 55 who pay in lump sums or in five- or ten-year installments. The average cost of a coffin, a bronze marker, and the lot is about $1,200, which may or may not include the liner and the registration paperwork.

The average purchaser of this so-called "preneed" package is 63 years old and, according to actuarial tables, has a life expectancy of 80. For the payment, which roughly equals the cost of the package if it were purchased today, the buyers get a kind of life insurance policy that guarantees the cemetery lot and specified extras, at some time in the future. The casket, funeral service, and other arrangements can also be prearranged in the same way. What it amounts to is that the client can lock in tomorrow's burial lot at today's prices. Most of these policies provide that if the buyer is in good health when the application medical questionnaire is filled out, the lot will be provided if death comes before all payments are made. SCI says the client gets "a sound, inflation-proof product." In 1983, estimated sales of the preneed packages were $40 million, at an average price of $1,600.

Skeptics of the plan say that Service Corp. will find that inflation and rising costs will force it to provide funerals or lots at a loss in the future. But SCI's president, B. B. (Ben) Hollingsworth does not agree. "Over 80 percent of the expenditures are fixed overhead costs; things like hearses and buildings. We need them whether we have one funeral or a hundred. The other 20 percent has been rising by only about 5 percent a year." But the preneed business is also very profitable. SCI invests all the money it receives from the plan and takes the earnings as income. The chart in Exhibit 19-1 compares earnings from preneed investments with those from the rest of the company's operations. Exhibit 19-2 shows promotional information for the preneed option.

COMPETITION AND THE FUTURE

While funerals are usually conducted no matter what the method of interment, the need for cemetery burial space varies widely, depending upon what method is used. And just as it does for other types of products on the market, competition and changes in market conditions may have serious implications for the sale of cemetery lots.

While cemeteries will be with us for some time to come, the volume of business available to them has dropped sharply. For one thing, the number of deaths is relatively steady considering that the population is rising. And the death rate (deaths per 1,000 population) is falling. Exhibit 19-3 shows actual deaths and the rates from 1955 to 1983.

A formidable threat to cemeteries is the increase in the number of Americans who are choosing cremation over traditional burial. In the past 25 years, the proportion of cremations has grown from 3.5 percent to nearly 12 percent, and it is expected to double again by 2000. Although this method has been around for many years, it has been fought vigorously by conventional funeral directors and cemetery organizations. In 1972, the tiny Telophase Society (named for the last stage in the development of living cells) performed cremations in San Diego, Calif., for a modest $250, including scattering the ashes at sea. Under pressure from the California Funeral Directors Association, the state legislature came close to passing restrictive legislation aimed at Telophase. Proponents claimed that Telophase did not live up to health and safety standards, a charge vigorously opposed by San Diego County's director of public health. Because of public opposition to the legislation, which provided that crematoriums would have to operate as standard mortuaries, the bill did not pass. Today, there are over 15,000 crematoriums in the United States.

Although the number of cremations has grown considerably (245,000 in 1985), they still account for a relatively minor percentage of all body dispositions. Of this figure, the West Coast accounts for nearly 40 percent, and the East Coast another 33 percent. This total is quite low when compared to other countries. In Japan, 84 percent of the bodies are cremated; in the United Kingdom, 59 percent; and in Australia, 40 percent, Some analysts predict that the U.S. figure will reach 25 percent by the year 2000.

The rather slow diffusion of this innovative service in the U.S. funeral industry is the result of a number of factors. The major one is concerned with traditional cultural, moral, and religious attitudes of many Americans toward death and the rites associated with it. Some religious groups forbid cremation outright, and the attitudes of others range from reluctant tolerance to encouragement.

HIGH-TECH INTERMENT

Although cremation may change some parts of the traditional funeral and burial ceremonies, the ashes are usually "buried" in a mausoleum or other space provided in a cemetery. But a new method proposed by the Celestis Group of Melbourne, Fla., may change even that. This consortium of morticians and former Kennedy Space Center engineers is pursuing a new commercial venture that will memorialize deceased persons through space flight, and the U.S. Department of Transportation has already approved the proposal and given preliminary clearance for the first space burial missions.

For $2,500 to $3,000, plus a $500 cremation cost, the ashes of an individual can be launched into space by a Conestoga booster, shown in Exhibit 19-4. Once in the Earth's Van Allen radiation belt, the spacecraft carrying about 5,000 cremated bodies will orbit the Earth for an estimated 63 million years. The ashes will be sealed into the craft, rather than scattered into space. This space burial satellite will have a highly reflective outer surface as a marketing technique so that friends and relatives of the deceased can see the space craft pass overhead on clear nights. If this venture proves to be successful, Celestis hopes to offer future flights with Earth escape trajectories that would send the space craft beyond the Moon and into deep space.

In order to make the flights profitable, Celestis had to develop a new technique for cremation that would reduce the weight and container size of ashes from a human body. Through a "recremation" process, they were able to fit the ashes into a capsule about three-eights of an inch in diameter and under 2 inches long. To break even, 5,000 capsules at a fee of $3,000 each will have to be carried on each flight.

Space burial will be marketed to the funeral trade by Celestis and morticians would market it in the same way they do cremation memorials or cemetery mausoleum space. Celestis will also establish a toll-free number for those who want to sign up for the first flight. The firm will also accept advance reservations, perhaps even through a preneed plan, much as cemetery lots are sold.

THE FUTURE

As one cemetery owner put it: "There aren't many impulse buyers in the cemetery business. Dad never gets up in the morning and says to Mom, 'It's a nice day, let's go look at some cemetery lots.'"

Generally, this type of business is slow, and costs have soared. Thus, marketing is critical to the sale of lots, and an understanding of how to sell to prospective buyers is vital. The only successful strategy is to persuade people to make arrangements and buy a burial lot before they die. To do this, all the standard marketing tactics are used, including TV, radio, and newspaper ads, as well as direct-mail solicitations. An example of one such advertisement is shown in Exhibit 19-5. But personal selling is considered by most cemetery owners to be the most effective, and commissions often total between $22,000 and $50,000 a year. One salesman watches for funerals, then contacts everybody in the neighborhood while they have the product in mind. Another says, "Three out of every four people I call on won't let me in. You have to talk your way in so they will listen to you. We have the most undesirable product there is, but it's a necessary one."

Analysis Questions

1. Using a basic consumer behavior model, trace a decision to buy a cemetery lot through the search process (a) when buying before death (preneed) and (b) when survivors are buying after a death.

2. Based on SCI's preneed sales, will this be a major factor in cemetery lot

sales? (You can calculate the number of lot sales from data in the case.) Is a preneed buy the best financial deal? Explain.

3. What cultural factors do you think inhibit the use of cremation in the United States? Do you think the proportion will really rise to 25 percent by 2000? Explain your reasoning using consumer behavior concepts.

4. Which cultural factors must the Celestis Group overcome in order to sell space interment? Do you think they can get enough reservations to make the flight? Why?

THE PROFIT CEMETERY

EXHIBIT 19-1

Service Corporation International Preneed Earnings versus Earnings from Rest of Company

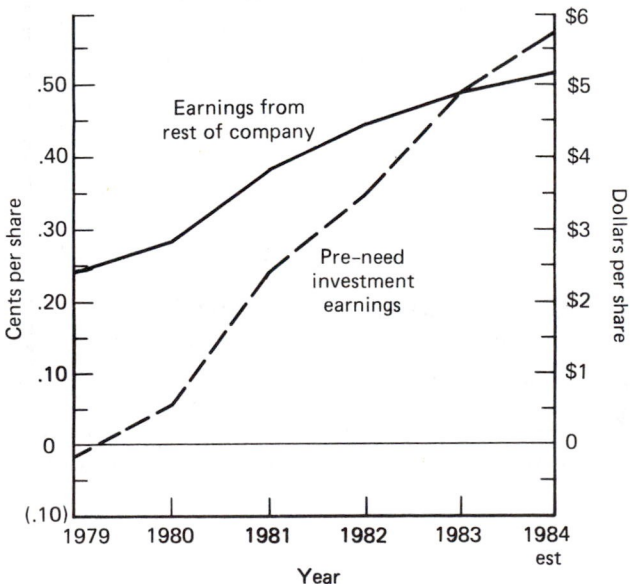

Source: Reproduced by courtesy of Service Corps International

THE PROFIT CEMETERY

EXHIBIT 19-3

Number of Deaths and Death Rates Per 1,000 Population, 1955 to 1983

Year	Number of Deaths	Percentage Incr/Decr	Rate Per 1,000	Annual Change
1955	1,528,000		9.3	
1960	1,712,000	+12.04%	9.5	+.2
1965	1,828,000	+6.70	9.4	−.1
1970	1,921,000	+5.08	9.5	+.1
1975	1,892,000	−1.50	8.8	−.7
1980	1,986,000	+4.9	8.7	−.1
1981	1,987,000	+0.005	8.7	NC
1982	1,975,000	−0.60	8.6	−.1
1983	2,010,000	+1.8	8.6	NC
1984	2,020,000	+0.049	8.6	NC
1985	2,037,000	+0.084	8.7	+.1

THE PROFIT CEMETERY
EXHIBIT 19-4

Conestoga II Booster

Source: Courtesy of Space Services, Inc.

EXHIBIT 19-5

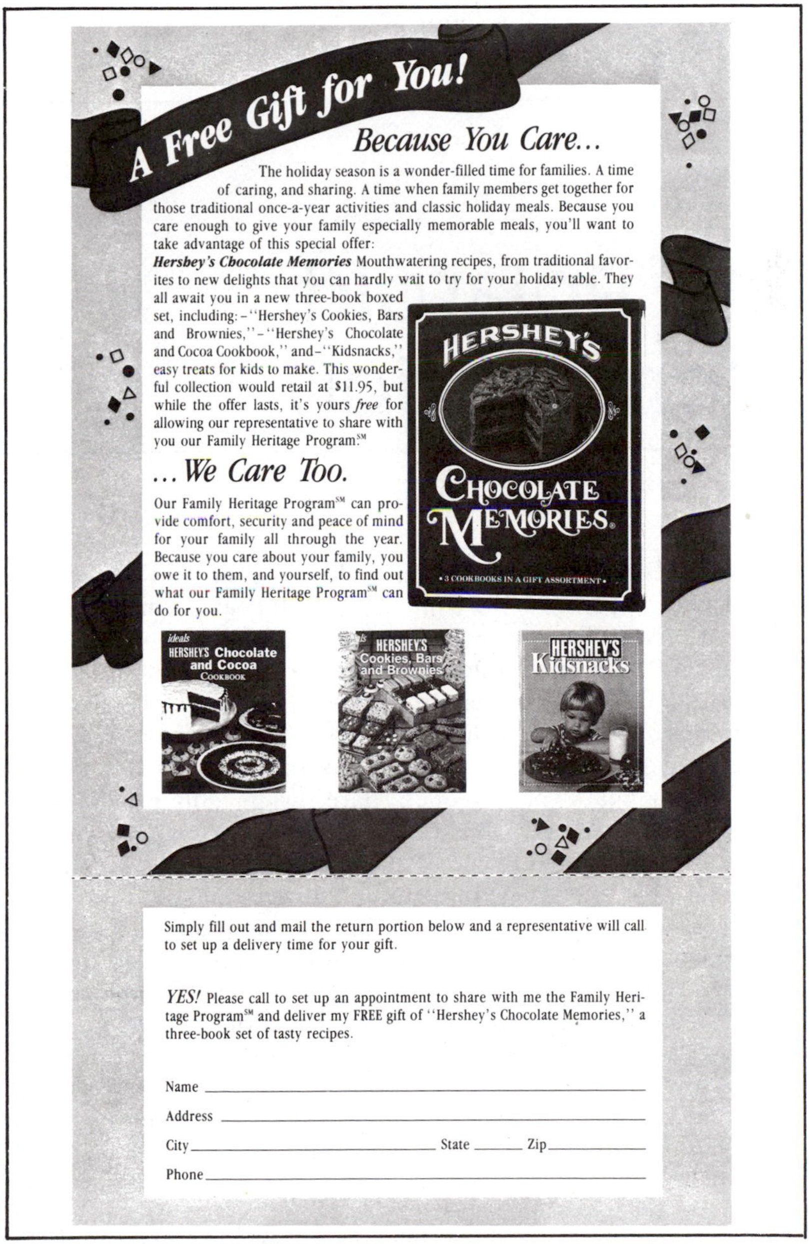

A Free Gift for You!

Because You Care...

The holiday season is a wonder-filled time for families. A time of caring, and sharing. A time when family members get together for those traditional once-a-year activities and classic holiday meals. Because you care enough to give your family especially memorable meals, you'll want to take advantage of this special offer:

Hershey's Chocolate Memories Mouthwatering recipes, from traditional favorites to new delights that you can hardly wait to try for your holiday table. They all await you in a new three-book boxed set, including: –"Hershey's Cookies, Bars and Brownies," –"Hershey's Chocolate and Cocoa Cookbook," and –"Kidsnacks," easy treats for kids to make. This wonderful collection would retail at $11.95, but while the offer lasts, it's yours *free* for allowing our representative to share with you our Family Heritage Program℠

...We Care Too.

Our Family Heritage Program℠ can provide comfort, security and peace of mind for your family all through the year. Because you care about your family, you owe it to them, and yourself, to find out what our Family Heritage Program℠ can do for you.

HERSHEY'S CHOCOLATE MEMORIES®

• 3 COOKBOOKS IN A GIFT ASSORTMENT •

ideals HERSHEY'S Chocolate and Cocoa Cookbook

HERSHEY'S Cookies, Bars and Brownies

HERSHEY'S Kidsnacks

Simply fill out and mail the return portion below and a representative will call to set up a delivery time for your gift.

YES! Please call to set up an appointment to share with me the Family Heritage Program℠ and deliver my FREE gift of "Hershey's Chocolate Memories," a three-book set of tasty recipes.

Name __________

Address __________

City __________ State _____ Zip _____

Phone __________

Source: Reproduced by courtesy of Service Corps International

Case 20

The Polaroid Corporation

The Polaroid Corporation has been called one of the most successful single-product companies in the United States. It began nearly half a century ago when W. Averill Harriman, a political figure in the Roosevelt administration; James P. Warburg, a financier; and several others provided Edwin Land with $375,000 to form a research company. The new Polaroid Co. was to find a means of polarizing light. But Land was not seeking this technology for use in cameras or photography, but as the basis for new automobile headlight lenses that would reduce glare, while still providing normal illumination. Unfortunately, the auto producers were not too interested in the lens. But World War II did create a demand for optic lenses that Land's company was able to produce in quantity and profitably.

After the war, the flow of lens orders dried up and, along with other highly specialized military contractors, the company was on the verge of bankruptcy. But, in the nick of time, Edwin Land announced he had discovered a near-magic process that would permit a camera to take a picture, develop it inside the camera, and turn out a photo print all in a matter of a few minutes. Sold first in 1948, the camera was advertised as an "instant" device, and it became an instant success, due mainly to its unique technological features. This early model is shown in Exhibit 20-1. It attracted hordes of innovators who wanted to be the first to own and demonstrate its captivating legerdemain. But it was also aided by the application of an important marketing technique—pricing. Its price was neither a skimming one that might restrict sales nor a penetration one that might cheapen its image; rather, the price was about half way between the two. Then, whether by clever marketing design or by a series of technological innovations, new features were added, prices were reduced, and sales volumes increased over the ensuing 35 years. Exhibit 20-2 lists the major product improvements for the instant camera. By 1971, Polaroid had grown to a $500 million firm, primarily due to its single product for which there had been no prior demand until its introduction.

DECLINE OF THE INSTANT CAMERA

In 1985, the Polaroid Corporation was facing serious problems. For practically all of its corporate life it had been a one-product company. Even after Kodak moved into the instant camera market in the late 1970s, Polaroid maintained its leadership, protected by a host of patents on instant photography technology. The market for instant cameras blossomed in the 1970s with the introduction of cheap color models and the popular Polaroid SX-70, with its Pronto counterpart a few years later. In the banner year of 1978, Polaroid sold 9.4 million instant cameras to Kodak's 4.5 million. Exhibit 20-3 shows sales of the two competitors from 1973 through estimates for 1985, and Exhibit 20-4 shows the decline in sales of Polaroid instant cameras and film.

The blossoming of the 1970s was short-lived. Polaroid's sales slipped 1.1 percent in 1979, and by 1984 they had dropped to 3.5 million cameras. During this period, Polaroid held on firmly to over two-thirds of the market—but this is two-thirds of only 45 percent of the 1978 sales.

Most analysts attribute the decline partly to market saturation, but mainly to changes in consumer preferences and needs. The most popular and fastest growing segment of the amateur photography market in the early 1980s was the 35mm single lens reflex camera, mainly the models selling for $100 to $200. These new models were more sophisticated, yet easy for amateurs to use, and the picture quality far outshown that of instant prints. Sales of these cameras in the United States nearly tripled, from about 1.2 million in 1976 to 3.5 million in 1980. Interestingly, however, many of the technological features on the new 35mms are the result of Edwin Land's extensive research in the Polaroid laboratories. Nonetheless, the 35mm models have had a direct appeal to the manipulative and practicality aspects of American culture. While many processes of the photo-taking operation are automatic, there are still enough adjustments for the amateurs to make, so they feel more in control. As one industry analyst put it, "Instant photography for amateurs, at least, has become old hat."

SOURCES OF PRESENT DIFFICULTIES

Today, the Polaroid Corp. is searching, more or less frantically, for new products or adaptations of present ones that can be sold in or out of the photography market. And this need was brought about by three elements, one inherent in the firm's long-term management and the others by an almost unforgivable failure to analyze the market.

The first involves the personality and business philosophy of Polaroid's president and founder, Edwin H. Land. His ideology is summed up in this quotation: "Our essential concept was—and mine still is—that the role of industry is to sense a deep human need, then bring science and technology to bear on filling that need. Any market already existing is inherently boring and dull." Because Land strongly opposed any moves into commercial photography or other areas of business, Polaroid's activities were restricted to the amateur market and tied to a single product line. So today, there are no other products to provide the income needed to pursue new interests, and what income there is is declining along with the demand for instant cameras. While Polaroid is aggressively trying to exploit its expertise in other markets, success seems to be several years away.

The second element was the judgment error Polaroid made when it failed to anticipate the peaking of demand in 1978 and its subsequent continuing decline. Instead, the company geared up to produce even larger quantities of instant cameras and saddled itself with unneeded capacity. This was certainly a major mistake for a firm that had created the product, marketed it for 40 years, and successfully held its own against Kodak's invasion into the instant camera market.

The third element was the Polavision fiasco, which all but dissolved the company's reputation as a technological leader in the amateur photography field and cost it millions in designing and marketing the product. Because of the importance of Polavision's failure, this source of the company's difficulties is described in more detail in the following sections.

THE POLAVISION ADVENTURE

In the late 1960s, Polaroid initiated a research program under the code name "Project Sesame," which was concerned with experiments that are conducted with film especially designed for viewing by shining light through it. At the time, most conventional film produced printed photographs that are viewed the same as other objects, by light shining on them. It was the "shining light through" concept that helped produce Polavision, a new instant movie system that took nearly eight years to bring to market.

Historically, the Polaroid Corporation has excelled in both technology and in marketing, but they failed in both when the new Polavision system was introduced in 1977. Under Land's direction, some $300 million was spent in research, development, and production to bring the system to market. Polavision was designed to take motion pictures with a special camera that developed them immediately for projection on a screen; it was a technological marvel that few consumers wanted.

The marvel had a few flaws. The camera was held by hand, and it used a very bright light that tended to frighten or annoy small children. Moreover, the movies were silent; there was no provision for sound, and the pictures themselves were quite grainy. When the instantly developed pictures were projected on the small 12-inch screen, they could only be seen clearly when the viewer was directly in front of it. Each instant movie film lasted only about two-and-a-half minutes, a short performance for the price. Although Polaroid was well aware of these flaws and imperfections, the company considered them to be trivial and introduced the system anyway.

There were other problems in addition to the design and technical deficiencies. Instead of trying to develop primary demand for the product through pioneering advertising where potential buyers are informed about the product and what it will do, Polaroid simply distributed it to the same channels that its SX-70 instant cameras used. While consumers knew the Polaroid brand and its regular products, they were uncertain about what Polavision actually did and how it worked. There was no easy way to demonstrate the system in the regular distribution channels, so that its advantages would be highlighted. This was particularly true in discount and drug stores where a large share of Polaroid's instant cameras have traditionally been sold. When consumers buy a $500–600 product, they want it demonstrated, and this was not possible in crowded camera departments, which are generally tended by part-time and often inexperienced salespeople. One Polaroid executive commented, "We learned we didn't know how to sell the system."

But Polaroid actually put out a considerable sales effort. A 1978 Christmas promotion promised a free personal delivery by Santa Claus to any purchaser of a Polavision system. About 3,000 buyers took advantage of the offer, and a battalion of Santa Clauses made the deliveries. If buyers did not want the personalized delivery, they could choose to take home their own Santa Claus suit along with the Polavision. And over 10,000 of them did. But the deficiencies in the system became all too apparent after it was used several times. Thus, the 13,000 innovators who took the risk of buying the product initially failed to become opinion leaders who should have been the information source that sparked the diffusion process. Consequently, the product gathered dust on retailers' shelves.

Not only were both technology and marketing faulty, but the company did not do its homework in researching the market itself or in forecasting demand. People had been shying away from home movies for many years. The photography trade's *Wolfman Report* indicated that 1.12 million 8mm movie cameras were sold in 1972, but that consumers bought only half that number, or 560,000 in 1978, so demand had been dropping for some time. Even if it missed this information, Polaroid should certainly have been able to predict the withering competition that was imminent from videotape cameras. The movies these cameras took could be viewed on a regular television screen, using a videocassette recorder, and the show they recorded lasted considerably longer than Polavision's two-and-a-half minutes. While Polaroid's film could only be used one time, videotape can be used over and over. But the most attractive feature is that sound may be recorded at the same time that the pictures are taken. In 1984, however, only 2.8 percent of U.S. households had a video camera, while 27.5 percent had a conventional home movie camera, as shown in Exhibit 20-5.

In 1979, Polaroid tried to correct some of the technological deficiencies in the Polavision system. They upgraded the film so that the pictures were not as grainy, and added a slow-motion and stop feature. But it was too late. Early in 1980, Polaroid quietly withdrew Polavision from the market, taking a hefty $68 million write-off in the 1979 fiscal year. As a result, total earnings for 1979 fell to $36 million from $118 million the previous year. And sales edged 1.1 percent lower, to $1.36 billion.

In mid-1981, the company introduced the Sun 600 series instant cameras that automatically combined ambient and electronic strobe light to eliminate shadows and harsh contrast. This was followed in 1983 by the 600 LMS with built-in flash and the SLR 680 with automatic focus. Several models in this series are shown in Exhibit 20-6. In late 1985, Polaroid announced the forthcoming introduction of the Series 7000 camera, which will produce "vastly improved photographs."

Most experts in the photographic field concede that while Polaroid's expertise and research improved the quality of both instant movie and camera prints and images, conventional prints are still much better. And the instant camera is old technology. Innovative research in photography, both amateur and commercial, appears to be concentrating on ways to store images electronically instead of on conventional film. Technology was on the threshold of this and other similar innovations when Polaroid introduced an outdated concept into a market geared for new innovative concepts.

Analysis Questions

1. What consumer behavior cultural concepts are likely to be involved in the marked consumer switch to 35mm cameras from the improved, simple, one-process Polaroid cameras?

2. Why did Polaroid market Polavision with all of its obvious deficiences?

3. How can you relate Polavision's failure to the concepts of consumers' changing needs and goals?

Source: Courtesy of Polaroid Corporation

POLAROID CORPORATION

EXHIBIT 20-2

Introduction and Major Improvements for the Polaroid Instant Camera

1948	First instant camera sold
1960	15 second picture and automatic exposure camera
1963	Color film and film cartridge
1965	Low priced swinger camera
1969	Cheap color camera
1971	Improved cheap color camera
1972	SX-70 pocket-sized color camera, film out in 1.2 seconds and 4 minute developing
1972	No litter, no-peel-apart film
1976	Pronto, low priced SX-70 model
1977	Polavision instant movie system
1979	Time Zero supercolor film for SX-70 models
1981	600 Series, auto-Strobe light and ultrasonic range system
1986	(Planned) Series 7000, vastly improved photos

POLAROID CORPORATION

EXHIBIT 20-3

Instant Camera Sales, Polaroid and Kodak, 1979–1985

	Sales in Millions of Units		
Year	Polaroid	Kodak	Total
1973	5.6		5.6
1974	5.6		5.6
1975	5.8		5.8
1976	6.1		6.1
1977	6.9	3.4	10.3
1978	9.3	4.5	13.8
1979	6.7	4.6	11.3
1980	6.4	3.7	10.1
1981	5.5	4.2	9.7
1982	4.0	3.2	7.2
1983	3.7	2.5	6.2
1984	3.5	1.1	4.6
1985	3.7	.9	4.6

POLAROID CORPORATION

EXHIBIT 20-4

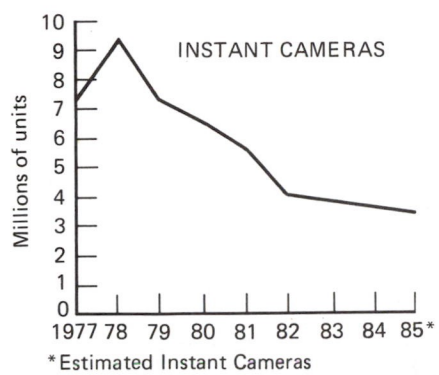

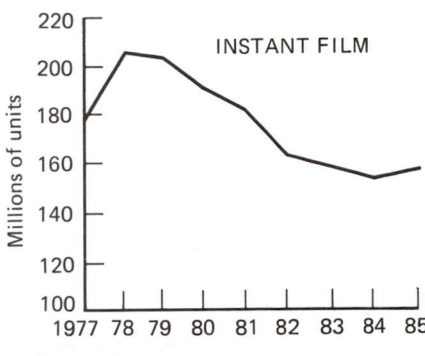

*Estimated Instant Cameras

POLAROID CORPORATION

EXHIBIT 20-5

Camera Types Owned by U.S. Households

Type	Percent Owning
Traditional still camera	93.2
Instant print camera	36.3
Home movie camera	27.5
Video camera	2.8

POLAROID CORPORATION

EXHIBIT 20-6

Source: Courtesy of Polaroid Corporation

Case 21

Radley Development Co., Inc.

John H. (Bud) Radley had just finished dictating the following memorandum to the divisional vice president for residential development of the Radley Development Co., Inc.:

MEMORANDUM

August 2

To: Charlie Shoburn
From: Bud Radley
Subject: Sales Strategy for Colonial Lakes

I have just looked over the sales report for Colonial Lakes and I am disappointed in what it shows, to say the least. Since we opened the development in May, we have sold only 14 units, and half of those are Lynwoods, the lowest priced, half-acre models. Even the heavy promotion on TV and in the *Evening Times* hasn't helped.

I know the competition is heavy from Suncrest and Wood Trails and there will be even more when Larchmont starts construction this month. The four or five other developments in the area are much lower priced and appeal to a different market, so I don't consider them as competition. But Colonial Lakes is the prestige property of the three now selling, yet we don't seem to be attracting prestige buyers and I wonder why. This may be our first high-priced develop-

---

ment, but neither of us are amateurs in this business. You will remember how fast Oak Hills sold out, even though it had a lot fewer amenities than Colonial Lakes has.

The builders are getting impatient with the delay and are calling me, complaining they can't get the revised plan from you for lot locations on the four house models. With sales as they are, I can understand why you want to wait. That's why I think we ought to do a little research to see if we can get a better handle on the problem here, and maybe change our sales promotion tactics. Please get our market research outfit to find out what our close competition is doing, who is buying from them, why the buyers bought from them, and if they looked at Colonial, why they didn't buy from us. We can also get some information on the 14 who already bought in Colonial and why they did. Maybe all this will tell us something new.

When you get the information, please set up a meeting with me to go over it.

BACKGROUND

The Radley Development Co. is a major developer of shopping centers, office complexes, and residential areas, with headquarters in a large midwestern metropolitan area. It is organized into three divisions: (1) retail development and shopping centers (2) office and commercial development, and (3) residential development. Each of these is headed by a vice president and Charles Shoburn heads division 3.

Over the past 20 years, the firm has developed some 32 residential tracts, the largest has 1,500 homes and the smallest has 32. As indicated in Mr. Radley's memo, all these projects were targeted to blue- and white-collar families who worked in skilled factory jobs, as service technicians, in clerical jobs, and as working owners of small businesses. Generally, these developments offer two basic home models with some variations, on one-eighth to one-quarter acre lots. Colonial Lakes is the most recent project and is the firm's first venture into prestige residential properties.

CHARLES SHOBURN

When he received Mr. Radley's memo, Charles Shoburn was somewhat concerned with its tone and the clear implication that he needed some help. This was his first major development project since his appointment to head the residential development division a year ago and he was anxious to make it a success. But he was forced to admit that Mr. Radley was right and that he, Shoburn, should have been first to suggest the need for market research. Colonial's sales had been far below expectations and, to make matters worse, he heard that sales of the two closest competitors, Suncrest and Wood Trails, had been more than double those of Colonial Lakes in the past two months.

Mr. Shoburn had been in the real estate business for 15 years, ever since he graduated from the University of Illinois business school. He knew that both the business and its clients were changing. Prices of all types of homes were constantly climbing upward. Yet, many two-earner families were looking for homes in the $100,000–150,000 range as symbols of their success. These were upwardly mobile families who were anxious to move in social circles that would help them advance in their careers. They hoped that living in a high-status suburban development would provide these circles. Shoburn and his division designed Colonial Lakes to appeal to this market, but so far the market had all but ignored it.

DESCRIPTION OF THE DEVELOPMENTS

The three present developments, and the forthcoming Larchmont, were all located about 12 to 18 miles from the midwestern city of Occomac. It was a large industrial manufacturing city of 1.5 million, and had recently been successful in attracting several large producers of electronic components for computer and national defense applications. The resulting influx of high-salaried engineers and executives created a market for new, larger suburban homes away from the older, smoke-stack atmosphere of Occomac itself. The relative location of the developments is shown on the map in Exhibit 21-1. The pertinent data and major features of each one are shown in Exhibit 21-2. Exhibit 21-2 lists several models of homes, and an encompassing price range. Generally, models in similar price ranges are built in specific sections. In Colonial Lakes, for example, two basic models are available in the $115,000 to $125,000 range, on one-half acre lots in areas furthest from the lake. Similarly, $130,000 to $160,000 homes are nearer the lake, and the highest priced ones, up to $195,000, are lakeside. Options and extras can add considerably to the basic prices.

Colonial Lakes is situated in rolling hill country on former farm land. Young trees are planted along all streets and there is an impressive stone structure at the entrance. Many of the homes are set well back from the road, and a number of the higher priced models have pillared fronts. About half of the homes have lake frontage or direct lake view and individual access. There are several sand beaches for use by nonfrontage property owners.

Wood Trails is a more rustic type of development with wooded lots and emphasis on contemporary styles. Colonial and split-level models are also available, however. The roads are high-grade gravel, which residents feel is in keeping with the rustic atmosphere and discouraging to sightseers and speeding teenagers. It targets younger, health- and exercise-oriented families with its bicycle trails, pool, and racquetball courts. Its lake is man-made and swimming is not permitted, although boating and fishing is. About one-third of the lots have lake frontage.

Suncrest is a traditionally styled development similar to Colonial Lakes. It is situated on the east bank of the Feather River. Swimming is not permitted at the present time, but the State Department of the Environment expects that it will be in three to four years when pollution sources are cleaned up. Riverside land has been reserved for beaches when the ban is lifted. About 45 of the 122 lots have some river frontage, and many lots are wooded. Near the entrance is a clubhouse with a large restaurant, open to the public. Other club facilities, including boat docks, are reserved for Suncrest residents.

Larchmont will be the most prestigious, highest priced of the four developments. It is built on flat or gently rolling land, with many trees. A wide stream bisects the area and 200 feet of parkland has been reserved on either side. There are two vehicle and four foot or bicycle bridges over the stream. House styles include mainly colonial and Georgian, with some contemporary. It is targeted to professionals (physicians, attorneys, etc) and mid- to upper-range business executives and officers.

RESEARCH

Mr. Shoburn reviewed this information on the competition. He then checked with several of the largest real estate agencies, banks, savings and loan associations, and other sources to get an estimate of sales for these competitive developments. The estimate he prepared from these sources is shown in Exhibit 21-3, and includes the number of homes sold by model and price range. Keep in mind that the same model may be sold for several prices, depending on the extras and options the buyer selects. Apparently Mr. Radley had similar information, and that was what prompted his memorandum.

There was little doubt in Mr. Shoburn's mind that something about Colonial Lakes or its promotion either failed to attract prospective buyers or inhibited them from buying once they visited the site and the models. To get things started, he set up a meeting with Leslie Bensen, vice president of Occomac Market Facts, a firm Radley had used in the past. During the meeting, he explained his problem and they went over the information Mr. Shoburn had collected about the competitive developments. He also explained why the research information was urgently needed, and she agreed to get a proposal to him in two or three days.

Two days later he received the following proposal (abstracted) from her:

PROPOSAL TO RESIDENTIAL DEVELOPMENT DIVISION, RADLEY INC.

We will conduct personal interviews with as many purchasers of homes in the three competitive developments as we can. We say "as many as we can" because there are relatively few of them and, in our experience, some of the buyers may not wish to cooperate. Word will also get back to the other developers, who may try to discourage their residents from participating. We try to work with community associations, and we have techniques that should provide an adequate sample for your needs.

From today on, we ask you to try to get names and addresses of people who visit Colonial Lakes. You may want to assure them that no *salespeople* will call on them. We would also like to have similar information on any visitors in the past, if you can identify them. We will interview as many of them as possible, using the unstructured-direct technique.

We will obtain demographic data on all buyers we interview, and will provide a summary of the salient factors that emerge from the qualitative interviews. We will also summarize these factors from interviews with Colonial Lakes visitors who have not yet bought. We do not believe that demographics from this group will be particularly useful to you, so we will not collect them. Since this will be exploratory research (to determine what the problem is), we will not make recommendations as to what you should do.

Since we understand the urgency involved, the study will be completed in 30 days from the date you give us formal acceptance. The cost to accomplish what is described above will be $5,500.

Please notify us in writing of your acceptance and please include a retainer of 25 percent of the total fee.

Presented by:

Leslie Bensen

LESLIE BENSEN
Vice President

Mr. Shoburn quickly accepted the proposal and sent a copy to Mr. Radley, letting him know that his instructions were being carried out, and how soon to expect an answer.

In a little over three weeks, Ms. Bensen made an appointment to discuss the research report with Mr. Shoburn, and a summary of the findings in her report is in Exhibits 21-4 and 21-5. Two days later, they met with Mr. Radley and spent most of the afternoon discussing the implications of the data and information in the report. Shortly after five o'clock, Mr. Radley got up, stretched, and said, "I think it's quite clear what we have to do. Let's have dinner and see if we can put the details together."

Analysis Questions

1. What factors seem to be influencing sales in Suncrest in recent months? What do Exhibits 21-1 and 21-4 suggest?

2. Is Mr. Shoburn correct in his assessments of what prospective buyers are looking for in a home and the area in which it is located? What is Mr. Shoburn promoting in Colonial Lakes?

3. What major changes should Mr. Shoburn make in his overall approach to the market in relation to (a) advertising and promotion, (b) types of homes being offered in Colonial Lakes, (c) sizes of lots in Colonial Lakes, and (d) schools in Colonial Lakes district?

City of Occomac and Surrounding Territory

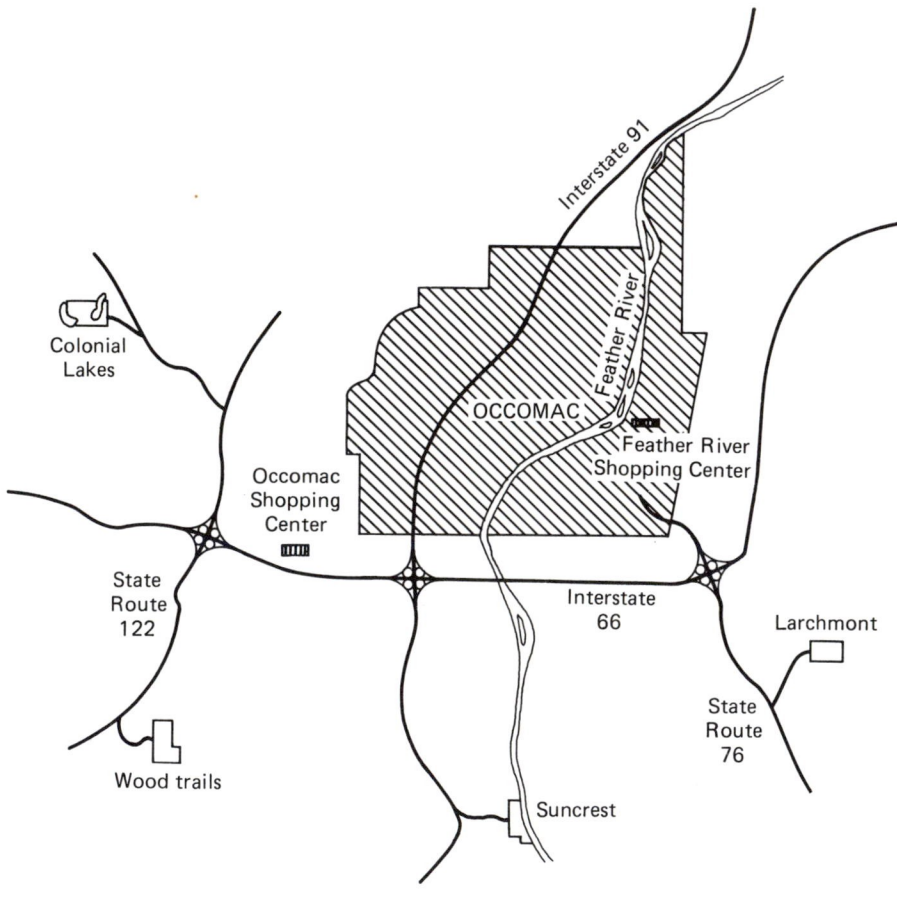

RADLEY DEVELOPMENT CO., INC.

EXHIBIT 21-2

Characteristics of the Four Developments

Development	# Home Models	Price Range	Sq. Ft. Range	Lot Sizes	Distance to City
Colonial Lakes (177 units) Expandable to 235 lots	4	$115,000– 195,000	1910– 3150	1/2, 1, & 2 acres	25 min. rush hour
Wood Trails (92 units)	3	$89,000– 142,000	1830– 2300	1, 2, & 4 acres	30–40 min. rush hour
Suncrest	3	$100,000– 158,000	2250– 2850	2, 3, acres	15–20 min. rush hour
Larchmont (109 units) Expandable to 127 lots	4	$135,000– 210,000	2540– 3200	2, 3, & 4 acres	35–40 min. rush hour

Development	Major Features	Distance to Schools	Distance to Shopping	Utilities
Colonial Lakes	Natural lake w/beaches Golf course Park Paved roads Tennis courts Swimming pool	1.7 mi. to Grade 5.2 mi. to High	Conv. Store 1.5 mi. Occomac Major Ctr. 6.7 mi.	City water sewers Underground utilities Cable TV
Wood Trails	Lake Swimming pool Large park Bike trails Tennis courts Racquetball Gravel roads	.5 mi. to Grade 8.4 mi. to High	Strip stores 2.4 mi. Occomac Major Ctr. 8.1 mi.	Well water Septic field Underground utilities
Suncrest	River location Swimming pool Clubhouse Restaurant Tennis courts Paved roads	4.0 mi. to Grade 7.4 mi. to High	Local stores 1.7 mi. Feather Major Ctr. 12.0 mi.	City water sewers Gas Cable TV
Larchmont	Golf course 2 Pools Security guards Tennis courts Park Paved main roads	3.4 mi. to Grade 6.1 mi. to High	General Store 2.0 mi. Feather Major Ctr. 7.9 mi.	Well water Septic field Underground utilities

RADLEY DEVELOPMENT CO., INC.

EXHIBIT 21-3

Sales of Homes and Approximate Prices, March through July

Development	March	April	May	June	July
Colonial Lakes (n = 14)	-	-	1-$127,500 1- 132,000 1- 129,750	3-$135,150 2- 125,000 1- 141,000 1- 137,000	1-$127,500 2- 132,000 1- 136,600
Wood Trails (n = 42)	1-$92,000	1-$ 97,300 2- 94,500 2- 101,600	3-$ 92,500 3- 98,000 2- 127,300 2- 119,900	3-$ 98,000 4- 119,000 3- 94,500 1- 128,500 2- 92,000	4-$123,000 4- 92,000 2- 101,600 2- 119,000 1- 132,200
Suncrest (n = 36)	-	2-$104,000 1- 110,750 1- 116,250	3-$110,750 2- 116,250 4- 125,000	4-$104,000 3- 116,250 3- 125,000 1- 132,500	3-$116,250 2- 120,100 4- 125,750 1- 132,000 1- 137,250 1- 140,100
Larchmont[a] (n = 3)	-	-	-	-	1-$155,500 1- 142,000 1- 174,500

[a] Preopening sales.

Selected Demographic Characteristics of Buyers of Homes in the Three Existing Developments

1. Colonial Lakes:

   Total buyers   14
   Interviewed   9 (64%)

Age of adult buyers listed on deed:	25–34	4
	35–44	12
	45–54	2
Occupations of buyers listed on deed:	Government	6
	Self-employed:	
	Retail	5
	Service	2
	Other	1
	Professional	1
	Work in home	2
Education:	High school	17.6%
	Some college	29.4
	College degree	29.4
	Graduate degree	17.6
	Other	6.0
Number of children:	Zero	28.0%
	One	41.4
	Two	22.6
	Three or more	8.0

2. Wood Trails:

   Total buyers   41
   Interviewed   30 (73%)

Age of adult buyers listed on deed:	20–24	1
	25–34	36
	35–44	16
	45–54	4
Occupations of buyers listed on deed:	Teacher	5
	Government	10
	Self-employed:	
	Retail	4
	Service	5
	Manufacturing	1
	Professional	2
	Work in home	11
	Military	2
	Clerical	7
	Technical	7
	Other	3

EXHIBIT 21-4 *(Cont'd.)*

Education:	High school	16.2%
	Some college	26.8
	College degree	36.6
	Graduate degree	18.3
Number of children:	Zero	45.0%
	One	36.7
	Two	15.0
	Three or more	3.3

3. Suncrest:

Total buyers   36
Interviewed   19 (53%)

Age of adult buyers listed on deed:	25–34	9
	35–44	25
	45–54	2
	55+	2
Occupations of buyers listed on deed:	Teacher	2
	Government	3
	Self-employed:	
	Retail	2
	Service	1
	Manufacturing	3
	Professional	9
	Religious	1
	Clerical	3
	Technical	4
	Political	2
	Retired	2
	Other	1
Education:	High school	10.9%
	Some college	18.9
	College degree	45.9
	Graduate degree	24.3
Number of children:	Zero	19.0%
	One	42.0
	Two	29.0
	Three or more	10.0

RADLEY DEVELOPMENT CO.

EXHIBIT 21-5

Abstracts of Major Points from Personal Interviews with Buyers and with Those Who Visited Developments but Did Not Buy

I. Of the 110 names given to us by Mr. Shoburn, we obtained information from 82. These potential buyers fall into the following categories (those who bought in Colonial Lakes are not included):

1. Have already bought in:

Wood Trails	21
Suncrest	13
Larchmont	1
Other develop	25
Still looking	22

2. Those still looking say they will probably buy in:

Colonial Lakes	3
Suncrest	6
Wood Trails	5
Larchmont	4
Other develop.	4

II. From our interviews with those who bought in each development, comments on why they bought or expect to buy, are summarized here:

1. *Colonial Lakes*: Liked the lake, particularly the beaches—can swim in natural water. City water and sewer. People already there seemed pleasant; like people we already know. Very pretty setting. Easy trip to city. Close to schools. Well-planned homes.

2. *Wood Trails*: Liked large lots and contemporary home styles. Not a "trimmed-up" development. Reasonably priced for what you get. Have friends and business associates living there. Lots of exercise facilities. Great bike trails for kids. Area school system has good reputation.

3. *Suncrest*: City services. Nice location by river; cool in hot weather. Some well-known people in city, and executives in my firm live there or are thinking about it. High school has highest SAT scores in metro area. Quick access to Occomac downtown. Clubhouse is good place to meet people. Like the wooded lots. Activities for children.

III. Why those who chose or are considering Wood Trails, Suncrest, or Larchmont did not choose Colonial Lakes:

Homes there now seemed to be smaller and on small lots. The people we talked to who live there were nice but they had pick-ups and campers in their driveway. Salespeople did not have information on the school system. Seems as though the leading people in Occomac are moving to Suncrest or Larchmont. There do not seem to be many houses going up in Colonial Lakes.

Case 22

Campbell's Soup and Nonsoup

"The Swanson TV dinner is junk food. It was great in the 1950s, but in today's world it doesn't go into the microwave, it doesn't represent variety or a good eating experience to my palate." These remarks did not come from a competitor in the frozen dinner business or from a food critic, but from R. Gordon McGovern, the 58-year-old president and chief executive officer of the Campbell Soup Co. And Swanson is one of Campbell's brands.

Until recently, Campbell was a stuffy, production-oriented company that produced what it could make easily and depended upon its name and distribution to attract customers. It did not venture much into market research to find out what people wanted to buy. This rather narrow outlook may have been because Campbells is a family-owned company, with nearly 60 percent of the stock owned by the Dorrance family. John T. Dorrance, Jr., who effectively controls 31 percent of the stock, retired as chairman in the fall of 1982. But today, the near insatiable demand of U.S. consumers for innovative convenience products, packaging, and preparation techniques has forced the company to heed the needs and desires of consumers in designing new products. It is sometimes difficult to understand the failure of large and successful firms to anticipate consumer demand. To help with this understanding, it is necessary to look briefly at the product history of Campbells and how decades of proliferation of basic staple goods have inhibited the firm's ability to innovate.

The brand and the product have melted together and achieved the connotation of a single word, *Campbellsoup*, in the language, with virtual brand insistence in the marketplace. It has monopolized the soup market in the United States for years, and holds a firm 80 percent share of the market, selling over two billion cans a year. Campbell's early strategy was to keep expanding the kinds of soup it offered. Thus, grocers had to either expand total shelf space to accommodate the new soups, or drop other brands of soup. Since Campbells was the favorite, and adding more kinds did not increase total soup consumption, they simply dropped competing lines.

The red-and-white can with a gold medallion has identified the company since its founding in 1897. More recently, it was the subject of a famous Andy Warhol pop-art production in the 1960s. Campbell's advertising, too, has been consistently clever and popular over the years. The cherubic "Campbell Kids" of the 1930s and 1940s were household figures, but were dropped in the late 1970s, only to be revived in 1984. The famous singing slogan "M-m-m-good" was hummed by more than one generation, and its replacement, "Soup is good food," emphasizes the soup's nutritional attributes and is equally well known.

But the company was not very innovative. Even its early acquisitions—Swanson, Pepperidge Farm, Franco-American, and Godiva—were just extensions of the soup line, with nothing in them to appeal to a different target market. The same policies continued into 1978 when Harold A. Shaub was president and chief executive officer. Faced with a continuing lawsuit begun by H. J. Heinz in 1976 which charged Campbells with monopolizing the canned soup industry, Campbells countercharged that Heinz attempted to monopolize the industrial ketchup market. Shortly thereafter, Schaub announced that his firm was testing ketchup in the Midwest. In May 1978, Campbells also acquired Vlasic Foods, Inc., with its lion's share of the pickle industry. But these products, too, were merely extensions of the old line, selling to the firm's existing markets. Nonetheless, the company was rock-solid financially with cash and short-term investments of $159 million and only $17 million of long-term debt.

A SHIFT TO MARKETING

In 1980, Gordon McGovern took the company helm and began changing its emphasis from production to marketing, and developing a new mission: "to be positioned with consumers as somebody who is looking after their well-being." He also split Campbell's traditional four production divisions into 50 "business groups" and delegated both responsibility and authority to the group managers for manufacturing and profits. "These moves are designed to bring the managers closer to the market," he announced.

Following up on his comments quoted earlier, in 1982 McGovern introduced LeMenu, high-priced frozen entrees offering such upscale fare as sirloin tips with mushroom gravy, broccoli with cheddar cheese sauce, and O'Brien potatoes. Campbells also tested other exotic menus, such as lobster thermidor and chicken cordon bleu. It promoted this line with commercials touting "LeMenu's carefully orchestrated foods," while on screen a string quartet played and a hand poured a glass of vintage wine. "You don't dare eat LeMenu without a vintage wine," intoned an aristocratic voice.

This was quite a change from 30 years before when Clarke and Gilbert Swanson developed their TV dinner. It was designed so Mom, Dad, and the kids could sit in front of the television and munch fried chicken or spaghetti (the favorites) from tin trays. The dinners were filling but not very appetizing. But consumers became wealthier, and wanted something lighter, more nutritious, and tastier. From 1979 to 1981, Swanson's sales dropped 16 percent, although the overall frozen dinner market was growing. More women were going to work and many of the burgeoning singles group did not want to cook for one.

As a result, sales of quality frozen dinners are increasing about 5 to 7 percent a year. The "TV dinner" tin tray has largely been replaced by plastic plates that look good enough to put on the table, and that can be used in microwave ovens. Campbells is also segmenting geographically by producing a salmon-based dinner for the Northwest and a barbecue dish for Texas. To provide a fish alternative for both the LeMenu and the Swanson lines, Campbells acquired Mrs. Paul's Kitchens, Inc. Under McGovern, Mrs. Paul's market share rose from 24 to 27 percent in just one year.

Prego spaghetti sauce was brought out regionally in 1981, with a $15 million advertising campaign, but not introduced nationally until 1982 with a $25 million budget. It turned out to be one of the company's biggest winners. Even though it was not in full distribution, its sales approached the $100 million mark in its first year, and by 1983 it was second in sales only to Ragu. But Ragu did not take the challenge lying down. Initially, Ragu offered coupons good for 75 cents off the regular Ragu, and then brought out new Homestyle spaghetti sauce, supported by a $20 million advertising campaign. Homestyle was followed in 1983 by Ragu Chunky Garden-Style sauce and a $22 million campaign. Prego is still number two.

Interestingly, Prego almost never made it to the market. In 1978, Campbell's policy provided that any new product had to show a profit in its first year, but Prego was not projected to be profitable until the third year. Straub changed the policy and launched the product in 1978. "In the ten years before Prego, Campbells had only two major new product successes— Chunky Soups and Hungry Man dinners—and both were nothing more than glorified extensions to the product line," said Marketing Vice President Herbert M. Baum. But by 1985, LeMenu and Prego together accounted for over $450 million of Campbell's $4 billion sales.

THE JUICE AND COOKIE FLOP

"Pepperidge Farm Star Wars cookies are a travesty. They do not fit the brand's high-quality, upscale adult image. And, at $1.39 a bag, it's a lousy value." Again, not a comment from a competitor or a cookie specialist but from R. Gordon McGovern, who ran Pepperidge Farm for 12 years before taking Campbell's top job. "But," he added, "I could be wrong." He wasn't.

Pepperidge Farm was founded in Connecticut in 1937 when Margaret Rudkin began baking whole wheat bread to help relieve her son's asthma. She started selling it locally, and word about its quality, taste, and health benefits soon spread. Before long, her kitchen grew into a large bakery, producing high-quality bread of various kinds. Campbell bought the company in 1961.

In the scramble for new products, Pepperidge Farm rushed Star Wars Cookies and apple juice into the market in 1983. But the quality image of the other bread-related products failed to rub off on the two new ones, and Pepperidge Farm eventually took them off the market. Another new product, a line of meat and cheese sandwiches baked in a crust called Delis, was phased out in late 1985. Initial sales were high, but customers did not rebuy. This was part of a product review in 1985 in which Richard A. Shea, the unit's new president, dropped 275 Pepperidge Farm products that were not doing well. He and his managers hope to return the firm to its basic attributes: "premium quality," "natural ingredients," "a bakery heritage," and "meeting consumer need."

Another continuing juice problem in the regular Campbell's line concerns Juice Works. Aimed at children, it consists of several fruit juice blends, with no sugar added. In the test phase, it was tried out on some 6,000 kids and they liked it. But it was introduced in the Northeast in the fall of 1984 in bottles and cans when competitors were using aseptic packages. Campbells unfortunately misjudged the importance of this packaging in the Northeast, even though it had tried it in other markets. Retailers balked at carrying the line because of the packaging and also because there were a number of other juice blends available. In the 1984 fiscal year, Juice Works sales were $24 million, $8 million below the forecast of $32 million. Scheduled to go national in the Spring of 1985, the product was delayed until 1986.

Campbells is also looking carefully at its traditional soup container. "The can isn't as user friendly as it used to be. It is being battered and beaten in consumer surveys," Anthony Adams, the company's research director is quoted as saying. But Frank Terwilliger, the packaging director, is concerned about the risk of using a new container that might cause problems. "Deep down, everybody [here] feels good about the can. We don't want to muck it all up by changing that good solid conservative image," he says.

But there are a lot of consumers who avoid using canned soup, particularly convenience-oriented singles. They do not like to use a can opener, mix the (sometimes gummy) soup with water, heat it, and then have to wash the pot, dish, and utensils. Besides, the metal can cannot be heated in a microwave oven, which is now used by an estimated one-third of U.S. households. Strangely, some younger consumers associate cans with old-fashioned preservatives and artificial ingredients. They also believe that cans do not keep the nutrients in. So Campbells is testing several alternative containers. One is a plastic microwavable bowl, with an easy-opening top. Another more conventional one is a plastic container shaped like a metal can and covered with the red-and-white label. But Mr. Terwilliger firmly rejected a plastic bowl that came with a small pouch containing what he described as a "silly little knife" to cut the plastic cover off the bowl. "It just looked dumb," he said.

THE CATERING KIOSK— TODAY'S TASTE

"My 83-year-old mother doesn't eat like my son. And my daughters eat differently than their parents, and we eat differently from the people around the corner," comments Mr. McGovern. Using this philosophy, Campbells is not only trying new products (334 of them since 1980) but completely new concepts as well.

The most recent test was quite different from conventional product preparation and retailing. The product is a line of freshly prepared entrees that are designed to upscale even today's upscale frozen "gourmet" entrees sold in stores. Designed especially for the working couple or single professional, the line includes 22 soups, salads, entrees, and desserts, some of which are named Veal Medallions with Baked Tomato and Kiwi, and Filet of Salmon with Basil Sauce. And none of them contain the preservatives and additives, such as monosodium glutamate, that are found in traditional frozen dinners. All can be reheated in a microwave or a conventional oven (20 minutes) and most of them contain fewer than 500 calories.

To retail these products, Campbells had to come up with a unique sales gimmick. They needed to be sure these "Today's Taste" products were not confused with frozen entrees, since they could not be taken home and popped in the freezer. They had to be heated and eaten right away if customers were to get the advantage of fresh preparation. But since the entrees were already cooked, consumers could also eat such things as salmon filet cold.

Catching the customer's eye was also important for this innovative product line, so Campbells designed a "catering kiosk," which is a free-standing refrigerated structure that houses the products. Photographs of the items are on the front side of the kiosk and the single-serving entrees, soups, and salads are stored on the other. Each item in the line comes in a plastic throw-away dish covered by a transparent plastic top, inside an attractive cardboard sleeve. Prices vary from $4.25 to $7.95 for the entrees, a bit above gourmet frozen dinners and a little below upscale carry-out food. The kiosk also has a side compartment called the "Chef's Corner" that contains spices, beverages, and sauces from small specialty producers, packaged under the Today's Taste label. Pamphlets describing the new products and their advantages, together with heating and serving suggestions, were available at the kiosks. The kiosk is depicted in Exhibit 22-1.

The single-serving packages are prepared daily at a catering facility just a short distance from the stores where the test is being conducted, and delivered directly to the kiosks. Today's Taste representatives personally examine and accept all shipments of food used in the soups, salads, and entrees to assure quality and freshness. All the ingredients are purchased locally, and the dinners are cooked and assembled under the supervision of trained chefs. The packages are delivered as soon as they are put together, and marked with a use-by date, four days later. In the test, however, unsold items were pulled in two days and given bacteriological tests for freshness.

THE TEST MARKET

Oddly enough, Today's Taste was test marketed in Washington, D.C., a metropolitan area that is almost never used for that purpose since its upscale demographics exclude it from the "typical American city" category. But upscale singles and working families are exactly what Campbells was looking for and it found plenty of them there. Also, the suburban counties of Montgomery, Maryland, and Fairfax, Virginia, are at the top of the list for per capita income in the United States and other expensive prepared foods have sold well there.

Campbells asked consumers about the design of the product packages and the kiosk itself. A number of people thought the burgundy sleeve with its white lettering "didn't look like a food package." But it was used anyway because Donna Haverstock, the senior manager for Campbell's consumer nutrition center, wanted something different from normal supermarket packaging that would set Today's Taste apart from other frozen dinners.

But the *Washington Post* reported that at least one supermarket manager in the area thought the line was not moving too well, and quoted a woman shopper as saying: "The prices are a little high. I wouldn't mind paying a dollar more than Lean Cuisine if it's good." Some of the items being offered and their prices are:

Pasta Primavera Salad	$1.85
Chicken Salad Jacques	$3.45
Chesapeake Style Crab Chowder	$2.85
Chicken Florentine	$4.65
Veal Marsala	$6.95
Spicy Shrimp & Vegetables	$5.95

The shopper's remark may suggest that the concept of Today's Taste may not be well understood, and the line may be perceived as just another high-priced assortment of frozen dinners. At one supermarket, "waiters" in tuxedos gave out free samples of the soups, salads, and entrees while explaining the concept of "fresh preparation." After the explanation, one consumer was not impressed. "It seems to me you're talking about heating up a dinner that may have been prepared yesterday. It sounds a bit like leftovers." In late 1985, after the test was completed, the manager of another Washington suburban chain store that participated said: "The products didn't move too well, and I don't believe it was price. The customers here are not price conscious at all. I'm not sure why we have sales at this store; we don't sell much more when we do. There was some other problem with Today's Taste and I'm inclined to think it may not have been promoted enough. People just didn't seem to understand what it was."

Campbells was careful throughout the test to soft-pedal its connection with Today's Taste. "We realize that when people hear the name Campbell they think of canned soup," says Ms. Haverstock. So it appears in small letters only on the back of the new product packages.

Analysis Questions

1. What type of innovation is the Today's Taste line?
2. What would be the diffusion process for the new line?
3. Do you think the Today's Taste managers are correct in minimizing Campbell's connection with the new product?
4. Do you think the Today's Taste concept will succeed?

The Catering Kiosk

Today's Taste

Case 23

The Merriwether Distillery

The Merriwether Distillery is one of the leading smaller firms in the United States producing a high-quality bourbon whiskey. This type of whiskey is distilled from a mash composed of at least 51 percent corn grain, with malt and rye. It was named for Bourbon County, Kentucky, where it originated in the eighteenth century, and it is considered to be the most distinctive American whiskey. The alcoholic strength of whiskey is known as its proof, which is double the percentage of alcohol. Pure, or absolute alcohol, is 200 proof. Most whiskey produced in the United States is 86 proof, which means it contains 43 percent pure alcohol, by volume. It may be called *straight* whiskey if it is distilled at 160 proof, then reduced to no more than 125 proof by adding water when it is placed in barrels for aging. U.S. regulations require that bourbon (and other whiskies) must not be distilled at more than 190 proof, and it must not be less than 80 proof when it is bottled. Thus, whiskey of less than 80 proof must be labeled *diluted*. Most whiskey sold in the United States is 80 or 86 proof.

EARLY HISTORY

In the early 1800s, two Merriwether brothers, John and Martin, built a small still on the banks of Clipper Creek in Kentucky near the Virginia border. They made "corn" whiskey, distilled from about 80 percent corn grain, which they grew on their hilly, rocky farms. It was mostly for their own use, but before long they were supplementing their meager farm income by selling part of their production to nearby neighbors. Over the years, the families multiplied and by the middle of the century, there were no less than two dozen small stills scattered in the mountains operated by Merriwethers or close relatives by marriage to the clan. Ostensibly small hill farmers, they all made their living from the clandestine distilleries.

After the Civil War, four from this group—three Merriwethers and one Jenkins (a first cousin)—decided to pool their resources and build a legitimate commercial distillery. Not only was the government becoming more aggressive in its insistence that the alcohol taxes be paid, but the "mason jar" market was a limited one. As the country grew and expanded, so did the distillery. And by so doing, the area around it became a prosperous corn farming center supplying the raw material. Initially, the distillery made standard corn whiskey, but it soon became apparent that the larger urban markets wanted a less bucolic and better tasting product, so the Merriwethers began making their first bourbon in 1875. By 1880, they produced 350,000 gallons of an increasingly well-known and high-quality bourbon. They expanded the market to all parts of the country, including the burgeoning West.

By 1917, when Prohibition put an end to their whiskey production, Merriwether had about 10 percent of the U.S. bourbon market, a share they quickly regained after Prohibition's repeal in 1933. By 1934, with total bourbon production reaching 35 million gallons, Merriwether had 16 percent of the market, or 5.6 million gallons. See Exhibit 23-1 for consumption of the several types of alcoholic beverages for selected years.

In the late 1970s the firm was still firmly in family hands and the product line had expanded to include a blend under the Wethermay brand, Crestway Dry Gin, and Crestoff Vodka. The Old Merriwether bourbon, however, continued to be the most popular seller, accounting for 75 percent of sales in 1979.

RECENT CHANGES

In 1978, Seth Merriwether was stricken with a heart attack and died. He had been president of the firm for nearly 30 years, and it had been a period of stability and steadily increasing earnings. His death was a blow to both the firm and the family. After a considerable amount of family squabbling, Seth's grandson, John McGowan, was installed as president and chief executive officer. The family heaved a collective sigh of relief and settled back for another long period of prosperity.

John was in his early thirties and had shown an avid interest in the firm, both the business and the technical aspects, since he first toured the distillery at the age of eight. He earned his MBA from a large eastern business school in 1969, and came to Merriwether in 1972 after three years with a large building materials conglomerate. After short periods in the production, aging, and accounting departments, he moved into marketing in 1976 where he became part of the three-man sales force. There, John was a little disappointed because the job did not seem to have much challenge. The wholesalers he called on seemed to be more interested in hunting and fishing stories or anecdotes about the mountain people back at the distillery than they were in the product. Mostly, they gave him the same orders at each call, with quantities building up only slightly over the years. They were not particularly concerned about promoting Old Merriwether because that would simply reduce sales of other brands and bring some retaliation. He did notice, however, a quiet but persistent note in conversations with the wholesalers that some changes seemed to be brewing in the liquor business.

Shrewdly, John felt that these undercurrents might be the rustlings of something more serious, so he began to look at information on production and consumption of the various liquor products on the market. Data on these products are shown in Exhibit 23-2. Merriwether's marketing people watched the bourbon market closely, and John knew that bourbon's share of the whiskey market during the period from 1960 to 1976 rose slightly, from about 14.2 to a peak of 18.5 percent in 1973, dropping slightly to about 18 in 1976.

START OF THE PROBLEM ERA

When he assumed the presidency in 1978, John McGowan saw clearly the direction the distilled liquor market was taking. After four years of relatively flat sales, a spurt in 1977 appeared to have lost steam in 1978. Beer consumption was rising steadily, and wine was erratic although sales reached an all-time high in 1977. Most disturbing of all the data was the slight sales decline of the long-time leader in liquor brands, Seagrams 7 Crown Blended Whiskey. Although still in first place in 1976, it showed signs of being edged out by Smirnoff Vodka. Moreover, other vodkas, Bacardi Rum, gin, and Canadian Mist, a light Canadian whiskey, showed the highest percentage gains from 1976 to 1977. The trend certainly appeared to favor the lighter liquors, but it remained to be seen whether the rise in popularity would be sustained over the next few years. He knew that consumption of lighter scotch whiskies increased in the Northeast and on the West Coast, and that one producer, Brown and Forman Distilleries, produced a clear bourbon called Frost 80/80, which they hoped would attract those following this trend. It was not what consumers wanted, though, and it was dropped soon after its introduction.

Realizing that Merriwether had to be prepared in the event the trend toward lighter distilled liquors continued, Mr. McGown started production of a premium brand of both gin and vodka, as well as an 80 proof, lighter bourbon at a market price 15 percent lower than that of Old Merriwether. Despite a substantial advertising budget, only the vodka attracted the attention of the market and was able to woo customers from other national brands. In 1980, the gin and light bourbon were dropped.

One major problem that all distilled liquor producers faced was an array of state government restrictions on advertising. Their products could be advertised in newspapers, magazines, billboards, and other media but they could not use televison. Beer and wine makers could, however, although they could not show anyone actually consuming the beverage in an ad. Even with this restriction, the ability to use visual media was a distinct advantage. Another problem facing producers was the wide variation in state laws that control liquor advertising. Six states do not permit price to be shown in an ad. Holiday packages cannot be used in two states and a woman may not be depicted in two states. Exhibit 23-3 lists these and some of the other advertising constraints placed on distilled liquor advertisements.

The downward trend for sales of whiskies and bourbon in particular continued into the 1980s. In the late 1970s, Seagrams Seven Crown Blended Whiskey, which had long been the undisputed leader in distilled liquor sales, lost its coveted first place to Smirnoff Vodka. In turn, Smirnoff was replaced by Bacardi Rum in 1981, and it still retains the lead. See Exhibit 23-4 for relative ranks of the leading brands in recent years.

THE FUTURE COURSE

At the Spring 1985 meeting of the Merriwether Board of Directors, Seth Merriwether III, vice president for marketing, showed the 1984 data on whiskey sales, along with that of directly competing distilled products, wine, and beer. He noted that, while the third-place Seagrams 7 Crown Blend was the highest ranked whiskey, the Canadian Mist brand had skyrocketed from eighth to sixth place since 1981. The one bright spot on the horizon was the rise of Jim Beam Bourbon to fifth place, the highest spot bourbon had held in recent years. But the picture is still bleak for distilled liquor producers. There has been a steady drop in overall consumption, with a decline from 437.7 million gallons in 1982 to 431.1 in 1983. And to make matters worse, the bourbon share of this declining market dropped from 13.8 to 13.2 percent in those two years. Seth said that consumption patterns are also changing, and the spread of bourbon drinkers is narrowing. Today, 21 percent of U.S. households consume 89 percent of the bourbon, a much smaller proportion than in past years.

He also pointed out that singles, as a group, are exerting more influence in the distilled liquor market, and they account for one out of every five dollars spent on those products. But as they grow older, marry, and change their life-styles, their household consumption of distilled products drops sharply, and they tend to drink wine, beer, or no alcoholic beverages at all. The downscale age group is more health and weight conscious. They believe that alcohol is not only fattening but detrimental to health. They also perceive lighter colored liquors as lighter in caloric content as well, and that wine and beer contain less alcohol per drink. One distiller, Seagrams, has run a series of ads comparing the amount of alcohol in similar portions of the three beverages. One such ad is shown in Exhibit 23-5.

Another disquieting change in the liquor market is the appearance of more specialty products in the ranks of the "Top 60" sellers. Until 1977, Kahlua, a coffee-flavored liqueur from Mexico, appeared in forty-fifth place while Southern Comfort moved up to thirty-third. Since then, Amaretto di Saronno and Bailey's Irish Cream have entered the race, with Bailey's moving up rapidly from last place in 1981 to thirty-fifth in 1983. No new liqueurs have entered the Top 60 since 1981. Exhibit 23-6 shows the rise in specialty product consumption since 1976.

Mr. McGowan observed that the figures do not tell all the story, and gave an overview of the liquor market. A few years ago, Merriwether's competition came from other bourbons and whiskies in the market. Then bourbon began to lose some of its market share to rum, vodka, scotch, and lighter whiskies. Today, the problem is multifaceted. Many consumers see scotch as a status, prestige product and blends as bar whiskies. Bourbon is perceived as more of a mixing drink for the middle classes, where most of the taste changes are occurring. He pointed out that since Old Merriwether is a mid-range brand with no real uniqueness except quality, it is difficult to promote new uses for it. Today, there seem to be both tangible and intangible deterrents to sales. Wine, for example, is not only a cocktail drink but it may be served with meals as well. It is also a highly versatile beverage in other ways. It comes in three basic types—red, white, and rose—while bourbon comes in only one. There are sweet and dry wines, appetizer and dessert wines, still and sparkling wines. Wine diluted with fruit juices or carbonated water is becoming popular and many new types are being marketed. And for the younger market—the one bourbon producers seem to be losing—wine also has a lore. Knowledge of it bestows a certain status on the holder. It can also be tasted, discussed, compared, and laid down in the cellar as an investment. Unfortunately, with the possible exception of scotch, most distilled liquors have little, if any, conversational value. One research group predicted the shift away from bourbon and scotch to vodka, rum, and gin because younger consumers were seeking instant gratification and it took some time to become accustomed to the heavier "brown" liquors. Also, this group was less concerned with drinking the conventional thing.

Nevertheless, wine sales also seem to be flattening and the trend seems to be toward consumption of less alcohol, or none at all. Some have suggested that social drugs of various kinds are substitutes for alcoholic drinks, but there does not seem to be widespread acceptance of them for social occasions.

Mr. McGowan concluded by pointing out the changes in our culture that have influenced consumption of many foods and beverages. He noted that not only are health and weight major factors, but there are social concerns as well. The ravages of drunk drivers have brought about more stringent laws and penalties, which, in turn, have caused many people to drink less or change what they drink. While these are recent phenomena and may be only fads that will fade away before long, Mr. McGowan urged his market research people to go beyond the facts and figures to see what kinds of basic changes are occurring in the population and social structure that influence liquor consumption. What they find out will help in charting the course of the Merriwether Distillery for the next several years.

Analysis Questions

1. The data in the case and exhibits show what is happening in the liquor market but not why. What social factors that have emerged in our society in the past five to ten years have influenced liquor consumption? Consider personal, legal, and political ones.

2. Mr. McGowan suggests that wine is a very versatile beverage. Why do you think wine has become so popular so rapidly? What personal and population factors are likely to be involved? Does wine possess any social factors other than its "drinkability"?

3. Why have some special liquors become so popular since 1977?

4. What should Mr. McGowan do?

MERRIWETHER DISTILLERY

EXHIBIT 23-1

**Sales of Alcoholic Beverages for Selected Years, 1960–82
(millions of gallons)**

	1960	1970	1975	1976	1978	1979	1980	1981	1982
All Distilled	316	370	414	422	437	447	449	449	438
Whiskey	84	240	247	249	231	221	165	162	153
Beer	95	135	158	161	176	184	193	195	194
Still wines	148	204	207	244	313	326	340	363	365

MERRIWETHER DISTILLERY

EXHIBIT 23-2

**Share of Distilled Liquor Market by Product Type
for Selected Years, 1970–83
(Percent of Market Share)**

	1970	1971	1973	1979	1980	1981	1982	1983	1985
Whiskeys									
Bourbon	22.8	21.7	18.5	14.6	13.9	13.5	13.8	13.2	11.8
Scotch	13.0	13.6	13.6	13.1	12.9	12.9	11.4	11.3	10.0
Canadian	9.0	9.5	11.3	12.0	12.5	12.4	12.9	13.1	12.9
Blends	19.8	18.2	14.7	9.0	8.6	8.5	7.9	7.9	7.4
Other	0.3	0.3	0.5	0.4	0.3	0.3	0.4	0.3	0.3
Total Whisky	65.1%	63.6%	59.1%	49.5%	48.5%	47.9%	46.8%	45.8%	42.4%
Nonwhiskey									
Vodka	12.4	13.3	15.6	18.8	19.0	19.1	20.0	20.2	20.5
Gin	9.9	9.8	10.1	9.7	9.5	9.6	9.5	9.5	9.0
Cordials	4.9	4.9	5.6	7.6	7.8	7.9	8.6	8.9	11.2
Rum	2.9	3.2	3.6	6.9	7.1	7.6	7.4	7.7	7.9
Brandy	3.5	3.7	3.9	3.9	4.1	4.2	4.2	4.2	4.6
Other	1.3	1.5	2.1	3.6	4.0	3.7	3.5	3.7	4.4
Total Nonwhisky %	34.9%	36.4%	40.9%	50.5%	51.5%	52.1%	53.2%	54.2%	57.6
Total Consumption (millions of gallons)	369.9	382.5	404.4	447.5	449.4	448.8	437.7	431.1	416.3

Source: Impact Magazine

MERRIWETHER DISTILLERY

EXHIBIT 23-3

Advertising Restrictions on Distilled Liquor in 1978

Restriction	State
No local liquor advertising	Mississippi Oklahoma
Price may not be shown in advertisements	Arkansas Georgia Wyoming Minnesota Maine Iowa
Only specified sizes of bottles may be shown in ads	Florida Kentucky
Cannot refer to price savings or use the word "sale"	Michigan Montana Virginia Washington N. Carolina Ohio Oregon Pennsylvania West Virginia
Holiday packaging not permitted	Alabama Utah
Cannot say "No extra cost"	Massachusetts South Dakota

MERRIWETHER DISTILLERY

EXHIBIT 23-4

Top Eight Liquor Brands, 1979–83
(Sales in Thousands of Cases)

Year	Rank	Brand	Sales
1979	1	Smirnoff Vodka	8,300
	2	Bacardi Rum	7,200
	3	Seagrams 7 Crown	6,100
	4	Seagrams VO	3,825
	5	Canadian Club	3,816
	6	Jim Beam Bourbon	3,825
	7	Popov Vodka	2,816
	8	Gordon's Gin	2,615

EXHIBIT 23-4 (*Cont'd.*)

1980	1	Bacardi Rum	7,600
	2	Smirnoff Vodka	6,100
	3	Seagrams 7 Crown	5,800
	4	Seagrams VO	3,800
	5	Canadian Club	3,600
	6	Popov Vodka	3,100
	7	Jim Beam Bourbon	2,950
	8	Jack Daniels Bourbon	2,800
1981	1	Bacardi Rum	7,750
	2	Smirnoff Vodka	6,000
	3	Seagrams 7 Crown	5,675
	4	Seagrams VO	3,675
	5	Canadian Club	3,450
	6	Jack Daniels Bourbon	3,300
	7	Jim Beam Bourbon	3,075
	8	Canadian Mist	2,850
1982	1	Bacardi Rum	7,825
	2	Smirnoff Vodka	5,750
	3	Seagrams 7 Crown	5,175
	4	Jack Daniels Bourbon	3,325
	5	Seagrams VO	3,250
	6	Canadian Mist	3,175
	7	Jim Beam Bourbon	3,100
	8	Canadian Club	2,950
1983	1	Bacardi Rum	7,675
	2	Smirnoff Vodka	5,700
	3	Seagrams 7 Crown	4,900
	4	Canadian Mist	3,350
	5	Jim Beam Bourbon	3,200
	6	Jack Daniels Bourbon	3,175
	7	Seagrams VO	3,050
	8	Canadian Club	2,850
1985	1	Bacardi Rum	7,650
	2	Smirnoff Vodka	5,875
	3	Seagrams 7 Crown	4,500
	4	Canadian Mist	3,700
	5	Jim Beam Bourbon	3,375
	6	Jack Daniels Bourbon	3,150
	7	Popov Vodka	2,800
	8	Seagrams V.O. Canad.	2,775

Source: Impact Magazine

IT'S TIME AMERICA KNEW THE FACTS ABOUT DRINKING.

12 oz. of beer, 5 oz. of wine and 1¼ oz. of liquor all have the same alcohol content.

It's time ABC, CBS and NBC let the facts be heard.

We submitted TV commercials to the networks which simply stated the facts of alcohol equivalency, and they have refused to put them on the air. Network policy bars advertising for distilled spirits. But these announcements are not commercials for products...ours or anyone else's. The message here is the fact of equivalence. A fact people have a right to know. A fact we want to tell.

It's Time All Of Us Were Heard.

We share the concern of other public spirited groups who believe that the popular misconcep-

tions about beverage alcohol can be dangerous. The National Institute on Alcohol Abuse and Alcoholism urges every American to know the facts of equivalency.

The American Automobile Association incorporates the facts of equivalence in its driver safety and alcohol education programs.

The Motor Vehicle Departments of California and New Jersey explain the facts of equivalence in their drivers' manuals. And the National Football League, the Insurance Information Institute and Citizens for Highway Safety, to name a few others, are also publicizing the facts.

This message is *that* important.

The facts are, there is the same amount of alcohol in a 12 ounce can of beer, a 5 ounce glass of wine, and a 1¼ ounce serving of 80 proof whiskey, vodka, gin or rum. To be exact, the typical serving of beer contains 0.54 ounces of alcohol. The typical serving of wine contains 0.55 ounces of alcohol. The typical serving of spirits contains 0.50 ounces of alcohol.

THE HOUSE OF SEAGRAM
© 1985, THE HOUSE OF SEAGRAM, N Y

Source: Courtesy of Jos. E. Seagram & Sons

MERRIWETHER DISTILLERIES

EXHIBIT 23-6

Ranks of Distilled Specialty Liquours, 1976–83
(Sales in Thousands of Cases)

Year	Rank of 60	Brand	Sales
1976	35	Southern Comfort	900
1977	33	Southern Comfort	1,025
	41	Kahlua	850
1979	27	Kahlua	1,175
	31	Southern Comfort	1,150
1981	23	Kahlua	1,500
	29	Southern Comfort	1,150
	46	Amaretto	700
	60	Bailey's Irish Cream	525
1983	19	Kahlua	1,550
	29	Southern Comfort	1,050
	35	Bailey's Irish Cream	900
	46	Amaretto	675

Source: Impact Magazine